أَرْسَلْنَاكَ إِلَّا
رَحْمَةً لِّلْعَالَمِينَ

*"And We have not sent you except as
a Mercy for the Worlds."*
[21:108]

THE
MIDDLE
COMMUNITY

The Messenger of Mercy: A Call in Makkah

Written by Dr. Sarfaraz Hussain Shah
Design by Jawad Shah
Illustrations by Afshin Amini

1st Edition, October 2022

THE MESSENGER OF MERCY

Volume I:
A Call In Makkah

Dr. Sarfaraz Hussain Shah

About the Author

Dr. Sarfaraz Hussain Shah (born 1990) is a British medical practitioner with a lifelong interest in literature, world history and the interpretation of the Noble Qur'an. He is proficient in several languages including classical Arabic. He has been writing poetry since the age of nineteen, specialising in didactic poetry and historical epics. He is also a founding member and current trustee of *The Middle Community*. He began writing the Messenger of Mercy in October 2015 whilst still at medical school. After seven years of research, writing and revisions, the poem was completed in 2022 in the Holy city of Makkah itself along with his first ever 'Umrah.
Contact: sarfaraz@middlecommunity.org

About the Middle Community

The Middle Community is a registered charity that was established in August 2021 by a group of Muslims with the aim of helping the needy and striving for greater inter and intrafaith harmony. We do not preach to people when we provide aid to them nor do we discriminate against anyone. We believe we are all equals in humanity, and are opposed to sectarianism and intolerance in all its forms. We are involved in running food banks, working with youth, organising conferences and producing literature. 100% of all proceeds from this book will directly go towards furthering the charitable goals of the Middle Community *Insha'Allah*.

For donations, enquiries and further information please visit:
www.middlecommunity.org

Registered Charity number: 1195305

Contents

Introduction

بِسْمِ اللهِ الرَّحْمٰنِ الرَّحِيْم

In the Name of Allah, the Merciful, the Most Merciful.

This book is an epic poem which describes the blessed life of Prophet Muhammad (ﷺ) from the start of his Mission until the *Hijrah* in the thirteenth year. It is intended to be comprehensive and yet concise; to make use of elevated language appropriate to the form, but without sacrificing clarity. It does not require a great deal of previous knowledge in order to understand, but supplementary information has been included in the following pages: original maps, lineage charts and some brief background information before the poem begins.

The main text consists of thirteen chapters, each corresponding to one year. The events have been arranged chronologically to the extent that has been possible for us to determine. There is no fixed metre but it generally follows a regular alternating structure and rhyme scheme which was devised specifically for the unique requirements of this work. At the end of this book can be found further material: short biographies of individuals mentioned in the text, a glossary of unfamiliar terms and a bibliography section. To keep it concise, we have chosen to restrict the glossary and biographies to only those terms and personalities found in the poem itself and not the supplementary material.

Any benefit found herein is from Allah (ﷻ) and any mistakes or shortcomings are from ourselves. Whatever we have written has been

1

based on historical sources, striving to remain impartial and accurate. Our sources are listed in the bibliography section at the end of this book. We have relied more on the earlier accounts than the later ones, especially the accounts of Ibn Hisham, Ibn Saad, and At-Tabari. However, we have referred to each referenced book in some way - sometimes to a larger and sometimes to a lesser extent. It may be noticed that the authors are from very different eras, cultural backgrounds and schools of thought. We have done so in order to broaden our insight through making use of the sincere efforts of others. Our intention has been to include only the best of whatever we have found, and to avoid the trappings of bias, strife and exaggeration. Even so, there will inevitably be things that some readers may disagree with. It is quite possible that the fault is with us, so we will wholeheartedly encourage you to research further.

We have not included every narrated event we have come across, nor have we included the entirety of details mentioned. At times, we have contented ourselves with mere reference or summary, while at times we have continued at length. This is to maintain the structure and to avoid losing the reader's attention. There are certain events and incidents about which the particulars, such as the dates are not well established. For cases such as these, the dates have been approximated on the basis of whatever resources were available to us. There are still other incidents, about which the scholars have differed. An example of this is the *Mi'raaj*. Some say it took place in the 10th year, while others say it was in the 12th year of the Prophetic Mission. We have chosen one over the other, according to our best judgement. And Allah (﷾) knows best.

In some cases, we avoided discussing certain points entirely due to the extent of the controversy surrounding them. Our aim is for this work to be inclusive and bring people together, not to stoke conflict and division. This only applies in those cases where there is no decisive answer. Throughout the course of the poem, we have included some portions of the words of the Prophet (ﷺ) and his contemporaries. We have taken these words from the sources, however we recommend that you take all quoted speech only as an approximate indication of the meaning, rather than to be a verbatim transcript of what was said. We have observed that the Noble Qur'an has also used this style of expression in relating events.

Where we have included some parts of the Verses of the Qur'an itself within the text, we have endeavoured hard to express the meaning of the Verses as accurately as possible. The intention is to draw the mind of the reader into remembering those Verses and understanding why they were revealed. However, given the use of poetry, we do not and cannot claim that our translations are perfect or complete, and we seek refuge with Allah the Almighty from changing the Words of His Book.

A note on transliterations

Although for the most part, we have replaced Arabic terms with their English equivalents wherever possible, there are still a considerable number of Arabic words used in this text; the pronunciation of which may be unfamiliar to English speakers. We will not emphasise too much on this point in this work. The interested reader should be able to clarify any pronunciations fairly easily. However, the following point might be helpful with phonetics: the use of apostrophes before or after a vowel (such as 'a, or a') is indicative of either a guttural sound (as produced by the Arabic letter ع: 'Ayn), or a pause.

A note on honorifics

(﷽) or (جَلَّ جَلَالُه):

> this says, *"Jalla Jalaaluhu"* which means "May His Glory be Exalted." It is used exclusively for Allah (﷽).

3

(ﷺ) or (صَلَّىٰ ٱللّٰهُ عَلَيْهِ وَآلِهِ وَسَلَّمَ):

This says, *"Sallallahu 'alayhi wa salam"* which means "May Allah send his peace and blessings upon him." It is used exclusively for Prophet Muhammad (ﷺ)

(ع) standing for (عَلَيْهِ ٱلسَّلَامُ):

This says, *"'alayhis-salaam"*, which means "Peace be upon him." We have used it for the Prophets and Angels.

Due to the nature of this work and for ease in formatting and readability, all honorifics have been omitted entirely from the poem itself. Similarly, we have not included any honorifics for anyone besides the three categories mentioned above in the supplementary text, though there are many who would be deserving of this, including various family members and companions of the Prophet (ﷺ). This should not be taken to imply a lack of respect on our part, and we encourage the reader to send the appropriate salutations upon them whenever they are mentioned.

اللَّهُمَّ صَلِّ عَلَى مُحَمَّدٍ وَعَلَى آلِ مُحَمَّدٍ

كَمَا صَلَّيْتَ عَلَى إِبْرَاهِيمَ وَعَلَى آلِ إِبْرَاهِيمَ إِنَّكَ حَمِيدٌ مَجِيد

"O Allah, send your blessings upon Muhammad and upon the family of Muhammad just as you have sent your blessings upon Ibrahim and upon the family of Ibrahim. Indeed you are the Praiseworthy, the Glorious."

Finally we turn to our Lord and ask Him to forgive us our faults, aid us in keeping our intentions pure, and accept and amplify our efforts. Ameen.

Dr. Sarfaraz Hussain Shah, M.D.
8th October 2022
12th Rabi'-ul-Awwal 1444 AH

Verses of the Qur'an

يَا أَيُّهَا النَّبِيُّ إِنَّا أَرْسَلْنَاكَ شَاهِدًا وَمُبَشِّرًا وَنَذِيرًا
وَدَاعِيًا إِلَى اللهِ بِإِذْنِهِ وَسِرَاجًا مُنِيرًا

*"O Prophet! Indeed We have sent you as a witness and a bringer of good
tidings and a warner. And one who invites to Allah by His permission,
and an illuminating lamp."* [33:45-46]

لَقَدْ جَاءَكُمْ رَسُولٌ مِّنْ أَنفُسِكُمْ عَزِيزٌ عَلَيْهِ مَا عَنِتُّمْ
حَرِيصٌ عَلَيْكُم بِالْمُؤْمِنِينَ رَءُوفٌ رَّحِيمٌ

*"There has certainly come to you a Messenger from among yourselves.
Grievous to him is your falling into distress, full of concern for you;
for the Believers kind and merciful."* [9:128]

وَإِنَّكَ لَعَلَىٰ خُلُقٍ عَظِيمٍ

"And indeed, you are of a great moral character." [68:04]

وَمَا أَرْسَلْنَاكَ إِلَّا رَحْمَةً لِّلْعَالَمِينَ

*"And We have not sent you except as
a Mercy for the Worlds."* [21:107]

فَبِمَا رَحْمَةٍ مِّنَ اللهِ لِنتَ لَهُمْ وَلَوْ كُنتَ فَظًّا غَلِيظَ الْقَلْبِ لَانفَضُّوا مِنْ
حَوْلِكَ

*"Thus it is due to mercy from Allah that you deal with them gently.
And had you been rough, hard hearted, they would certainly have
dispersed from around you..."* [3:159]

5

لَّقَدْ كَانَ لَكُمْ فِي رَسُولِ اللَّهِ أُسْوَةٌ حَسَنَةٌ لِّمَن كَانَ يَرْجُو اللَّهَ وَالْيَوْمَ الْآخِرَ وَذَكَرَ اللَّهَ كَثِيرًا

"Certainly you have in the Messenger of Allah an excellent exemplar for him who hopes in Allah and the Latter Day and remembers Allah much." [33:21]

إِنَّ اللَّهَ وَمَلَائِكَتَهُ يُصَلُّونَ عَلَى النَّبِيِّ ۚ يَا أَيُّهَا الَّذِينَ آمَنُوا صَلُّوا عَلَيْهِ وَسَلِّمُوا تَسْلِيمًا

"Allah and His angels send blessings on the Prophet. O you who believe! Send your blessings on him, and salute him with a becoming salutation." [33:56]

لَقَدْ مَنَّ اللَّهُ عَلَى الْمُؤْمِنِينَ إِذْ بَعَثَ فِيهِمْ رَسُولًا مِّنْ أَنفُسِهِمْ يَتْلُو عَلَيْهِمْ آيَاتِهِ وَيُزَكِّيهِمْ وَيُعَلِّمُهُمُ الْكِتَابَ وَالْحِكْمَةَ وَإِن كَانُوا مِن قَبْلُ لَفِي ضَلَالٍ مُّبِينٍ

"Certainly did Allah confer great favour upon the Believers when He sent among them a Messenger from themselves, reciting to them His Verses and purifying them and teaching them the Book and wisdom, although they had been before in manifest error." [3:164]

وَأَطِيعُوا اللَّهَ وَالرَّسُولَ لَعَلَّكُمْ تُرْحَمُونَ

"And obey Allah and the Messenger that you may obtain mercy." [3:132]

قُلْ إِن كُنتُمْ تُحِبُّونَ اللَّهَ فَاتَّبِعُونِي يُحْبِبْكُمُ اللَّهُ وَيَغْفِرْ لَكُمْ ذُنُوبَكُمْ ۗ وَاللَّهُ غَفُورٌ رَّحِيمٌ

"Say: If you love Allah, then follow me: Allah will love you and forgive you your faults. And Allah is Forgiving, Merciful." [3:31]

Traditions

إِنَّمَا بُعِثْتُ لِأُتَمِّمَ صَالِحَ الأَخْلاقِ

"I was sent to perfect good manners."
[Sahih al-Bukhari #273]

إِنَّ مِنْ خِيَارِكُمْ أَحْسَنَكُمْ أَخْلاقًا

"The best among you are those who have the best
manners and character."'
[Sahih al-Bukhari # 3559]

اعْبُدُوا الرَّحْمَنَ وَأَفْشُوا السَّلَامَ

"Serve the Most Merciful, and spread greetings of peace."
[Sunan Ibn Majah #3694]

إِنَّ اللَّهَ رَفِيقٌ يُحِبُّ الرِّفْقَ وَيُعْطِي عَلَيْهِ مَا لاَ يُعْطِي عَلَى الْعُنْفِ

"Allah is Gentle and loves gentleness,
and He grants reward for it that He does not grant for harshness."
[Sunan Ibn Majah, #3688]

مَنْ يُحْرَمِ الرِّفْقَ يُحْرَمِ الْخَيْرَ كُلَّهُ

"Whoever is deprived of gentleness is deprived of
goodness in its entirety."
[Sahih al-Bukhari # 3687]

مَا رَأَيْتُ أَحَدًا أَكْثَرَ تَبَسُّمًا مِنْ رَسُولِ اللهِ صَلَّى اللهُ عَلَيْهِ وَسَلَّمَ

"I have never seen anyone who smiled
as much as the Messenger of God (ﷺ)."
[Tirmidhi #3641]

وَكَانَ رَسُولُ اللهِ صلى الله عليه وسلم إِذَا سُرَّ اسْتَنَارَ وَجْهُهُ، حَتَّى كَأَنَّهُ قِطْعَةُ
قَمَرٍ، وَكُنَّا نَعْرِفُ ذَلِكَ مِنْهُ.

"Whenever the Messenger of God (ﷺ) was happy,
his face used to glitter as if it were a piece of the moon,
and we used to recognise it from his face."
[Sahih al-Bukhari #3556]

فَلَرَسُولُ اللهِ صلى الله عليه وسلم أَجْوَدُ بِالْخَيْرِ مِنَ الرِّيحِ الْمُرْسَلَةِ

"The Messenger of God (ﷺ) was so generous
that he was faster than the swiftest wind in this regard."
[Sahih al-Bukhari #3554]

مَنْ رَآهُ بَدِيهَةً هَابَهُ، وَمَنْ خَالَطَهُ مَعْرِفَةً أَحَبَّهُ

"Whoever unexpectedly saw him would
stand in awe of him, and whoever accompanied him and
got to know him would love him."
[Shama'il Muhammadiyah, #6]

لَمْ أَرَ بَعْدَهُ وَلاَ قَبْلَهُ مِثْلَهُ

"I have not seen anybody like him,
neither before nor after him."
[Sahih al-Bukhari # 5908]

The State of The World Prior to the Prophet (ﷺ)

ظَهَرَ الْفَسَادُ فِي الْبَرِّ وَالْبَحْرِ بِمَا كَسَبَتْ أَيْدِي النَّاسِ لِيُذِيقَهُم بَعْضَ الَّذِي عَمِلُوا لَعَلَّهُمْ يَرْجِعُونَ

"Corruption has appeared in the land and the sea on account of what the hands of men have wrought, that He may make them taste a part of that which they have done, so that they may return." [30:41]

The population of the world at the start of the Sixth century is about 210 million people. It is a century of change: battles rage, great empires are built and razed, and entire populations are transformed in ideology. In 536 AD, following a series of huge volcanic eruptions in various regions throughout the world, a volcanic winter begins. A huge cloud of ash blocks out the sun and darkens the skies for more than a year and a half. The world is full of famines due to crop failures, droughts and one of the most significant global cooling events in human history. Then in 541 AD, the first pandemic of the bubonic plague starts to spread throughout North Africa, Europe and the Middle East, killing tens of thousands of people. Finally, towards the end of the century, smallpox spreads from India into Europe. In short, between the natural disasters, wars, famine, disease, oppression and moral decline, it is an era of suffering and hopelessness; where the people of the world are in desperate need of mercy and are crying out for a saviour.

9

The Roman Empire

After centuries of expansion and domination, the Roman Empire is becoming too large to manage effectively by a single ruler, so in 286 AD, it is first divided into an Eastern and a Western half by Emperor Diocletian. Diocletian also begins the worst period of persecution that the community of Christians has ever faced. The pagan emperor despises monotheism and does everything in his power to try to eradicate the faith.

However, his brutal efforts fail, and only a few years later a succeeding Emperor, Constantine I, converts to Christianity in 312 AD. Constantine combines parts of the Roman traditions and culture with Christianity to make it more palatable to the population. During his reign, the Council of Nicaea takes place in 325 AD: in it all but two bishops reach the consensus that "Christ is Divine in nature".

By 392 AD, Christianity becomes the official state religion when the old pagan religion is outlawed by Theodosius I. The Western Roman Empire falls in 476 AD, but the Eastern Roman Empire (or Byzantine Empire as it would later be known) remains intact. Emperor Justinian helps re-establish the might of the Roman Empire during his forty-year long rule which ends with his death in 565 AD. Anatolia, Syria, Palestine, Egypt, North Africa, Greece and parts of Italy are all part of the Empire. Heavy taxation of the poor helps fund the many meaningless amusements and luxuries enjoyed by the rest.

In 610 AD, Heraclius arrives with a fleet at Constantinople, now the capital of the Roman Empire and the world's largest city. He deposes the unpopular Emperor Phocas who had himself overthrown his predecessor in a mutiny only a few years earlier. Under Heraclius, the Roman Empire thrives: a fact not ignored by the Persians. The Roman-Persian wars begin the same year, with the Romans suffering a series of heavy losses at the start - the worst of which is the Sack of Jerusalem in which "the True Cross" and other ancient relics are taken away.

Europe

After the fall of Western Roman Empire and the sacking of Rome itself, various Germanic tribes including the Franks, Ostrogoths, Visigoths and Vandals vie with one another for control over the former Roman territories in Western Europe. Much of the Italian peninsula is under the rule of the Ostrogoths who had gained independence in 554 AD. It is then conquered by the Lombards in 568 AD. Compared to the past, there is little in the way of philosophy, innovation, literary or intellectual development, even in Greece which had once been the centre of learning. Meanwhile the Slavic tribes begin to dominate parts of the Balkans and Eastern Europe.

Britain

The Celtic natives of Britain gradually lose ground to the Angles and the Saxons: two invading Germanic tribes which they had already been fighting for over a century. Various kingdoms are founded. Pope Gregory of Rome sends a monk named Augustine as a missionary to Canterbury. Augustine converts King Ethelbert of Kent, and establishes in 597 AD what would become the Church of England, thus beginning the process of converting the pagan population of the British Isles to Christianity.

The Persian Empire

In Persia, the Sassanid dynasty is at the peak of its power. Zoroastrianism is the main religion and involves a symbolic reverence of fire in temples which they say represents God but is not God per se. Manichaeism and other ideologies are also followed throughout various parts. Khosrow I rules for nearly fifty years and establishes its economy, military and infrastructure before his death in 579 AD. Khosrow "Parviz" II becomes the ruler at the time of the Prophetic mission and regards himself more as a god than a king. He and the Persian nobility live lives of unparalleled opulence and splendour with endless greed. Meanwhile, the population by and large live in abject poverty and degradation. There has been intermittent conflicts with their regional rivals, the Romans, at various points throughout the last few centuries. However, Khosrow II wants to establish absolute authority over everyone and begins a new invasion with the aim of all-out war. During the initial phase he manages to deliver some decisive victories and conquers much of the Roman territory including Jerusalem which he sacks in 616 AD.

India

The powerful Gupta Empire, which had once consolidated twenty-one different kingdoms and made major contributions to mathematics, astronomy and medicine, collapses in 467 AD. The Indian subcontinent is once again carved into various feuding kingdoms, and a period of general intellectual, creative, social and moral decline begins. By the year 570 AD, people in many parts of India are divided into a caste system which degrades the lower classes and deifies the upper classes. Women now have few rights if any, and practices such as widows being forced to throw themselves onto the burning pyres of their dead husbands are common. Most of the people are polytheists with varying traditions and beliefs. However, Jainism and Buddhism have both also been practised in the region since their origination a thousand years earlier. Over the course of centuries, Buddhism slowly spreads to other states by means of monks and traders.

China

Emperor Wen establishes the Sui Dynasty in 581 AD and reunites the fractured Northern and Southern dynasties after a series of wars and purges. The Emperor then converts to Buddhism and popularises it throughout China. Taoism, Confucianism, various folk religions and philosophies are also followed by many. Huge construction projects and a disastrous war with the Goguryeo Kingdom of Korea take a toll on the economy and foment rebellion. The Sui are overthrown and replaced by the Tang Dynasty in 618 AD, which will remain dominant for nearly three hundred years.

East Asia

Korea is in its "Three Kingdoms" period. Intermittent conflicts between each of the three major regional powers have been ongoing for the last few centuries. However, shifting alliances between them and external states such as the Chinese dynasties and Japanese Empire lead to huge social and dynastic upheavals. By 552 AD, the people of all three Kingdoms are now mostly following Buddhism.

In Japan, the majority of the population follow the polytheistic Shinto religion with a belief in venerating ancestral spirits. However, Buddhism starts to gain traction after being introduced by the Koreans. It gains official acceptance by the Japanese Emperor by 589 AD, taking on a syncretic form among the general population.

Central Asia

The first Turkic Khaganate is founded by the Göktürks around 552 AD. They follow a religion called Tengrism which incorporates elements of shamanism and animism into its otherwise monolatric worship of a 'sky god'. They are fierce nomadic warriors. They conquer the Mongolian plateau but external threats and in-fighting cause this to split into a eastern and a western half by 602 AD. Their eastern half repeatedly battles with the Sui dynasty before being defeated by the Tang dynasty. Their western half supports the Eastern Roman empire against the Sassanids.

The Americas

In North America, there are various hunter-gatherer, fishing and farming settlements. Beliefs vary from tribe to tribe, but generally have a strong pantheistic focus on spirits and the natural world. Some have the belief in a single supreme spirit guiding to good, while there are other lesser spirits charged with various tasks.

In Mesoamerica, Teotihuacan is a major metropolis: the sixth largest city in the world at this time. They have constructed huge stepped pyramids, palaces and elaborate temples. The people follow an agricultural lifestyle and a polytheistic religion. In South America, the Mayan civilisation is at its peak. They follow a highly ritualistic religion combining elements of animism, ancestor worship and polytheism. Ceremonies of human sacrifice are common. There is a long-running war between two powerful city states: Tikal and Calakmul, as well their allies. This culminates in Tikal being defeated and its king ritually sacrificed in 572 AD. Tikal enters a period of decline while Calakmul for the time being gains ascendancy. Further conflicts continue to occur.

Egypt

Once a major world power in its own right, Egypt for the last few centuries has been a mere province under the Roman Empire, which uses it and most of North Africa as a bread basket to feed their Empire. Pagan practices and sites of worship are banned by the Roman Emperor Justinian in 527 AD and Christian missionaries are sent to the region as he solidifies his control over it. In contrast to the Byzantine Orthodox version of Christianity, the Coptic Christians set up their own Church which is not the first theological difference they have had with Rome or Constantinople. Monasticism is prevalent among many Christians in Egypt. During the Roman-Persian wars, Egypt falls into the hands of the Sassanid dynasty of Persia in 614 AD. It would later be recaptured by the Romans under Heraclius, and thereafter the Arab Muslims.

East Africa

Nobatia is a kingdom in the location of historical Nubia, south of Egypt. They mostly follow the Egyptian pagan religion, in particular the Cult of Isis, until 543 AD when they convert to Christianity. Similarly other neighbouring kingdoms such as Makuria and the Blemmyes also embrace Christianity by the end of the Sixth century. They would eventually become Muslims after the advent of Islam.

Abyssinia

Although beliefs vary in other regions, the Abyssinian Kingdom of Axum in particular is predominantly Christian at this time. Christianity had been introduced by the missionary Frumentius who became its first Bishop in 330 AD when he converted the King Ezana. Ezana expanded its borders and influence considerably. The Axumite Empire eventually would control much of Yemen and be involved in trade as far as India. Ashamah or An-Najashi (Negus) as he is also titled, is the ruler at the time of the emergence of Islam, and he is known for his justice and personal piety. He has good trade relations with the Arabs of Makkah.

Central, West and Southern Africa

Many different ethnic groups, tribes, and kingdoms exist throughout the rest of the African continent with their own languages, cultural practices and unique beliefs. Various folk religions are practised: for the most part animistic, pantheistic or polytheistic in character. Monotheism is generally absent however. Ancestor worship, shamanism and beliefs in supernatural spirits are common. Most things are passed down through the oral tradition so written scriptures are almost unheard of.

Yemen

The original Arabs come from Yemen (*Al-Yaman*), as the descendants of Ya'rub ibn Qahtan. They travel throughout the Arabian peninsula and interact with the descendants of Ibrahim (ﷺ) and Isma'il (ﷺ).

In the 11th century BC, The Kingdom of Saba (Sheba) is one of the wealthiest and most powerful in the region. Following Queen Bilqis of Saba's meeting with Prophet Sulayman (ﷺ), she and her entire people become monotheists. Afterwards, they construct the Great Dam of Maarib which enables them to irrigate the barren desert. They are blessed with fruits and prosperity for over a thousand years. However subsequent generations become ungrateful and become worshipping idols once again. The Dam bursts causing hugely destructive floods and the end of the Kingdom.

Later, one of the Himyarite Kings called Asad Abu Kurayb (known by his title of Tubba) during a campaign against the Romans, learns of the coming of a future Prophet in Arabia and he expresses his belief in him. He even travels to Yathrib and encourages the people there to support this coming Prophet. He is the first to cover the Kaaba with the *Kiswa* (cloth). Although Tubba himself believes, many of the people after him become Disbelievers and are destroyed by Divine Punishment.

By 523 AD, the Jewish King Dhu-Nuwas comes to power in Yemen, and begins to brutally persecute the Christians throughout Southern Arabia. He throws thousands of Believers into a huge pit of fire: an event the Qur'an makes direct reference to (85:4-11). King Kaleb of Axum assists Emperor Justinian in putting an end to Dhu-Nuwas.

In the year 570 AD, Abraha, a tyrannical governor who replaced Dhu-Nuwas, rises up with an army that includes war elephants and marches to Makkah with the aim of demolishing the Holy Kaaba. He does this because he has constructed an elaborately decorated church in Yemen, which he hopes will replace the Kaaba as the site of pilgrimage for all Arabs. His plot is thwarted when a Divinely-sent flock of birds pelts his army with hardened clay, decimating them and sending them back in confusion. Abraha dies on the way back and the Kaaba remains safe.

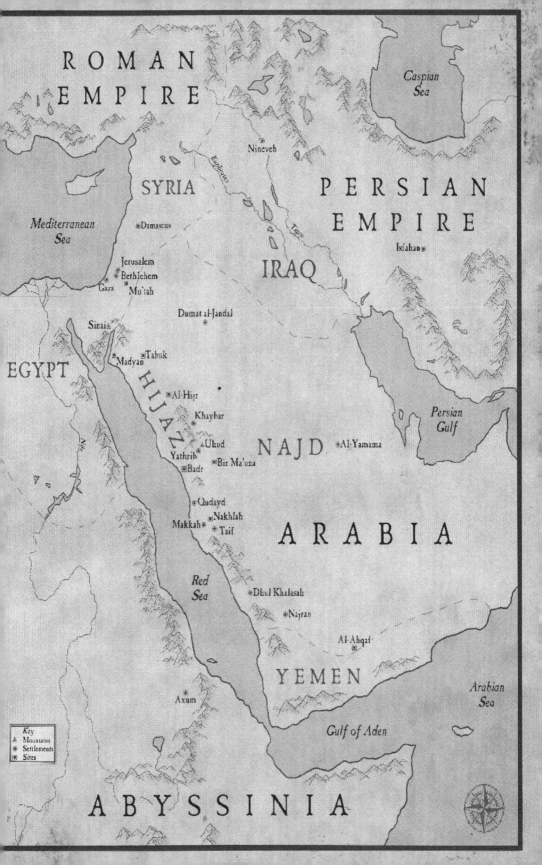

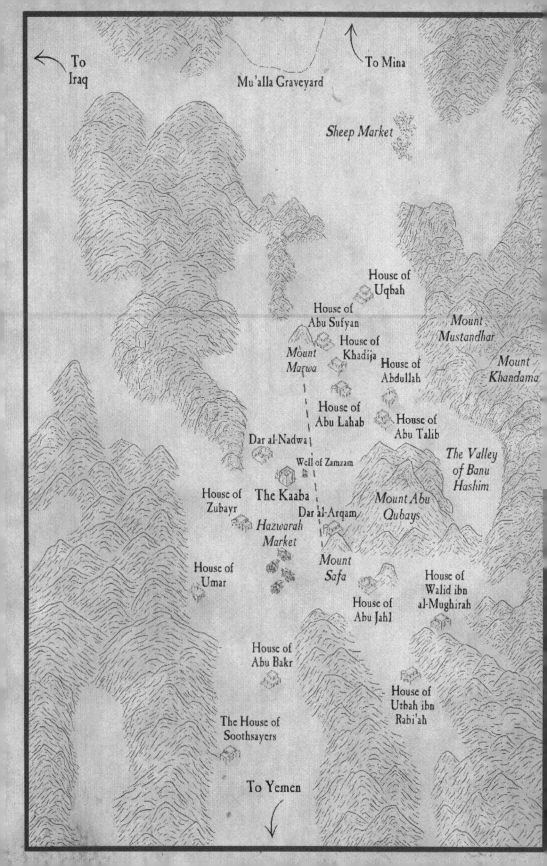

The State of the Arabs in the Jahiliyyah Times

هُوَ الَّذِي بَعَثَ فِي الْأُمِّيِّينَ رَسُولًا مِنْهُمْ يَتْلُو عَلَيْهِمْ آيَاتِهِ وَيُزَكِّيهِمْ وَيُعَلِّمُهُمُ الْكِتَابَ وَالْحِكْمَةَ وَإِن كَانُوا مِن قَبْلُ لَفِي ضَلَالٍ مُّبِينٍ

"It is He who has sent among the unlettered a Messenger from themselves reciting to them His Verses and purifying them and teaching them the Book and wisdom - although they were before in clear error." [62:2]

We will now proceed to give a brief description of what Arabia was like at the start of the Prophetic mission. Understanding this is crucial as it will provide the appropriate context for what follows.

Their Religion:

Idol Worship:

The majority of people were polytheists. They would worship idols that they constructed in various images. However, unlike most other nations, they lacked a complex mythological framework for understanding these supposed gods - in most cases they were nothing more than names, roles or fictitious lineages they had invented. A great number of the pagan Arabs actually affirmed the existence of Allah (﷾) and recognised the fact that He was the Creator of the Heavens, the Earth and themselves. They believed that His Power was the greatest out of all deities. Yet at the same time they justified the existence of idols by claiming they were necessary intercessors or disposers of affairs.

Makkah which was a city founded on pure monotheism, had become the main centre of idol worship. All in all, a total of 360 idols were placed in and around the Kaaba during times of pilgrimage. These were sourced from tribes and clans throughout the entire Arabian peninsula. Placed prominently in front of the Kaaba was *Hubal*, an idol in the form of a man. On the mountains of As-Safa and Marwah they had placed two figures of stone: a male they called *Isaaf* and a female they called *Na'ilah*. Despite claiming that these idols were two people who had been turned to stone as a punishment for committing indecency in the Kaaba itself, they would touch each idol for blessings as they performed the rites of passing between the two mountains. There were also three notorious idols that they claimed were the "daughters of Allah". These they named al-Lat, al-'Uzzah, and Manat. Each of them had a major shrine where their adherents would visit, make prayers and place offerings.

The shrine of al-Lat was looked after by the Banu Thaqif in the city of Ta'if. This made their chiefs gain great wealth and influence, second only to the Makkans. The cult of al-'Uzzah was based near the Valley of Nakhlah, between the two mighty cities of Makkah and Ta'if. The idol was placed upon a tree they considered sacred. The Quraysh would journey there to offer sacrifices and seek blessings. They would also adopt names for themselves like "'Abd al-'Uzzah", meaning "servant of al-'Uzzah". As for Manat, it was placed in Qudayd, a place near to Yathrib. Its main devotees were the clans of Al-Aws and Khazraj.

Furthermore, different tribes and clans had their own 'gods'. Some would imitate former nations and adopt their traditions and gods, or the gods of their neighbours, the Persians and Romans. Some members of Banu Kalb were the worshippers of an idol named Wadd which they had placed in Dumat al-Jandal. Other tribes created shrines for Ya'uq, Yaghut, Suwa, or Nasr. These were all the names of idols that the destroyed nation of Prophet Noah (ﷺ) used to worship. The Arabs learnt their names and adopted them. There would also be the invention of hundreds of 'lesser gods', specific to a region, family or even a household.

Animism:

Some would worship the Sun and the Moon, Venus, or specific stars such as Sirius. Others would bow before particular trees, mountains or rocks. There were also communities of the so-called "Fire worshippers" with practices adopted from the Magians or Zoroastrians of Persia.

Other polytheists:

There were factions that worshipped the Angels, claiming they were the "daughters of Allah." Others would worship the Jinn, claiming that there was a kinship between them and Allah, or that they had a share in creation or that they knew the Unseen.

Atheism:

And among them were materialists who said they did not believe in God or the Day of Judgement at all. They claimed they had just come to be and would never be resurrected. These were generally not people of any great conviction or desire to change the thinking or practices of others. They simply wished to live their lives as they desired without any feeling of responsibility or accountability. They were often wealthy, considered themselves self-sufficient and therefore did not feel the need for worship. Culturally however, they were no different from the idol worshippers, and might on any given day also participate in their festivals or traditions. They were essentially followers of whatever and wherever their whims took them to.

People of the Book:

There were also small communities of Christians and Jews, but these were mostly found outside of Makkah. Both were called the "People of the Book" as they possessed Scripture. They were expecting the arrival of a Prophet in the near future - a Prophet who would destroy idolatry and establish monotheism throughout the Arabian peninsula. Some Jewish communities were established in Yathrib and in places like Khaybar. Christians could be found in monasteries throughout Syria and in places like Najran. A large part of the tribe of Banu Kalb were Christian as they lived near the frontiers of the Roman Empire and had interacted with them. Furthermore, across the Red Sea in Abyssinia was a well-known Christian kingdom named Axum with whom the Arabs had good trade links. A community named the Sabians also existed in Arabia, who it is said were followers of the *Zabur* (Psalms) revealed to Prophet Dawud (ﷻ). Or it has been said that they were the remnants of some communities who were upon the religion of Nuh (ﷻ).

The Upright Ones:

Scattered throughout Arabia and within Makkah were also some monotheists called *Hunafa*. They followed the upright religion of Ibrahim (ﷻ) and did not worship idols. These were few in number and they did not always proclaim their faith. They were generally people who adhered to strict principles and a certain code of conduct for themselves in contrast to others. The names of some of the more well-known of them are mentioned in books of history. Muhammad (ﷺ) was prior to the announcement of his Prophethood, a follower of the way of Ibrahim (ﷻ) and he refrained from all forms of injustice and indecency.

Their lifestyle:

Some of them lived bedouin lifestyles, travelling from place to place with their tents in search of pasture for their animals. They largely survived on milk, dates and meat. Others had settled in cities and towns around sources of water. Sheep, goats, cows, camels and chicken were their main livestock. Some near the coast were fishermen while others grew some limited crops or would forage, hunt, raid or trade. They were able to acquire pomegranates, figs, grapes, olives, raisins, honey, oil, barley or wheat flour at times. Their main mode of transport was camels which enabled them to traverse the harsh deserts between their settlements, although some also had horses or mules.

They wore light cotton clothing, cloaks, headdresses, turbans and sandals suitable for their environment. They prized gold and silver, silk, gemstones, fine mats, perfumes and spices which they could acquire through trade. They themselves produced some textiles, perfumes, cheese, clarified butter, leatherwork but not much else. They slept on mats stuffed with palm leaves and used utensils of pottery. They collected water from wells and stored it into vessels and skins. They did not have latrines but would relieve themselves out of sight outdoors, using stones to clean themselves then covering up the area.

Their characteristics:

The following traits would be found rampant in society as a whole, not necessarily in every person or applicable to every clan. However, a sign of the times was that things were allowed to deteriorate this far, and there was almost no one forbidding people from unworthy acts. They would drink intoxicants and lose their senses, gamble in excess and lose life savings. All forms of indecency were prevalent and not shunned. There was for many no concept of chastity. They would take pride in, and even advertise immorality. Children would be born not knowing their fathers. Others would be killed fearing poverty. They would eat carrion, and did not abstain from many harmful kinds of meat.

Grudges and wars would last generations, often starting over the most trivial things. Killing and pillaging the weaker ones was seen to add to honour and prestige, and the only deterrence from it was the threat of retaliation from a powerful clan or tribe. There were feelings of extreme zealotry and pride. Racism towards people from other lands, disdain between tribes, elitism among various classes and hatred for the followers of other faiths. Honesty was a rare thing to find among people. Lying had become second nature to most. Trust was the rarest of commodities. Whoever would be left in charge of anything would take it for himself. The marketplaces were notorious for fraud. Merchants would charge exorbitant rates to strangers, cheat customers in weight and measure, embezzle funds from their employers, and swear false oaths in order to sell defective goods.

However, it should be noted that the pre-Islamic Arabs did possess some good traits. The harsh climate in which they lived made them patient, brave-hearted, and generous to guests. They took pride in providing water and hospitality to pilgrims. They loved their freedom and did not tolerate the rule of outsiders. Thus, for the most part they rejected the influences of other societies. They were active people who valued physical strength and skills like horse-riding, wrestling, swimming, swordsmanship and archery. Although very few of them had learned to read, they had sharp minds with keen memories. They were eloquent speakers who could compose and memorise poetry easily. In fact at the time of the Revelation of the Qur'an, their skill with words had reached a point where they were considered to have reached the very pinnacle of linguistic expression. Such was the importance they gave to this, that they collected seven of the greatest poems from different eras and had them hung on the wall of the Kaaba itself to celebrate them. They never imagined these could ever be surpassed.

Their Practices:

They would organise several market fairs each year where poets, wrestlers and merchants would compete with one another. They would have an abundance of superstitious practices. They would beat, brand, starve, mutilate or burn alive camels, cows and sheep, and hope thereby for rain, healing or reward. They would not allow some animals to be milked, and forbid others from bearing any burden as they had set these aside for their idols. They would claim that certain meat was lawful for the men but not the women in some cases, but lawful for both of them in other cases. They would visit soothsayers and fortune tellers. They would obtain potions, charms, amulets and spells from those involved in black magic and sorcery. Some would seek news of the unseen from the Jinn, while others would call on them to offer protection. Or they would use divining arrows to make decisions or gain 'certainty'. All of this was from their own invention and not any Divine Revelation.

During the time of Hajj - the yearly pilgrimage - they would not enter their houses from their doors but from holes they made in the back, as they considered this a sign of piety for some reason. If people could not afford the expense of special uniforms for pilgrimage, they would make them circumambulate the Kaaba entirely unclothed, and claim that God had ordered this indecency. In any case, their worship would often be nothing more than whistling and clapping, or clinging and rubbing themselves against idols, or the throwing of perishable offerings onto altars that would soon be swarming with flies. And they knew that their forefather, Ibrahim (ع), never used to do any of these things.

Their society:

There was no emphasis on learning or reflection. Nor were these a people possessing the spirit of great curiosity and scientific invention. For the most part, they did not keep written records but preserved their history through oral traditions and poetry. Their civilisation was deemed primitive by their neighbours, the Romans and the Persians - both of whom had little interest in them as their environment was harsh and seemingly lacking in resources.

Justice did not exist in any real sense. Wealth determined status, and position overrode all considerations. There was no legal system, only the rule of force. The rich lived lavish lives of luxury, while the poor would be left to suffer in misery. Giving food to the impoverished was not encouraged. The orphans would be mistreated, and their wealth would be misappropriated by their supposed guardians.

Raiding was a lifestyle for many of them. Slavery was rife and those who unfortunate enough to become enslaved would often be treated worse than animals. Even a free born person from a noble house could easily end up a slave if they were kidnapped as a child, or if bandit slave-traders captured them on a journey. No slave owner would be questioned about their behaviour towards their slaves. Sometimes, a slave might be freed, but they would generally remain attached or allied to their former household or clan as they would not be able to survive by themselves without support. Or sometimes they might if their masters took a particular liking to them, be adopted as a son. Once their masters made the announcement, they were considered to be the real son of that person from that point on and the two would inherit from one another. And this was largely done because having many sons were considered as a source of pride, whereas daughters were for them a burden.

A man could marry an unlimited number of wives, and in some cases would even marry their close relatives. The men would not be asked about how they behaved with their women. Women were treated harshly and most had no place of importance in society. Some fathers would bury their infant daughters alive out of a feeling of shame. Those that did make it to adulthood were often treated as nothing more than objects of desire or a means of competing in the production of children. Instead of allowing them to inherit, women would themselves be inherited like property. If a woman became a widow, everything she owned could be taken from her by her relatives and she might be expected to remain for the rest of her days weeping for her husband. However, depending on her circumstances and family, she might also remarry. There were no guarantees for anyone in this society, nor was there any kind of advocacy or any movement for change.

Some Important Tribes of Arabia

يَا أَيُّهَا النَّاسُ إِنَّا خَلَقْنَاكُم مِّن ذَكَرٍ وَأُنثَىٰ وَجَعَلْنَاكُمْ شُعُوبًا وَقَبَائِلَ لِتَعَارَفُوا ۚ إِنَّ أَكْرَمَكُمْ عِندَ اللَّهِ أَتْقَاكُمْ ۚ إِنَّ اللَّهَ عَلِيمٌ خَبِيرٌ

"O mankind! Indeed We have created you from a male and female and made you peoples and tribes that you may know one another. Indeed, the most noble of you in the sight of Allah is the most righteous of you. Indeed, Allah is Knowing and Acquainted." [49:13]

Tribes of Old:

Banu 'Aad:

One of the destroyed nations of former times, most likely from the region of Al-Ahqaf in Southern Arabia. They came after the People of Prophet Nuh (ع). They built incredible cities like Iram, full of lofty pillars. Prophet Hud (ع) was sent to them but they refused to abandon idol worship, arrogance and oppression. When they crossed all limits they met their end by Divine Punishment: a furious wind and sandstorm came over them; breaking their bodies into pieces and leaving their cities buried under sand.

Banu Thamud:

One of the destroyed nations of former times, often identified as being from the region of Al-Hijr in Northern Arabia. They were the successors who came after the People of 'Aad. They used to carve their houses into the mountains. Prophet Salih (ع) was sent to them but they

27

refused to abandon idol worship, extravagance and tyranny. When they crossed all limits they met their end by Divine Punishment: a sudden earthquake and lightning blast that left them motionless in their homes. The other Arabian tribes knew of them and would regularly pass by their ruins during their journeys.

Banu Jurhum:

They were an ancient tribe that originated from Yemen. They came across Lady Hajrah (ع) and her son Isma'il (ع) in the Valley of Bakkah. When they saw the Well of Zamzam, they requested permission to settle there. The city of Makkah was thus founded and Jurhum became the custodians of the Kaaba when it was built. In time, Prophet Isma'il (ع) married from among them. However, eventually their descendants became unruly and they were forced out by the Banu Khuza'ah. Before they left, Jurhum destroyed the traces of the Well of Zamzam, so that its location became forgotten. It was centuries later when it was rediscovered by 'Abdul Muttalib.

Nabatu (Nabateans):

They were an ancient tribe of bedouins who lived in Northern Arabia and the Levant region from at least the time of Ibrahim (ع) Resembling the Banu Thamud in some respects, they were a polytheistic people who built the incredible stone city of Petra in around the First Century BC. They had wars with the Romans and the Kingdom of Judaea. Gradually over the following centuries, they had left their nomadic warlike lifestyles entirely and become an agricultural civilisation allied to the Romans. They converted to Christianity in the Fifth century AD.

Western Arabia:

Banu Khuza'ah:

For several centuries, they were the custodians of Makkah and the Holy House, after having expelled Banu Jurhum from that role. It is said that 'Amr ibn Luhay, the chief of Banu Khuza'ah was the first to introduce

28

polytheism to the Arabs of Makkah. He brought back idols from his journeys to Syria and used his position and wealth to encourage pilgrims to do the same. Eventually the Kaaba was surrounded with idols, and people left the religion of Prophet Ibrahim (ع). The Banu Khuza'ah lost their position as custodians when they were replaced by the Quraysh, but they remained around Makkah and in the surrounding regions. One of their well-known subclans was the Banu Mustaliq.

Banu Quraysh:

They were the descendants of Fihr ibn Malik. Fihr is said to have led the defence of the Kaaba against Yemeni tribes who wished to destroy it. From among his descendants was Qusayy ibn Kilab who brought together the scattered descendants of Fihr and gained power in Makkah. They established themselves as the custodians of Makkah after defeating Banu Khuza'ah. At the time of the Prophet's (ﷺ) mission, Quraysh's important subclans included Banu Hashim, 'Abd Shams, Umayyah, Taym, Zuhrah, Nawfal, Asad, 'Abd ad-Dar, Makhzum, 'Adiyy, Sahm, and Jumah. Prophet Muhammad (ﷺ) was from this tribe, specifically belonging to the clan of Banu Hashim, but was also related to other clans. Surah Quraysh of the Qur'an is named after this tribe: it recounts how Allah (ﷻ) aided them in the past and provided them with security in their land and an abundance of blessings and sustenance. However, a large part of the Quraysh were ungrateful, rejected Islam and opposed the Messenger (ﷺ) until after the Conquest of Makkah. After the Prophet (ﷺ) passed away, the caliphate remained in the hands of the Quraysh for a long period of time.

Banu Thaqif:

A tribe based around the city of Ta'if. They had great wealth and influence to the extent that they were regarded as the closest rivals to Quraysh. They had created a large shrine for an idol named al-Lat, which pilgrims would flock towards throughout the year. This tribe behaved very cruelly towards the Messenger of Allah (ﷺ), rejecting his invitation to Divine Guidance, and stoning him. Even so, he regarded them as his own people and prayed for their forgiveness. After the Conquest of Makkah, and the unsuccessful Siege of Ta'if, their chief, 'Urwa ibn Mas'ud at-Thaqifi accepted Islam. He was highly regarded throughout Arabia due to his great wealth and influence. He expected that his people would follow him in embracing the Faith, but instead they killed him. The Banu Thaqif also plotted to kill the Messenger of Allah (ﷺ) but failed to do so. Eventually, they sent a delegation of their chiefs to him and submitted. The Messenger (ﷺ) ordered them to demolish the temple of al-Lat and to break all their idols.

Banu Hawazin:

A large group of bedouin tribes that occupied the regions between Makkah and Yathrib. From among them was Banu Sa'ad, the clan of Halimah the wet nurse of Muhammad (ﷺ). He lived among them during the first years of his life. The Banu 'Amir and Banu Thaqif were also branches that originated from this tribe but went on to form their own identities while remaining close. During Muhammad's (ﷺ) teenage years, Banu Hawazin fought against the Quraysh and its allies in what came to be known as the Fijar war. This took place over four consecutive years at Ukaz with eight separate days of battle. A peace treaty was eventually effectuated with them, and the Banu Hawazin paid blood money. After the Conquest of Makkah, Banu Hawazin raised forces against the Muslims. Prophet Muhammad (ﷺ) and his followers fought against them at Hunayn. The Believers emerged victorious after a tense battle. He then placated the hearts of his vanquished foes with good treatment.

Banu 'Amr ibn 'Awf:

They had settled around Quba and had already accepted Islam by the time of the Hijrah. They were the first ones to offer the Prophet (ﷺ) hospitality when he arrived.

Banu Ghifar:

A tribe found in the South West of Yathrib. It is said that some of the members of this tribe were not polytheists but instead followed Judaism. They had a reputation for being fierce highwaymen who would pillage caravans for a living. The first person to accept Islam from them was Abu Dharr al-Ghifari, and he went on to guide many others.

Banu Qaylah:

A tribe of Arabs of Yemeni origin that settled in Yathrib. They were initially under the rule of the Jewish tribes. Banu Qaylah gained rule of Yathrib a century prior to the start of the Prophetic mission. After that differences began to appear among them and they became divided into opposing clans: Al-Aws and Khazraj. This culminated in the Battle of Bu'ath where Al-Aws gained a narrow victory after seeking assistance with the Jewish tribes. That took place seven years after the start of the Prophetic mission. The animosity between them continued to grow. In response Khazraj went to Makkah seeking the assistance of Quraysh. When they met Prophet Muhammad (ﷺ) they saw in him a solution not just to their war, but to all their problems, and so they embraced Islam. Eventually the entirety of Banu Qaylah - Al-Aws and Khazraj - accepted Islam and became known as *"Al-Ansar"*, meaning the Helpers. The Messenger of Allah (ﷺ) emigrated to their city along with the Believers from Makkah. The Ansar opened their homes to them, shared their wealth and supported them in every battle with their own lives. After the Conquest of Makkah, the Prophet chose to remain with them instead of returning to the city of his birth.

Banu Sa'ida:

A subclan of Khazraj. They were mostly idol worshippers but accepted Islam after their chief Sa'ad ibn Ubadah became a Muslim. After the lifetime of the Prophet (ﷺ), it was at their *Saqifah* (meeting hut) that Abu Bakr was selected as the first caliph.

Banu Najjar:

The Prophet (ﷺ) was related to this clan through his grandmother. Some of them were Jews but most were polytheists. They had all accepted Islam by the time of the Hijrah. When their chief As'ad ibn Zurarah died, Prophet Muhammad (ﷺ) became their chief. Abu Ayyub al-Ansari was from this clan - and it was at his house that he (ﷺ) stayed. Masjid an-Nabawi was built in their garden.

Banu 'Awf:

A Jewish tribe settled in Yathrib. They were Arabs who had accepted Judaism. They made a mutual defence treaty with the Prophet (ﷺ) after his emigration, mostly retaining their religion.

Banu Al-Harith:

A Jewish tribe settled in Yathrib. They were of Yemeni origin. They made a treaty with the Prophet (ﷺ) after his emigration, mostly retaining their religion.

Banu As-Shutaybah:

A Jewish tribe settled in Yathrib. They made a mutual defence treaty with the Prophet (ﷺ) after his emigration, mostly retaining their religion.

Banu Nadir:

A Jewish tribe settled in Yathrib. They sided with Al-Aws during the Battle of Bu'ath. After the Hijrah, they made a mutual defence treaty with the Prophet (ﷺ) for the protection of Madinah. Banu Nadir ended up breaking this treaty and betraying the other inhabitants of Madinah by siding with their enemies and plotting for their destruction. Therefore, after the Battle of Khandaq in which their plot failed, the Prophet (ﷺ) ordered the Believers to lay siege to their fortress. Eventually the Banu Nadir fled without any fighting taking place, and settled in other areas. Surah Hashr was revealed about their expulsion.

Banu Qaynuqa':

A powerful Jewish tribe settled in Yathrib. They sided with Khazraj during the Battle of Bu'ath. They had made a mutual defence treaty with the Prophet (ﷺ), but they broke the terms, siding militarily with the enemies of the inhabitants of Madinah and inciting civil unrest. For this they too were expelled.

Banu Qurayzah:

A Jewish tribe settled in what was then known as Yathrib. They sided with Al-Aws during the Battle of Bu'ath. They had made a mutual defence treaty with the Prophet (ﷺ), but broke it during the Battle of Khandaq when they sided with the invading Quraysh against the people of the city of Madinah. Following the victory of the Believers at Khandaq, Banu Qurayzah took up positions in their strongholds. The Believers laid siege to them, and following their surrender, a judge of their own choice judged them according to their own laws for betrayal. Thus, only their leaders who had broken their pacts, plotted a war and those who had spilt blood were executed. The rest of them were exiled from Madinah.

Central Arabia:

Banu 'Amir ibn Sa'sa'ah:

Not to be confused with Banu 'Amir ibn Lu'ayy, a clan from Quraysh. Banu 'Amir ibn Sa'sa'ah was an important tribe from the region of Najd, and was a branch of the Banu Hawazin. They were among the last to accept Islam in the lifetime of the Prophet (ﷺ). Some of them later battled with Abu Bakr during the Ridda wars.

Banu Hanifah:

A tribe based in Al-Yamama in the region of Najd. They gave the worst and most ugly reaction of any tribe when they were invited to Islam. They remained antagonistic until the final years of the Prophet (ﷺ)'s life, when they finally submitted. After he passed away, they quickly became apostates under the leadership of the false prophet Musaylimah the Liar. They were defeated in the Battle of Al-Yamama during the Ridda wars. They re-embraced Islam, but a portion of them apostated again when they joined the extremist Khawarij movement.

Banu Tamim:

A very large tribe localised around the region of Najd. Many of them lived a bedouin lifestyle, raising animals. Among them existed pure, clear-minded people whose belief was firm; but also from this tribe came a great number of ignorant and stubborn ones whose characteristics made them inclined towards extremism. Most did not accept Islam until after the Conquest of Makkah. After the lifetime of the Prophet (ﷺ), some of them renounced their Faith, supporting Musaylimah the Liar, or joining the extremist Khawarij movement.

Banu Asad ibn Khuzaymah:

Not to be confused with the Banu Asad of Quraysh. They were the inhabitants of Qatan in the region of Najd. They were known to be fierce warriors. Prior to accepting Islam, they were involved in several plots and conflicts against the Prophet (ﷺ). They later migrated to the region of Iraq, where some of them played an important role in later events: siding with 'Ali at Jamal and with Husayn at Karbala.

Northern Arabia:

Banu Kalb:

A bedouin tribe based around North-western Arabia and Syria. Its members were mostly Christian, but some were pagan: the worshippers of an idol named Wadd, and they had established a well-known shrine at Dumat al-Jandal. This was eventually demolished and the pagans among them accepted Islam, while the Christians for the most part retained their faith.

Banu Sulaym:

A tribe based in Northern Arabia, especially around the region of Harra. They were allied with Quraysh and were hostile to Islam. They were involved in the attack on Muslim missionaries at Bir Ma'una and were part of the aggressive confederates in the Battle of Khandaq. They finally accepted Islam after the Conquest of Makkah.

Southern Arabia:

Banu Azd:

This was a major tribe originating in Yemen but with many sub-branches. They were the inhabitants of Saba until the Maarib Dam collapsed, after which they dispersed. Azd of Shanu'a, Khuza'ah, Aslam, Al-Aws and Khazraj are some later offshoots of this tribe.

Himyar:

They were mostly former polytheists who converted to Judaism about two hundred years before the birth of the Prophet (ﷺ). The righteous King who was known as *Tubba*, was from them. They had ruled much of Yemen for about six hundred years. They referred to God by the name "Rahman-an". After the rule of the oppressive Dhu-Nuwas, their Kingdom was conquered in 525 AD by the Abyssinian Axumites who were Christians. After that, the governor Abraha ruled over them and established a grand cathedral trying to rival Makkah. In the time of the Prophet (ﷺ) several envoys were sent to them until they accepted Islam in the 8th year of Hijrah.

Banu Hamdan:

This was a major tribe in Yemen who were known for their courage and indomitable spirits. Among them were polytheists, Christians and Jews. Khalid ibn al-Walid was sent to them in the year 9 AH and he remained among them preaching for six months but did not gain any acceptance from them. Then the Messenger of Allah (ﷺ) sent 'Ali ibn Abi Talib to them in the year 10 AH and it is reported that the entire tribe accepted Islam in a single day at his hands. The Messenger of Allah (ﷺ) was delighted by this news and prayed for blessings upon them. Years later, Banu Hamdan supported 'Ali in the Battle of Siffin and composed a significant part of his army.

Madhij:

They were a large tribe of Yemeni origin, found throughout Southern and Central Arabia. They were famed for their martial prowess, and were particularly skilled in terms of horse-riding and archery. Following the Banu Hamdan becoming Muslims, Madhij also accepted Islam at the hands of 'Ali ibn Abi Talib.

Banu Kindah:

A tribe that was from Southern Arabia in the region of Yemen, although they had Northern branches too. Among them were Christian and Jewish clans as well as idolaters. They had various kings who once held considerable power throughout Central Arabia including in Al-Yamama, but eventually they lost their influence and retreated back to Yemen. The Prophet (ﷺ) approached them when they attended one of the fairs near Makkah. However they refused outright to support the Prophet (ﷺ) or to submit as Muslims at that time. They finally accepted Islam towards the end of the Prophet's (ﷺ) lifetime.

Previous Messengers of God

قُلْ مَا كُنتُ بِدْعًا مِّنَ الرُّسُلِ وَمَا أَدْرِي مَا يُفْعَلُ بِي وَلَا بِكُمْ ۖ إِنْ أَتَّبِعُ إِلَّا مَا
يُوحَىٰ إِلَيَّ وَمَا أَنَا إِلَّا نَذِيرٌ مُّبِينٌ

"Say: I am no new thing among the messengers, nor do I know
what will be done with me or with you. I only follow that which
is revealed to me, and I am but a plain warner." [46:9]

The *Rasul* (Messenger) is a guide whom Allah (ﷻ) has sent to a people who have disbelieved with a *Message* in order to bring them out of the manifold darknesses of ignorance into the light of Guidance. The word Nabi (Prophet) is often thought to be synonymous but according to some scholars, it refers to the one who receives Revelation and is sent to a people who have believed in order to keep them firm upon the Laws and Guidance given to them by the Rasul. Thus, every Messenger is a Prophet, but not every Prophet is a Messenger. According to the traditions, there have been 124,000 Prophets sent in total to mankind - 313 of them were Messengers, and 5 of them were establishers of a new system of Law. The stories and examples of some of them have been mentioned in the Qur'an. They have clear parallels with the life of the final Messenger (ﷺ). Here we will relate a few of them.

Nuh (Noah/Nauach)

He is said to have been the first Messenger to be sent to the children of Adam (ع). The people of his time had begun to worship idols that they had named Wadd, Suwa, Ya'uq, Yaghut and Nasr. These were likely the names of some pious people who had passed away. Nuh (ع) came to them with clear signs and invited them to worship Allah (ﷻ) alone and to reject all falsehood. His preaching might have been effective had it not been for the wealthy chiefs of his people whose arrogance turned them aside. Most of the people obeyed these chiefs instead of the Divine Guidance that was brought to them. Nuh (ع) remained patient despite the abuse and rejection he faced each day. After nine-hundred and fifty years of preaching day and night, openly and in secret, only a group of around eighty people believed.

Finally, Nuh (ع) was ordered by Allah, the Exalted and Wise, to build an ark and to take the necessary livestock with him. Once it was complete and all the Believers boarded, a large flood was sent upon the unjust and they all drowned. Nuh (ع), his family and the Believers, were all saved. Nuh (ع) then established a new city and a *Shar'iah*, a system of Law as commanded by God. The communities that formed from the descendants of these survivors remained upon it for a long duration. They gradually spread out to different parts of the earth.

Hud

He was from among the descendants of Nuh (ع). He was the Messenger sent to the tribe of 'Aad in the Al-Ahqaf region of Southern Arabia. 'Aad were given a great deal of wealth and physical prowess. However, they misused these things; spending extravagantly on monuments of pride and acting oppressively to those weaker in physical strength. Worst of all, they denied the very Lord who created them and instead began to associate partners with Him. Hud (ع) preached to his people about the Oneness of God and told them to abandon idol worship, injustice and arrogance. The people called him a 'liar', 'a sorcerer' and 'insane' and they persisted in their tyranny despite clear Signs and a long duration of preaching. Hud was instructed to warn them of an approaching chastisement. In the end, only a few believed and left the city with Hud (ع). The rest were destroyed by a furious sandstorm which obliterated all traces of their city which was named Iram.

Salih

He was a Messenger from among the descendants of Nuh (ع). He was sent to the tribe of Thamud in the area of Al-Hijr in Northern Arabia. Salih (ع) was well-regarded by his people due to the excellence of his lineage, his qualities and his character, so they had all expected he would become a man of great position and importance. However, when he began to preach the Oneness of God and called on them to abandon idol worship, they called him a liar and rejected him. This went on for a long time until they demanded a miraculous Sign, and it was shown to them. Even so, they transgressed all bounds after that and called Salih a 'magician'. Instigated by nine chiefs of different clans, they eventually plotted to kill Salih in a secret attack one night, then to deny it so his clan could not take revenge. But their plot was brought to naught. After providing a final warning to them, God commanded Salih (ع) to leave the city along with his family and the few who were Believers. Then the unjust ones were destroyed by a powerful earthquake after three days just as Prophet Salih (ع) had warned them.

Ibrahim (Abraham/Abram)

He was from among the descendants of Nuh (ع). He was a Messenger of Allah (ﷻ) whose call to monotheism reached far and wide. He was first sent to the people of Mesopotamia and their tyrannical king, Nimrod. Those people rejected the worship of Allah (ﷻ), and Ibrahim (ع) rejected the worship of their idols and everything they worshipped besides Allah (ﷻ). Despite overcoming them each time with convincing arguments, the people remained obstinate. Then, desiring to kill him, they threw him into a very large fire. When Ibrahim (ع) miraculously emerged from it unharmed, the people drove him out and exiled him from the city of his birth. Ibrahim (ع) continued preaching for a lifetime throughout different lands - Egypt, Canaan and Arabia. Some scrolls of wisdom were revealed to him, and he was commanded by God to establish a new *Shari'ah*, a system of Law. Eventually in his old age, he was given two sons, Isma'il (ﷺ) who was the ancestor of a large section of Arabs, and Ishaaq (ﷺ) who was the ancestor of the Jews. Both of them were Prophets and possessed great virtues. He built the Kaaba with Isma'il (ﷺ), and Masjid al-Aqsa with Ishaaq (ﷺ). The rites of Hajj - *Tawaaf*, *Sa'i*, stoning the pillars and sacrificing an animal - were established after various noteworthy incidents in the lives of Ibrahim and his family (ﷺ). Prophet Ibrahim (ﷺ) prayed for the security and providence of Makkah, for monotheism and leadership to remain among a section of his progeny, and for a future Prophet to appear among them to purify and guide them.

Lut (Lot)

He was the nephew of Ibrahim (ﷺ), being the son of his brother, Haran. He was one of the few who believed in him while he was in the city of his birth, and when he was driven out, he performed *Hijrah* alongside him. He helped Ibrahim (ﷺ) in his mission and displayed the highest degree of patience and sincerity in doing so until Lut (ﷺ) himself was given wisdom and appointed to Prophethood. He was sent as a Messenger to the People of Sodom and Gomorroh: a people who were involved in idol worship, banditry and unprecedented indecency. Lut (ﷺ) remained preaching among them for many years, but they did not accept the Divine Guidance that was brought to them. After they crossed all limits, Lut (ﷺ) was finally ordered to leave alongside his family, and the transgressive people were destroyed.

Isma'il (Ishmael/Yishma'el)

He was the long-awaited firstborn son of Ibrahim (ﷺ) who had reached old age by that time. Lady Hajrah, the mother of Isma'il (ﷺ), had been a slave. When Isma'il (ﷺ) was born, Allah the Almighty and Wise, commanded Ibrahim (ﷺ) to leave both of them in a desolate valley without water that was named the Valley of Bakkah. It was the place where Adam (ﷺ) had laid the foundations of the Most Ancient House of worship, and it was visited by all the Prophets (ع) after him. While his mother was searching frantically for water between two hillocks named As-Safa and Marwah, Isma'il (ع) kicked his heels on the ground, and a spring of clear water sprung forth from underneath him. Lady Hajrah made a structure around it and it became known as the Well of Zamzam. People settled in that area thereafter, and the city of Makkah was thus founded. Isma'il grew to become a righteous man, who was patient and true to his promise. He was also known to be a skilled archer. He married from among the Banu Jurhum, and his descendants thus became "Arabicised".

One day, Ibrahim (ع) came to Makkah to visit Isma'il (ع) and repeatedly saw a dream where he was sacrificing him. Therefore, Isma'il (ع) submitted immediately to that, knowing that the dreams of Prophets were true visions through which God may send His commands. However, once they had both submitted and passed the test, Isma'il (ع) was saved miraculously and a ram appeared sacrificed in his place. Isma'il (ع) was appointed to Prophethood and Messengership, tasked with promoting the worship of Allah (ﷻ) among the people of Arabia. He helped his father rebuild the walls of the Kaaba so that masses of pilgrims would come visit it for the purpose of worshipping Allah (ﷻ).

Ishaaq (Isaac/ Yishaaq)

He was the second son of Ibrahim (ع). His mother was Lady Sarah, the wife of Ibrahim (ع), who had been barren before the Angel Jibreel (ع) came to give them the good news of Ishaaq's (ع) miraculous birth. Ishaaq (ع) lived a righteous life. He continued preaching the Oneness of God to the people of Canaan and kept them firm on the Faith of Ibrahim (ع). He built Masjid al-Aqsa along with his father, forty years after the construction of the Kaaba. Prophethood was given to his son Yaqub (Jacob/Israel) (ع) and a great many of his descendants after him.

Yusuf (Joseph/Yosef)

He was the son of Yaqub (ع), grandson of Ishaaq (ع) and great-grandson of Ibrahim (ع). He was born in the land of Canaan. Yusuf (ع) was exceptionally handsome and was the most beloved child of his father, which brought about jealousy in his elder brothers. They faked his death and sold him into slavery. Yusuf (ع) was brought to Egypt where he was tested in many ways before being released from a prison where he had spent many years. He was then appointed to a position of great authority. His brothers who had betrayed him came to him seeking provisions at a time of famine, not recognising him. When Yusuf (ع) revealed himself to them, they felt ashamed and afraid. However, he then extended to his brothers one of the finest ever examples of forgiveness and generosity, and they finally acknowledged and recognised why Allah (ﷻ) had given him superiority over them. Then he invited his entire family to settle in Egypt with him with honour and dignity. They were known as the Bani Israel.

Shu'ayb

He was a Messenger from among the descendants of Ibrahim (ع) and was sent to the people of Madyan in Arabia. These people lived in a region of thicket and worshipped trees. Shu'ayb (ع) continued preaching among them for many years, ordering them to give up worship of all except Allah (ﷻ), to establish justice in their marketplaces instead of cheating people of their rights, and to refrain from ambushing travellers in every path. The people called Shu'ayb (ع) a 'liar', and a 'heretic'. They tried to compel his followers to return back to the ways of paganism. Since Shu'ayb (ع) belonged to a powerful clan who protected him, the Disbelievers refrained from harming him physically. Eventually, they forced Shu'ayb (ع) and his followers to leave the city. The Disbelievers were immediately destroyed by a severe punishment after him and they were left motionless in their homes.

Musa (Moses/Moshe)

He was a Messenger from among the Bani Israel and was born in Egypt during their period of enslavement. The tyrannical Pharaoh had a dream warning him of the end of his rule by the hands of someone from the Bani Israel so he plotted to kill all their newborn males. However, by the Plan of Allah (ﷻ), Musa (ؑ) ended up being raised in the palace by the Pharaoh himself and his wife Asiya, who was secretly a Believer concealing her faith.

Musa (ؑ) grew to be a righteous man who would go out to help the needy and protect the weak from oppression. One day, he defended a man from the Bani Israel against an oppressive soldier of the Pharaoh. The soldier ended up dying from that single strike, although that had not been the intention of Musa (ؑ). When the Pharaoh sensed in him a danger and plotted to kill him, Musa (ؑ) left the city of his birth and went to Madyan where he remained for ten years.

At the age of forty, he received his first Divine Revelation atop Mount Sinai. He was ordered to go back to Egypt along with his brother Harun (Aaron) and preach to the Pharaoh and his community. They remained there for a period of time, displaying clear Signs to them one after the other. However, the people, except for a few, only increased in disbelief and rebellion, accusing him of being a 'liar', 'insane' and a 'magician'. Eventually, as they intended to kill him and his followers, Musa (ؑ) and the Bani Israel left in the middle of the night, and were pursued by the Pharaoh and his army. Allah (ﷻ) miraculously split apart the sea for Musa (ؑ): his followers were all saved, while the Pharaoh and his army were all drowned. Later, the Ten Commandments, some Scrolls of Wisdom, and the *Taurat* (Torah) were revealed to Musa (ؑ), and he established a new system of Law. He continued preaching to the Bani Israel despite facing various trials from them including disobedience, hypocrisy and rebellion from many of them. However, through his continued efforts, and the efforts of successive Prophets after him, many members of the Bani Israel remained on Guidance for a long duration after him.

Ilyas (Elijah/Elias)

He was a Messenger from among the Bani Israel, sent to the Kingdom of Israel. Their king, Ahab, had married a pagan woman who introduced idol worship to the Bani Israel. The cult of Baal quickly became the national religion, and the teachings of the former Prophets were forgotten. Ilyas (ﷺ) came to them with convincing arguments and clear signs, but those with positions of authority continued in their rejection and forced Ilyas into exile. Each of those met humiliating deaths soon after him, and the rule of authority was taken away from them.

Yunus (Jonah/Yonah)

He was a Messenger from among the Bani Israel. He was sent to the Assyrian city of Nineveh in Northern Mesopotamia. This was a very large metropolis with a population exceeding one-hundred thousand people, most of whom were polytheists. Yunus (ﷺ) continued preaching among them without any of them accepting him. Yunus (ﷺ) was told to warn them of a coming punishment. After warning them, he left in a state of anger before the final command of God had come, instead of waiting until the last moment. After him, the people saw the signs of their imminent destruction and the entire city came out of their homes and began to repent. By this point, Yunus (ﷺ) had already travelled far away on a ship and was being put to trial by God due to his haste. Yet he too repented and praised his Lord with sincerity whilst being confined within a whale, so he received Divine Mercy. When he returned to his city, he found the people in masses declaring that there was none worthy of worship but God alone, and that Yunus (ﷺ) was the Messenger of God. They remained firm on the Truth for a long time after him.

44

'Isa (Jesus/Yeshua)

He was a Messenger from among the Bani Israel. He was sent to the Jews and to the Romans ruling over them. He was born miraculously to the Virgin Mary. He announced his Prophethood whilst still a newborn and defended his mother from slander. He lived a devout life of worship and was compassionate towards people. At around 30 years of age, his Prophetic Mission began, the *Injil* (Evangel) was revealed to him, and he was commanded by Allah (﷽) to establish a new system of Law. Although 'Isa (ﷺ) had shown many miracles proving that he was a true Prophet of God, he was mostly only accepted by the humble and weak of society, while the rich, powerful and supposedly learned rejected him.

The Disbelievers from among the Bani Israel and the Romans called him a 'liar', a 'magician', and 'heretic' and plotted to kill him. Their plot was frustrated when Allah (﷽) raised His Messenger, 'Isa (ﷺ) up to Heaven alive. 'Isa (ﷺ) had twelve disciples who had pledged to support him in his Mission. He had already informed them that there would be a period of time after him in which there would be no new Prophet until the Final Messenger that was to come, whom he referred to as *'Ahmad.'* He described his signs and characteristics so they would recognise and obey him. 'Isa (ﷺ) only ever referred to himself as a slave and Messenger of God. His earliest followers all accepted this and were Unitarian believers in only one God. After he was raised up, some confusion arose among his community and with the passage of time, they became divided into various sects each with their own ideologies. Some of them claimed that 'Isa the son of Mary (ﷺ) was in fact "the son of God". Others began to claim that he was part of God himself: some putting forward a Binitarian view and others later, a Trinitarian view. The truth of the matter would soon be clarified by the Final Messenger (ﷺ).

Ancestors of Muhammad (ﷺ)

وَإِذْ قَالَ إِبْرَاهِيمُ رَبِّ اجْعَلْ هَٰذَا الْبَلَدَ آمِنًا وَاجْنُبْنِي وَبَنِيَّ أَن نَّعْبُدَ الْأَصْنَامَ

"And when Ibrahim said: My Lord! make this city secure,
and save me and my sons from worshipping idols." [14:35]

The lineage of the Messenger of Allah (ﷺ) has been reported as follows: He is Muhammad ibn **'Abdullah** ibn **'Abdul-Muttalib** ibn **Hashim** ibn **'Abd Manaf** ibn **Qusayy** ibn Kilab ibn Murrah ibn Ka'b ibn Ghalib ibn **Fihr** ibn Malik ibn Nadr ibn **Kinanah** ibn Khuzaymah ibn Mudrikah ibn Ilyas ibn **Mudhar** ibn Nadr ibn Ma'ad ibn **'Adnan**. We have provided some brief details about the more prominent among his ancestors. We have not provided the lineage beyond 'Adnan, as this is as far as the correct names and order are known by us with certainty.

'Adnan

He was from the descendants of Isma'il (ع). He was a common ancestor for most of the Arabs found in Central, Western and Northern Arabia. He was the twentieth ancestor of Prophet Muhammad (ﷺ).

Mudhar ibn Nadr

He was the great-grandson of 'Adnan. His descendants formed the Mudhar tribe, the most important and influential of the four major branches of the 'Adnani Arabs.

47

Kinanah ibn Khuzaymah

He was a descendant of Mudhar. Kinanah was a man greatly esteemed by his people for his excellent qualities. His descendants, the Banu Kinanah, formed the largest, most powerful and respected Mudhari tribe from which the later tribes descended.

Fihr ibn Malik

He was a descendant of Isma'il from the line of 'Adnan. He led the defence of Makkah, rallying warriors from Banu Kinanah against aggressive tribes from Yemen who had come with the intention of destroying the Kaaba - the House of Allah (﷾). He looked after pilgrims to Makkah and due to his virtues attained a reputation of great respect and honour among all the Arabs.

Qusayy ibn Kilab

He was a descendant of Fihr. It is said his real name was Zayd. He brought together the Banu Fihr who had been scattered around different parts of Arabia, and settled them in Makkah. They, now known as Banu Quraysh, established themselves there, increasing in power until they replaced the Banu Khuza'ah as Custodians of Makkah and the Kaaba. As their leader, Qusayy put in place various traditions such as feeding and giving water to the pilgrims. These became highly revered posts after him, divided up between his sons and the subsequent clans that formed from their descendants. He built *Dar An-Nadwah*, which was later used as the official congress hall for all matters of importance.

'Abd Manaf

He was the son of Qusayy. His real name was Al-Mughirah. His elder brother was 'Abd ad-Dar. A disagreement took place after their father's death, regarding the rights and responsibilities each would take. It was eventually decided that 'Abd ad-Dar and his descendants would inherit the house of Qusayy named Dar an-Nadwa, which was the place for all official assemblies, whereas 'Abd Manaf and his descendants would have the honour of providing food and drink for the pilgrims to the House of Allah (ﷺ). 'Abd Manaf had many children and enjoyed great prestige during his life due to his wisdom and generosity. He was regarded as the foremost personality of Makkah and he lived an honourable life. He was buried in the Mu'alla graveyard in Makkah.

Hashim

He was the son of 'Abd Manaf. His original name was 'Amr, but people referred to him by the title *"Hashim"*, meaning "the one who crushes". This was given to him due to his practice of crushing bread and generously providing food to pilgrims. Hashim travelled extensively and was a far-sighted man with excellent business acumen. It was he who established trade links between Makkah and the surrounding Kingdoms, leading to the two great trade caravans referred to in Surah Quraysh of the Qur'an: the caravan of winter to Yemen and the caravan of summer to Syria. Hashim was thereafter held in much honour for the wealth he brought and prominence he thus brought to Makkah.

However, he did face two challenges before he ultimately became recognised as the foremost chief of Makkah. The first was a matter related to inheritance and the division of posts. Hashim formed an alliance with some of the clans, that was named "The Scented ones' as it was solemnised by dipping their hands in perfume. Against them were "The Alliance of the Confederates", composed of some of the other clans. Ultimately, it was settled peacefully. The second was a rivalry between him and Umayyah (the son of his twin brother 'Abd Shams), due to the latter's jealousy of his position. Umayyah called for a neutral judge to judge between them but Hashim was judged to be better in his qualities, deeds and character. Umayyah thus went into exile to Syria for a decade, thereby planting the seeds of animosity between their respective descendants (*Banu Hashim* and *Banu Umayyah*), which would lead to considerable conflict later on. Hashim died at the age of 33, after falling sick during a journey. He was buried in Gaza in Palestine.

'Abdul Muttalib

He was the son of Hashim. His real name was Shaybah. He was raised in Yathrib by his mother, but after the death of his father he came to Makkah. The people saw him accompanying and serving his uncle Al-Muttalib and assumed he was his slave, so they referred to him as "'Abdul Muttalib". Even after the reality was made clear, the name stuck and he continued to be called this in an affectionate manner. His fine qualities and outstanding traits soon earned the respect and admiration of the people of Makkah, and he went on to become the foremost of chiefs and leaders among them. He re-discovered the long-lost Well of Zamzam after having a dream in which he was ordered to dig at a certain place. Abraha's attempted attack on the Kaaba in the Year of the Elephant took place during his time as the leader of Makkah. He showed unshakeable Faith at that time and informed Abraha that Allah (ﷺ) would personally defend His House, which is exactly what happened.

'Abdul Muttalib had many sons including Al-Harith, Az-Zubayr, Abu Talib, 'Abbas, Abu Lahab, 'Abdullah and Hamza. Shortly after rediscovering the Well of Zamzam, at a time when he had only one son to defend him, he vowed that if he was given ten sons he would sacrifice one of them for the sake of Allah (ﷺ). When many years later it ended up being so, he remembered his vow. The name of 'Abdullah was drawn out in successive lots. The people resisted this and 'Abdul Muttalib himself was reluctant to sacrifice his most beloved son, but he had made a vow to Allah (ﷺ). Seeking a solution, he was advised to draw lots between increasing numbers of camels and 'Abdullah. Finally, when the number of camels reached 100, the lots repeatedly came in favour of the camels instead of 'Abdullah. 'Abdul Muttalib then sacrificed the 100 camels instead of his son. A year later, 'Abdullah married Aminah bint

Wahb. 'Abdul Muttalib thus became the grandfather of Muhammad (ﷺ) and raised him from the age of six until his own death two years later.

'Abdullah

He was the second youngest and most beloved son of his father 'Abdul Muttalib. He possessed fine qualities and a pure and honourable character. Just like Prophet Isma'il (ﷺ), he was very nearly sacrificed by his father out of obedience to Allah (ﷻ), but then ransomed by a great ransom. After this event, he married Aminah bint Wahb, a lady equally virtuous. 'Abdullah died suddenly from an illness whilst on a journey, shortly before the birth of their son, Muhammad (ﷺ). He was brought to Yathrib where he was buried.

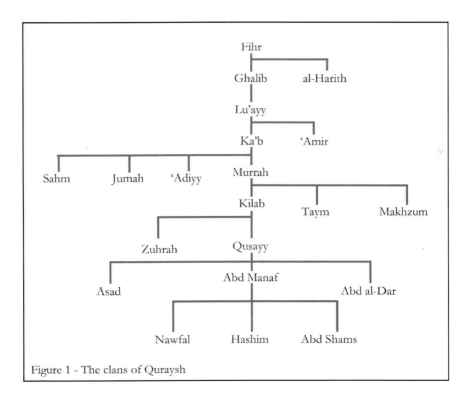

Figure 1 - The clans of Quraysh

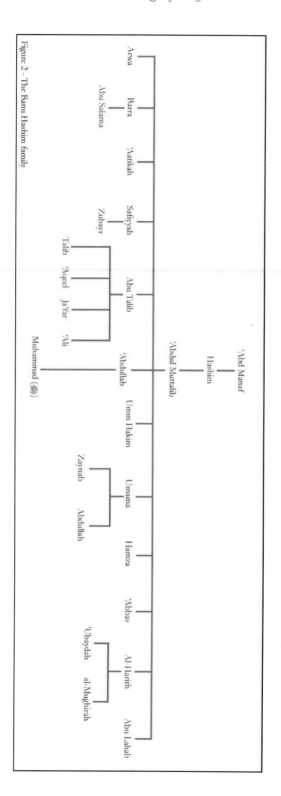

Figure 2 - The Banu Hashim family

How the Prophet (ﷺ) was Related to his People

وَهُوَ الَّذِي خَلَقَ مِنَ الْمَاءِ بَشَرًا فَجَعَلَهُ نَسَبًا وَصِهْرًا ۗ وَكَانَ رَبُّكَ قَدِيرًا

"And it is He who has created man from water, then He has made for him relationships of lineage and marriage, and your Lord is Ever-Powerful." [25:54]

Allah the Exalted and Almighty chose Muhammad ibn 'Abdullah (ﷺ) above all people. He created him with a character that was well-loved by them, and placed him among a lineage that was well-known and respected. He created closeness between him and other people such that every clan and tribe would in turn come to claim him as their own.

Lineage:

On his father's side he was from the clan of **Banu Hashim** of the tribe of **Quraysh**. He was the son of 'Abdullah ibn 'Abdul Muttalib ibn Hashim ibn 'Abd Manaf ibn Qusayy. He was a cousin to **Banu 'Abd ad-Dar**, **Banu Al-Muttalib** and **Banu Nawfal** since these clans were descended from the other children of 'Abd Manaf.

He was also a member of:

- **Banu Zuhrah** through his mother Aminah bint Wahb, the wife of 'Abdullah.
- **Banu Makhzum** through his paternal grandmother, Fatima bint 'Amr, the wife of 'Abdul Muttalib.

53

- The tribe of **Banu Qaylah**, the clan of **Banu Khazraj** and the family of **Banu Najjar** through his great-grandmother, Salma bint 'Amr, the wife of Hashim. He was thus related to the people of Yathrib and also to the **Bani Israel** since she was among the descendants of Prophet Ishaaq (ﷺ).

- **Banu Hawazin**, through his great-great grandmother, 'Aatikah bint Murrah, the wife of 'Abd Manaf.

- **Banu Khuza'ah** through his great-great-great grandmother Hubbah ibn Hulail, the wife of Qusayy ibn Kilab.

Going back further, he belonged to the group of **'Adnani Arabs**, the branch of **Mudhar** and the line of **Banu Kinanah**. Thus, the vast majority of people he came into contact with could consider Muhammad the Messenger of Allah (ﷺ) as their own relative.

Marriage:

At the age of twenty-five, Muhammad (ﷺ) married an honourable lady named Khadija bint al-Khuwaylid. She was from the Qurayshi clan of **Banu Asad ibn 'Abd al-'Uzzah**. She remained his only life partner for the next twenty-five years, until her death. She was the very first person to accept Islam. Afterwards, following the Hijrah and certain battles, it became increasingly important to create peace between different people. Among other reasons, the Prophet (ﷺ) married in order to strengthen ties between him and other tribes and clans. This would give them the honour of being part of the Prophet's (ﷺ) family, and would go a long way in placating their hearts after conflict. He married these women:

- Sawdah bint Zam'ah, linking him to **Banu 'Amir ibn Lu'ayy**.

- 'A'isha bint Abu Bakr, making him more closely related to **Banu Taym**.

- Hafsah bint 'Umar, making him more closely related to **Banu 'Adiyy**.

- Juwayriyyah bint al-Harith, reconciling him with **Banu Mustaliq**,

- Safiyyah bint Huyayy, creating a bridge with **Banu Nadir** and **Banu Harith**.

- Umm Habiba bint Abu Sufyan, further relating him to **Banu 'Abd Shams**,

- Maymunah bint al-Harith making him more closely related to **Banu Makhzum**.

- Umm Salamah bint Abi Umayyah, also relating him to **Banu Makhzum**.

- Zaynab bint Khuzaymah, making him more closely related to **Banu al-Muttalib**.

- Zaynab bint Jahsh, linking him to the tribe of **Banu Asad ibn Khuzaymah**.

It was not the case that these marriages were merely political or for the sake of convenience. The strengthening of ties between clans and tribes was one of the blessings that Allah the Most High had placed in these marriages. However, in most of these cases there were several other reasons why the Prophet (ﷺ) married these particular women. Some he married in order to provide support for them after they became widowed - and thereby encourage other believers to do likewise.

Nor can it be said that the Prophet (ﷺ) married out of a desire for women. He had remained monogamous by choice throughout his entire youth. Furthermore, it should be noted that despite having so many wives, the Prophet (ﷺ) maintained the rights of all of them, treated them in the best manner with the utmost affection, respect and dignity. They were even given the title of *"Ummuhat al-Mu'mineen"* which means "The Mothers of the Believers" to indicate their special status.

Description of the Prophet (ﷺ)

الَّذِينَ آتَيْنَاهُمُ الْكِتَابَ يَعْرِفُونَهُ كَمَا يَعْرِفُونَ أَبْنَاءَهُمْ

"Those whom We have given the Book recognise him as they recognise their sons..." [2:146]

His face:

His face was large and slightly oval in shape; neither very fleshy nor very round. His skin was light brown in tone; neither extremely pale nor very dark. His eyes were large and deep black in colour. He had long eyelashes and eyebrows that were thick and curved. His teeth were white and beautiful. His hair was dark and reached up to his earlobes, but was neither straight nor extremely curled. His beard was thick, full and always well-groomed.

His body:

Whenever he stood among a group of people, he appeared to be the greatest of them in stature, but he was neither extremely tall nor short. His height was somewhere in the middle. His build was strong and muscular. His joints and limbs were large and well-formed. His skin was very soft and delicate and a pleasant scent emanated from it. His neck was long and fine. His body was not full of hair, but he had a fine line that ran from his chest to his navel. On his back, between his shoulder blades was found a mark known as *Khatam an-Nabuwwah* which means "the Seal of Prophethood." This has been described as an egg-shaped arrangement of hairs, and it was a sign referred to in previous Scriptures that clearly identified him as the Final Prophet of God.

His voice:

His voice was somewhat deep and resonant, but not coarse or harsh in any way. When he spoke it was in a measured tone. Every word was distinctly enunciated and could be clearly heard. He did not speak too fast or too slow. He was eloquent: he was not excessively talkative nor was he taciturn. He did not raise his voice except for matters of great importance, and when he addressed people he did so in a way full of warmth and compassion.

His clothing:

He dressed in simple clothing. His dignity was apparent, though he would not wear silk or gold or any other outwards symbols of his status. He would wear the same kinds of garments as the ordinary people and did not seek superiority over them in this respect. His preferred colours were green and white. Often he would be seen with a cloak around his shoulders. He would place a turban on his head: sometimes green or white or black in colour. He wore a silver ring on his right hand. He would wear sandals that he would often mend himself.

His habits:

He would wear perfume of a pleasant scent. He was always well-groomed and was a man of exceptional cleanliness. He would clean his teeth and perform ablution many times a day. He would wake up before dawn and remember God. He would work throughout the day and meet the needs of his family. He would sleep in the early part of the night and rise in its middle to remember his Lord. He would fast often, and would ask for forgiveness frequently for himself and his community.

His manners:

His happiness could be seen from his face. He would not laugh loudly but his smile would broaden. When he spoke to anyone, he would turn his entire body towards them and listen attentively. He was never shameless, but always behaved with respect and shyness. He did not speak harsh words or discuss unworthy things. He would visit the sick and spend time with the elderly. Whenever he came across an orphan he would treat them with the greatest of affection. When he was asked for something he would not refuse.

His characteristics:

He was cheerful in disposition, generous of heart and fearless in spirit. In times of trial, he was patient and he did not lose his bearing or dignity. In times of blessings, he was thankful and increased in humility. He was the most truthful of people and the kindest of them. When he was silent, he commanded respect. When he spoke, he would be heard. He was very perceptive, far-sighted and excellent in judgement. His heart was not attached to worldly things, but he associated with people, socialising with them, attending their gatherings and alleviating their concerns. He was aware of all matters relating to his people: he was the most eloquent of them in their language, the most informed of them of their history and genealogies, and the most acquainted of their strengths and weaknesses. He was not vengeful, but forgave easily. There was no one who entered his presence except that they felt honoured, no one who spoke to him except that they were heard, and no one who listened to him except that they were guided.

The Messenger of Mercy

His Titles

Muhammad (ﷺ) was known throughout his life by many names and titles. These include:

- **Abul Qasim** - The Father of Al-Qasim
- **Mustafa** - The Chosen one
- **Hamid** - The one who Praises
- **Ahmad** - The Most Praiseworthy
- **Al-Mahi** - The Effacer (of falsehood)
- **As-Sadiq** - The Most Truthful one
- **Al-Amin** - The Most Trustworthy one
- **Al-Aqib** - The Final one
- **Al-Muzzammil** - The Wrapped up (in his Cloak)
- **Al-Muddatthir** - The Covered up
- **As-Sayyid** - The Master
- **At-Tahir** - The Pure one
- **Al-Kamil** - The Perfect
- **Muhyi** - The Restorer of (spiritual) Life
- **Mansoor** - The one who is Helped
- **Al-Hadi** - The Guide
- **Ra'ufun** - The Kind one
- **Khayrul Khalq** - The Best of creation

- **RasulAllah** - The Messenger of Allah

- *NabiAllah* - The Prophet of Allah

- *Al-Ummi* - The Unlettered/From Ummul Quraa'

- *Nabi-ur Rahmah* - The Prophet of Mercy

- *Rahmatullil 'Aalameen* - Mercy to the Worlds

- *Nurullah* - The Light of Allah

- *At-Tayyib* - The Good

- *As-Siraaj al-Muneer* - The Illuminating Lamp

- *Al-Hashir* - The Gatherer

- *Habibullah* - The Beloved of Allah

- *Khatimul-Anbiya* - The Seal of the Prophets

- *Al-Mudhakir* - The Reminder

- *As-Shahid* - The Witness

- *Al-Bashir* - The Bringer of Glad Tidings

- *An-Nadhir* - The Warner

- *Ad-Da'i* - The Caller

- *'Abdullah* - The Servant of Allah

- *As-Shaafi* - The Intercessor

- *Sayyidul Mursaleen* - Master of the Messengers

- *Imaamul Muttaqeen* - Leader of the Pious

- *Ta-Ha* - its meaning is not clear to us

- *Ya-Seen* - its meaning is not clear to us

The Hijri Calendar

The Islamic or "Hijri calendar" is a twelve-month lunar calendar. As it is based on the cycles of the moon, the number of days in each month are not fixed, but can vary from 28, 29, or 30 days from year to year. It is the same system as was used by the pre-Islamic Arabs and the names of the months are the same.

It is now named 'Hijri' because the base year (i.e. year 1) is the year that Prophet Muhammad (ﷺ) performed 'Hijrah', or emigration from Makkah to Madinah. A number followed by the letters B.H. (*Before Hijrah*) or A.H. (*Anno Hijrah*, the Year of Hijrah) indicates how many years before or after the Hijrah a given event took place. Prior to this system being adopted during the caliphate of 'Umar, the second caliph, there was no standardised way in which the year was recorded. They would simply use any significant event as a point of reference for other years as they saw fit.

The months of the Hijri Calendar are as follows:
1. Muharram
2. Safar
3. Rabi' al-Awwal
4. Rabi' al-Akhir
5. Jumada al-Ula
6. Jumada al-Akhir
7. Rajab
8. Sha'ban
9. Ramadhan
10. Shawwal
11. Dhil-Qa'dah
12. Dhil-Hijjah

Of these, four of them are called the Sacred or Forbidden Months, as fighting is prohibited in them. These are Dhil-Qa'dah, Dhil-Hijjah, Muharram, Safar, and Rajab. Dhil-Hijjah was the most important month as it was when the *Hajj* or major annual Pilgrimage of Makkah took place. Dhil-Qa'dah, which was the month before it, and Muharram which was the month after it, were made Sacred so that pilgrims could safely travel to and from Makkah without fear of warfare, retribution or raids. Rajab which was separate from the others and located in the middle of the year was made Sacred because it was a month when the *'Umrah* or minor pilgrimage to Makkah would be performed by many.

This was a custom that had been present from the time of Isma'il (ع) and was for the most part strictly adhered to. A famous exception in the Jahiliyyah times was *Harb al-Fijar* War (The Sacrilegious War), which broke out in Dhil-Qa'dah at the annual fair of Ukaz.

The Qur'an (see Verse 9:36) and the Messenger of Allah (ﷺ) confirmed the importance of the Sacred Months and reiterated that fighting was forbidden in them except in very specific and exceptional circumstances of self-defence.

You may also note that throughout this text we have also used the Gregorian Calendar (which uses BC and AD). This uses the life of Prophet Jesus (ع) as a reference point, and should already be familiar to most readers.

Chronology

قُل لَّوْ شَاءَ اللَّهُ مَا تَلَوْتُهُ عَلَيْكُمْ وَلَا أَدْرَاكُم بِهِ ۖ فَقَدْ لَبِثْتُ فِيكُمْ عُمُرًا مِّن قَبْلِهِ ۚ أَفَلَا تَعْقِلُونَ

"Say: If Allah had desired (otherwise) I would not have recited it to you, nor would He have taught it to you; indeed I have lived a lifetime among you before it; do you not then understand?" [10:16]

Before the announcement of Prophethood

Birth: (53 BH / 570 AD)

12th (or 17th) Rabi' al-Awwal: In the Year of the Elephant (570 CE), fifty days after the attack on the Kaaba was miraculously averted, Muhammad (ﷺ) is born to Lady Aminah bint Wahb. His father, 'Abdullah ibn 'Abdul Muttalib had already passed away some weeks before on a journey. At the age of eight days old he is given to a wet nurse, Halimah, to be raised in the clear air of the desert where it is hoped he will grow healthy and strong and become eloquent in speech.

Age 6: (47 BH / 575 AD)

Muhammad (ﷺ) is returned to Makkah. He accompanies his mother on a journey to the city of Yathrib where they visit the grave of his father, 'Abdullah. Not long after this, his mother Aminah falls sick and also passes away. He is then taken into the care of his grandfather, 'Abdul Muttalib.

Age 8: (45 BH / 578 AD)

'Abdul Muttalib, the most respected chief of Makkah, passes away. Abu Talib becomes the guardian of his nephew, Muhammad (ﷺ), as well as the new chief of the clan of Banu Hashim.

Age 12: (41 BH / 582 AD)

Muhammad (ﷺ) travel to Syria with his uncle, Abu Talib. He meets a monk named Bahirah who recognises signs of his Prophethood and warns Abu Talib to keep him hidden from those who would have enmity towards him.

Age 15-19: (38-34 BH / 585-589 AD)

Dhil-Qa'dah: The Fijar war takes place at Ukaz during a month in which fighting is forbidden. It arises after a man from Quraysh kills a man from Banu Hawazin, and then various clans and their allies get involved in the ensuing conflict. It becomes prolonged and bloody. Abu Talib, being the chief of Banu Hashim, has to also take part as his allies came under attack. Muhammad (ﷺ), aged 15, is present but does not participate in the fighting. He witnesses the atrocities of that war and is affected by the needless loss of life. When the war comes to an end after four years of intermittent fighting, a peace treaty is made and blood money is paid to the side with the greater casualties.

Age 20: (33 BH / 590 AD)

Hilf-ul-Fudul (the alliance of the virtuous) is established. Al-'Aas ibn Wa'il, a rich man from Quraysh's nobility, defrauds a traveller from Yemen and refuses to return his goods. When he realises there is no one he can turn to for help, the man from Yemen shouts an appeal to the entire community of Makkah. Some members of Bani Hashim, Bani Zuhrah, Bani Asad, and Bani Taym meet together and conclude that something needs to be done to establish justice and hold people to account. They had just seen the evil effects of tribalism in the recent war, so they take a firm pledge to help every stranger needing help, and aid every oppressed person regardless of tribal affiliation. They then rush out to help the man to retrieve his goods. Among those present and who agree to this is Muhammad (ﷺ). At every opportunity he hastens towards this cause and through him the rights of many are restored. Soon he is known far and wide as Muhammad *al-Amin*: Muhammad, the Trustworthy one.

Age 25: (28 BH / 595 AD)

Muhammad (ﷺ) is employed to travel to Syria with a trade caravan. When he returns, his new employer, Khadija bint Khuwaylid becomes very impressed with his honesty and his great moral character. She ends sending a marriage proposal to him, which he accepts. Khadija and Muhammad (ﷺ) establish a happy and harmonious marriage together.

Age 35: (18 BH / 605 AD)

The Kaaba is rebuilt. When a flood damages some of the walls of the Kaaba, the Quraysh decide to rebuild it, insisting that only the purest money is used for it. Once its construction is complete, all that remains is to set the Black Stone in its place. Each clan vies for this honour and tempers flare to boiling point. Then, just as conflict seems inevitable, Muhammad (ﷺ) arrives and puts an end to their conflict with a solution acceptable to all. He places the Black Stone onto his cloak, and instructs a member from each clan to raise a part. When they carry it to its position, Muhammad (ﷺ) himself finally edges it into place.

The Makkan Period of the Mission:

Age 40: (13 BH / 610 AD)

Bi'that - the start of the Prophetic Mission. Muhammad (ﷺ) has been seeing true dreams and hearing declarations from the unseen that he is a Prophet. These have been increasing in intensity throughout Rajab and Sha'ban, and he spends most of the month of Ramadhan in meditation.

Ramadhan: The first Revelation of the Qur'an in the cave of Al-Hira. The Prophet (ﷺ) begins to invite certain individuals to Islam in secret. Khadija, Ali, Zayd, Lubabah and Abu Bakr are the earliest to testify.

Age 41: (12 BH / 611 AD)

Preaching continues in secret and the first Islamic centre is established in the house of Al-Arqam ibn Abil Arqam. The number of Muslims reaches forty.

Age 43: (10 BH / 613 AD)

Da'wat Dhul Ashirah: The Prophet (ﷺ) invites his clan of Banu Hashim to Islam. Abu Lahab shows his disbelief, while others profess their faith.

Age 44: (9 BH / 614 AD)

The first public proclamation. The Messenger of Allah (ﷺ) invites all the people of Makkah to Islam. Abu Lahab openly mocks this and Surah Lahab is revealed as a result. After he (ﷺ) continues with his mission, more and more people are attracted to Islam. The chiefs of Quraysh approach Abu Talib asking him to stop his nephew from preaching. The Prophet (ﷺ) refuses to stop and Abu Talib pledges to protect him under all circumstances.

Age 45: (8 BH / 615 AD)

Hamza, the uncle of the Prophet (ﷺ), openly declares his Faith. After a great deal of persecution on the early Believers, many of them emigrate to Abyssinia. The Quraysh pursue them but An-Najashi after hearing the Qur'an, refuses to give them up.

Age 46: (7 BH / 616 AD)

The persecution increases. 'Umar ibn al-Khattab intends to kill the Prophet (ﷺ), but ends up also becoming a Muslim. The polytheists of Quraysh are now afraid that they will be unable to contain the spread of Islam, so they continue to plot.

Age 47: (6 BH / 617 AD)

Muharram: The beginning of the boycott against Banu Hashim. A pact to straiten them economically is made against them by the other clans, which they write onto a parchment that they hang in the Kaaba itself. People refuse to buy, sell, intermarry or associate with them in any capacity - and it is implied that the next step will be violence. As a result of this, the Banu Hashim retreat to a narrow valley behind their houses for their own protection.

Age 48: (5 BH / 618 AD)

The Banu Hashim continue to suffer. Khadija spends her entire wealth to prevent them from starving. Meanwhile Abu Jahl and the other leaders of the pagans exert further pressure.

Age 49: (4 BH / 619 AD)

The end of the boycott. A quarrel arises among the Quraysh about whether to continue the boycott. The parchment is miraculously found eaten by ants except for the words "*Bismika Allahumma*" (In your Name, O Allah") just as the Prophet (ﷺ) has informed them would be the case. The pagans relent for a time and the Banu Hashim are allowed to return to their homes.

69

Age 50: (3 BH / 620 AD)

<u>Rajab-Ramadhan</u>: Abu Talib (26th Rajab) and then Khadija (10th Ramadhan) both pass away, within a short time of each other. The Prophet (ﷺ) names this year *'Aam al-Huzn*, "the Year of Grief". The persecution from the pagans intensifies upon him and Makkah no longer is a safe place.

The Prophet (ﷺ) visits Ta'if and preaches to them, but the people reject him and throw stones at him. When offered by God the opportunity for their destruction, the Prophet (ﷺ) prays for their forgiveness instead.

<u>Dhil-Hijjah</u>: Six people from Yathrib meet with the Prophet (ﷺ) and accept Islam. They then go back to their own people to begin preaching.

Age 51: (2 BH / 621 AD)

The Messenger (ﷺ) continues inviting surrounding tribes to Islam. He faces a lot of rejection and abuse from each of them but does not give up on their guidance.

<u>Dhil-Hijjah</u>: The First Pledge of Al-'Aqabah. Twelve men from Yathrib secretly meet with the Messenger (ﷺ) at a mountain pass and pledge their loyalty to his Divine mission. He sends Mus'ab as his representative to the people of Yathrib to help prepare the rest of the community for his eventual arrival.

Age 52: (1 BH / 622 AD)

<u>27th Rajab</u>: The Isra and Mi'raaj. The Prophet (ﷺ) is taken from Makkkah to Jerusalem, then raised to the Heavens in a single night. He is shown many Signs, speaks to the Lord of the worlds (ﷻ), and then the five daily prayers are given to him before he returns.

<u>Dhil-Hijjah</u>: The Second Pledge of Al-'Aqabah. Eighty-three new Muslims from Yathrib meet secretly with the Prophet (ﷺ) at a mountain

pass. They pledge their allegiance to the Divine Mission and invite the Prophet (ﷺ) to come to Yathrib as their leader.

Age 53 (Year of Hijrah / / 623 AD)

The order for emigration to Yathrib is given. The Believers proceed to emigrate in small groups at a time. The Messenger (ﷺ) himself remains in Makkah until almost everyone has gone.

28th Safar: The Quraysh plan to assassinate the Prophet but their attempt is thwarted. 'Ali volunteers to risk his own life by sleeping in place of him in his bed, while the Prophet (ﷺ) emigrates to Yathrib accompanied by Abu Bakr. The majority of the Believers have already emigrated. Spurred by Abu Jahl's promise of a reward, the entirety of Quraysh set off in pursuit after the Prophet (ﷺ) but are thwarted by the Divine Plan at every turn.

The Madinan Period of the Mission:

Age 53: (1 AH / 623 AD)

12th Rabi' al-Awwal: The Prophet (ﷺ) is given a warm welcome by its people and the city is renamed to *"Madinatun-Nabi"* – "the City of the Prophet (ﷺ)". He brings peace between two long-warring clans and establishes the first Masjid. This year is later known as the Year of Hijrah, after which all other years are reckoned in the Islamic calendar.

Age 54: (2 AH / 624 AD)

17th Ramadhan: The Battle of Badr. Led by Abu Jahl, the Makkan pagans attempt to destroy the nascent Islamic movement. Despite outnumbering the Muslims by a ratio of three to one, they are defeated decisively. Seventy Makkan pagans are killed and another seventy are captured. All but two of these prisoners are released through various means - and a number of them actually embrace Islam.

Age 55: (3 AH / 625 AD)

<u>7th Shawwal:</u> The Battle of Uhud. Under the leadership of Abu Sufyan, the pagans fight the Muslims once more. The Muslims are on the verge of victory, when some of them longing for worldly gain, ignore specific orders of Prophet Muhammad (ﷺ). This leads to them being defeated and the Prophet (ﷺ) himself is badly wounded. Hamza ibn 'Abdul Muttalib is martyred and his body is badly mutilated. In an act of vengeance and enmity, Hind, the wife of Abu Sufyan, chews his liver.

Age 56: (4 AH / 626 AD)

The Believers suffer two acts of betrayal. Seventy Muslim missionaries are attacked and killed by the Banu Lahyan, during their expedition of Bir Ma'una. Secondly, the Banu Nadir tribe breaks their pledge and is therefore expelled from Madinah.

Age 57: (5 AH / 627 AD)

<u>Shawwal:</u> The Battle of Khandaq. The Quraysh enlist the help of their allies from among the pagan Arabs and Jewish tribes in order to make an all-out attack on Madinah. However, news reaches the Prophet (ﷺ) who orders a defensive trench to be dug around the city. After a month-long siege, the Quraysh and their allies are defeated and disbanded, and they return back in disgrace.

Age 58: (6 AH / 618 AD)

<u>Dhil-Qa'dah:</u> The Treaty of Hudaybiyyah. The Prophet (ﷺ) signs a seemingly unfavourable ten-year peace treaty with the pagans of Makkah. However, the Divine Revelation calls it a "Manifest Victory": the truth of which gradually becomes clear, as they are free to preach to various tribes. Huge numbers of people now begin to accept Islam.

Age 59: (7 AH / 629 AD)

Dhil-Qa'dah: The Muslims perform 'Umrah to Makkah as was agreed.

Safar: The Battle of Khaybar. The Muslims lay siege to and gain victory against the pledge-breaking Jews of Khaybar.

Age 60: (8 AH / 630 AD)

1st Jumada al-Ula: The Battle of Mutah. An army of three thousand Muslims are sent north against the Romans who are planning an attack. They are confronted by an army of at least ten thousand soldiers. Zayd ibn al-Haritha, Ja'far ibn Abi Talib and 'Abdullah ibn Rawaha are all martyred. However under the leadership of Khalid ibn al-Walid the Muslims gain victory.

20th Ramadhan: The Conquest of Makkah. After the Quraysh unilaterally break the Treaty of Hudaybiyyah, the Messenger of Allah (ﷺ) is ordered to march to Makkah along with the Muslims who are now ten thousand in number. They camp at a place just outside of it. Abu Sufyan and the remaining chiefs of Quraysh seeing their numbers, realise that they can no longer resist. He and the rest of the polytheists at this point accept Islam. The Muslims enter Makkah peacefully whilst wearing the clothing of pilgrims. The Kaaba is cleansed from all the idols and every trace of polytheism is finally removed from the entirety of Makkah. Instead of taking revenge upon his enemies, Prophet Muhammad (ﷺ) forgives them, recounting to them the example of Yusuf (ع) to his brothers.

Shawwal: The Banu Hawazin, Banu Thaqif and their allies plan an attack against the Muslims. The Prophet (ﷺ) mobilises an army which includes many of his former enemies including Abu Sufyan. The Battle of Hunayn takes place in which most of the Muslims flee after an ambush and abandon the Prophet (ﷺ), but through the hands of a steadfast few the Muslims gain victory. The Hawazin and their allies are defeated

73

decisively and they too submit. The Prophet (ﷺ) then gives his former enemies the bulk of the spoils as a gift to root out what remains of rancour in their hearts.

Age 61: (9 AH / 631 AD)

Rajab: The expedition to Tabuk. In order to ward off an attack by the Romans, the Prophet (ﷺ) leads an army to Tabuk, a region at the frontier. After twenty days, they return without any conflict having taken place.

Age 62: (10 AH / 632 AD)

8th-10th Dhil-Hijjah: The Farewell pilgrimage. The Prophet (ﷺ) delivers a moving sermon to the pilgrims. He advises them of many important matters that they should remember.

18th Dhil-Hijjah: The event of Ghadir. The Messenger of Allah (ﷺ) on the way back to Madinah stops everyone to make an announcement in favour of 'Ali ibn Abi Talib.

24th Dhil-Hijjah: The event of *Al-Mubahala*. A group of Christians monks dispute with the Prophet (ﷺ), and accept a challenge for mutual imprecation. When the appointed time comes, they see that he has brought only his nearest family: Ali, Fatima, Al-Hasan and Al-Husayn, so they become afraid and back out of the challenge.

Age 63: (11 AH / 632 AD)

28th Safar (or 12th Rabi' al-Awwal): The Prophet (ﷺ) passes away after a brief illness. He returns to the Lord of the Worlds, having completed his illustrious mission.

The Teachings of Islam

رَبَّنَا وَاجْعَلْنَا مُسْلِمَيْنِ لَكَ وَمِن ذُرِّيَّتِنَا أُمَّةً مُسْلِمَةً لَّكَ وَأَرِنَا مَنَاسِكَنَا وَتُبْ
عَلَيْنَا إِنَّكَ أَنتَ التَّوَّابُ الرَّحِيمُ

"And, Our Lord, make us both submissive to You and (raise)
from our offspring a nation submitting to You, and show us
our ways of devotion and turn to us (mercifully), surely You
are the Oft-returning (to mercy), the Merciful." [2:128]

What is Islam? Islam means the state of peace achieved only through submission to God. This submission is expressed through both beliefs and actions. Whoever does this is called a 'Muslim', or 'one who submits.' Islam is therefore not a new religion, because every believing nation in the past that followed the Guidance sent to them by the Messengers of God were Muslims and on the way of Islam. The specific Revelations, Rites and Laws that were given to them differed in the details, but the core of their teachings remained the same.

When Muhammad (ﷺ) the Messenger of God was appointed to his Mission, he began by first calling people to the foundations of Belief. Then gradually over time, he was told to enjoin more Laws unto them, in accordance with their needs. Thus, Islam was established in two phases: most of the Beliefs were first declared in Makkah; and most of the Laws were later expounded in Madinah. During the thirteen-year period of preaching in Makkah, this is what Islam meant to the Muslims:

Beliefs:

◉ There is no god or object worthy of worship except Allah (ﷻ).

75

- Muhammad (ﷺ) is the Messenger of Allah (ﷻ).
- Many Messengers have been sent before him, calling to truth.
- The Day of Judgement is approaching soon.
- Every soul will be resurrected after death to be judged for their deeds.
- Paradise will be given to the righteous, and Hell to the Disbelievers.
- All people are created equal: the only distinctions between them are deeds and piety.
- All acts of superstition, indecency and injustice are wrong.
- All sins could qualify for punishment, but Allah (ﷻ) is Merciful.
- All acts of goodness will be rewarded, however small.

Actions:

- Purifying the body, mind and spirit
- Prayer and remembrance of God
- Recitation of the Qur'an
- Patience in times of trial and difficulty
- Forgiveness, and turning aside from the ignorant
- Eating only pure food that is lawful
- Dressing in a dignified manner
- Greeting each other with words of peace
- Giving alms to the poor and needy
- Looking after orphans and widows
- Visiting the sick and attending funerals
- Good treatment to relatives and neighbours
- Offering good hospitality to guests
- Freeing slaves, and behaving well with animals
- Inviting people towards the path of guidance

Year I

The First Revelation

It was a night like none he had ever seen,
When upon the Mountain of Light he ascended.
His eyes were expectant and his heart was serene,
That night the first rays of Revelation descended:
When he saw Jibreel, the Trustworthy, full of might,
And Al-Hira's cave dazzled with celestial light.

"Read in the Name of your Lord who did create!
He created mankind from a suspended clot.
Read! And your Lord in Generosity is Great;
He who taught man by the pen what he knew not."[1]

Those words of weight now inscribed upon his heart,
Muhammad went down from the Mount full of emotion.
His chest was shaking as though it would be torn apart,
And then he saw Jibreel once more upon the horizon,
Filling the space from Earth to Heaven raised up high
In whichever direction that he turned to in the sky.

Muhammad went straight to Khadija, his beloved wife,
"Cover me, O Khadija, please do cover me," he said,
"I have never before felt the likes of this in my life."
She brought a blanket and gently caressed his head.

"Be sure that your Lord shall never abandon you.
You are good to kin and you show guests hospitality,
You only speak the truth and are faithful to what is due;
Kind-natured and patient, you help in every calamity."
Then his agitation began to pass and he spoke to her,
"Indeed I have been appointed as Allah's Messenger."

He began describing to her what he had been shown,
Then Khadija stood up and declared immediately,
"None is worthy of worship except for Allah alone,
And you, O Muhammad, are His Messenger certainly."

---

[1] (Surah Al-Alaq (96): 1-5)

It was not long before 'Ali came upon that scene.
He watched them silently in awe and admiration,
Hearing the words they recited so pure and serene,
Praising God as they bowed and fell into prostration.
Though 'Ali often saw Muhammad and Khadija pray,
Yet never before had they established it in this way.

And when they were done and they had risen,
Their faces had become illuminated with beauty.
'Ali looked up to Muhammad, his beloved cousin,
"Could you please explain these actions to me?"

He replied, "We turn ourselves to our Lord
Who has chosen for us this way and Religion,
Just as He has sent many Messengers before
As the bearers of glad tidings and admonition.
And you, O 'Ali, to this path of mine I now invite,
So that you may follow the way that is most right."

He said, "Should I not with my father first consult?"
That entire night 'Ali spent in deep contemplation,
Reflecting upon the world and on its final result,
Till the next morning he rose with determination.

"My Lord did not ask anyone's permission
Before he created and nurtured me," he said,
"So why should I ask the approval of anyone
Before I believe in Him and what He has sent?"
Then to Allah he offered his complete submission,
And vowed to support the Messenger's mission.

'Ali at only ten years of age had attained maturity,
As he was someone Muhammad himself did raise.
He would try to emulate his cousin's personality,
And had never before any idol lowered his face.

Now whether all of Arabia stood with him or against him,
'Ali had decided that it would not alter his faith in any way,
But thanked Allah to be among the first to believe in Him,
Then asked to remain firm upon His path till his final day.

"Soon We will cast upon you a Word of weight.
Indeed most potent for governing is the night vigil,
And for speech, it is the way that is most suitable.
Indeed in the daytime you have a long occupation.
And remember the Name of your Lord frequently,
And devote yourself to Him with complete devotion."[2]

From then on, accompanied by only Khadija and 'Ali,
The Messenger of Allah would now establish prayer.
Early each day they would leave their home secretly
To stand among the mountain passes' open air.

They gazed from above upon the city of Makkah,
Where placed like a glistening jewel in its centre
Was the Kaaba - the Most Ancient House of Allah
That Ibrahim had built for mankind to remember.
But it was now filled with statues of wood and stone
By people who abandoned the worship of Allah alone.

It was this that Muhammad had been sent to rectify:
A Messenger of their own to recite unto them Signs,
"To teach them the Book and Wisdom and to purify",
Just as Ibrahim had supplicated for in former times.

And Zayd ibn Haritha, Muhammad's adopted son,
Who had previously been a slave that he had freed,
Soon heard the powerful words of the Revelation,
And became the third to accept the purest creed,
Followed by Umm Kulthum, Zaynab and Ruqayyah,
Along with Fatima, the Prophet's dearest daughter.

So his household would spend most nights awake,
Praising Allah, seeking His Guidance and Pleasure.
They would leave the comfort of sleep for His sake,
And then at dawn glorify Him in abundant measure.

---

[2] (Surah Al-Muzzammil (73): 5-8)

Then Abu Talib came across 'Ali praying one day,
"My son, what is this now upon which I see you?"
"Father, I believe in Allah and His Messenger's way,
I bear witness that the Message sent unto him is true,
And I pray to our Lord alongside him with sincerity."
"Stay with him for he only calls to good certainly."

Then Fatima bint Asad, who was Ali's mother,
And had raised Muhammad since his childhood,
Now came to recognise him as Allah's Messenger,
For she too had only ever seen him call to good.

New Revelation came in the hours before dawn,
"O you who are wrapped up, arise and warn!
And your Lord do magnify, and your garments
Keep free from stain. And uncleanliness forsake,
And do not give in order that you may gain,
But instead be patient for your Lord's sake."[3]

Faith had been confined to a single home so far,
But upon Khadija's personal recommendation,
The Messenger now spoke to Umm Fadl Lubaba,
And she too accepted Islam without hesitation.

Abu Bakr ibn Abi Quhafah arrived from a journey,
And was informed about the Messenger's mission.
He knew Muhammad was the noblest in ancestry,
And was the best of all men in character and vision;
Never would he be deceived and never had he lied,
So Abu Bakr immediately submitted and testified.

And of such prominence was the son of Abi Quhafah,
When he accepted Islam, he helped guide others too:
Talhah, Zubayr, 'Uthman ibn 'Affan and Abu 'Ubaydah,
Each of them recognised the Prophet's call was true.

---

[3] (Surah Al-Muddaththir (74):1-7)

Then 'Abdal 'Amr ibn 'Awf testified to the same,
Rejecting the worship of idols for one God alone,
And to "'Abd Ar-Rahman" he changed his name,
So that by the best of names he would be known.

Sa'ad ibn Abi Waqqas was seventeen years of age
When the Faith of Islam entered into his heart,
And his mother at this news became full of rage.
"O Sa'ad! With your ancestral way did you part?
By God, either this new way forsake and falsify,
Or I swear that I will not eat or drink until I die!"

"O my mother! Please do not do that," Sa'ad cried,
"As I cannot forsake this Faith of mine for anything."
So for days from food and drink Hamnah turned aside,
And though she became weak, she kept on refusing.

"Dear mother, my love for you is strong indeed,
But stronger is love of Allah and His Messenger.
I swear I would not, for anything, leave this creed,
Even if I had to lose you a thousand times over."
Recognising his resolve, Hamnah relented finally,
And she began to eat and drink again reluctantly.

Now their love of idols was not ancestral in reality:
Makkah was monotheistic for the longest duration,
Made by Ibrahim a centre of affirming Allah's Unity,
And his progeny kept far from every false adoration.

But as time went on and faith weakened gradually,
A chief rose up among them named 'Amr ibn Luhay:
He saw the religion that the Syrians followed earnestly,
And he liked the images to which they used to pray,
So he brought back to Makkah some idols for trade,
And in the Kaaba itself had a shrine for *Hubal* made.

Though some people opposed him, the masses listened,
For 'Amr ibn Luhay was well-known for his generosity,
And he promised rewards for every idol commissioned,
So they let him continue what he was doing with impunity.

83

Hubal was an image of a man made out of red agate,
Gold-handed where the stone had previously cracked.
Manat, in whose lifeless hands they claimed was fate,
Although even the power of speech it clearly lacked,
And from *al-Lat* and *al-'Uzzah* they would beg for might,
While these two heard nothing and possessed no sight.

Thus, Banu Khuza'ah used their influence as custodians
To steer the foolish people of Makkah towards idolatry.
They told them that it was Allah who made all decisions,
But these idols were merely means of gaining proximity.

It became a time of ignorance where the foolish prospered,
And virtues were shunned while vices spread undeterred,
Acts of brutality were taken as signs of strength and pride,
Many different forms of deception were considered wise,
Soothsayers and divining arrows became trusted guides,
And the truth became like an island amidst a sea of lies.

And although the Banu Khuza'ah were ousted eventually,
And the tribe of Quraysh replaced them as custodians,
The love of idols had into hearts become imbibed deeply,
And people continued to introduce new superstitions.

With clouded intellects and bodies nurtured on impurity,
Their treachery increased as corruption began to thrive,
Society continued to spiral into the depths of indecency,
Oppressing orphans and burying infant daughters alive,
Regarding women as nothing more than commodities,
As though they were not the other halves of humanity.

Instead of justice, a class system was established,
Dividing people on the basis of wealth and family:
A system that often oppressed and impoverished,
And at the heart of it all was the love of idolatry.

Thus, did chiefs and merchants become wealthy
As more and more of their inventions were sold,
And from *Ummul Quraa'* kept proliferating rapidly,
Until idols entered almost every Arab household.
And so whoever came to Makkah for pilgrimage,
Now found it a place polluted with great sacrilege.

And thus did the People of the Book stop visiting,
But continued reminding each other that someday,
An *Ummi* Prophet would rise up and begin reciting
A Book that guided people to a more righteous way.

They hoped and prayed, each and every generation,
And they passed down that knowledge successively:
"He is the one Moses spoke of from a Brethren nation,"
"And he is the one that Jesus called *'The Praiseworthy.'*"
So of his description they had each been apprised,
Until by Bahirah, then Waraqah he was recognised.

Khadija had brought Muhammad to her cousin Waraqah,
An elderly Christian monk who was well-versed in Scripture.
"You have in truth received the same angel sent unto Musa,
And you have indeed been chosen as this nation's Messenger."

Then Waraqah's smile flickered and a look of concern grew,
"If I could only live till the time they drive you out with enmity;
For never has anyone brought anything similar before you,
Except that they were treated with harshness and hostility."
Then only a few days later, Waraqah the sage passed away,
But his words upon Muhammad's heart continued to weigh.

Would his people truly reject his call and drive him away?
And what would become of them if they refused and denied?
He knew that there would be many great difficulties in his way,
And he would have to break down barriers of ignorance and pride.

Yet the prospect did not put him off, for each time he felt afraid,
He turned his face towards his Lord and asked Him for Guidance.
This was an opportunity for which he had his entire life prayed:
To correct the ills of his community he had long borne with patience.
Even if few people would support him, his Lord was his supporter,
And even if the way was uncertain, he would obey his Lord's orders.

So he said, "Avoid all that is evil, and follow all that is good.
Turn away from idols, O my people, and worship Allah only.
Take care to both earn and spend your wealth as you should,
And do not commit on earth any form of injustice or tyranny."

And in a distant place, that message was heard
By Jundub, better known as Abu Dharr al-Ghifari,
Who had chosen to live a simple life as a shepherd,
Amongst a tribe that was notorious for its banditry.
Abu Dharr had long rejected polytheism and idolatry:
One of the few to have ever done so in his community.

And Abu Dharr's brother had come to inform him
That he had he just seen in Makkah a man of nobility:
A claimant of Prophethood from the Banu Hashim,
Who, like Abu Dharr himself, was denouncing idolatry.

So Abu Dharr came to Makkah and behaved cautiously,
Waiting by the Well of Zamzam, concealing his intentions,
Until he met 'Ali, a young boy who offered him hospitality,
And brought him to the very one he had come to question.
And when Abu Dharr saw Mustafa's face he instantly knew,
That this man in front of him only ever spoke what's true.

Then Abu Dharr went and stood in front of the Kaaba.
"O people of the Quraysh!" he declared loud and openly,
"I hereby testify that there is no other god besides Allah,
And that Muhammad is His Messenger most certainly."

The pagans of Quraysh by those words became furious,
"Seize this brazen abandoner of religion!" they cried.
They began to beat Abu Dharr, savage and merciless,
And they would not have cared at all if he had died
Had 'Abbas not then intervened and taken up a stand,
"He is Ghifari! Your caravans pass through their land!"

"Had I not advised you to refrain from this?"
The Prophet would later ask Abu Dharr softly.
"O Allah's Messenger, it was a need from within,
And I have fulfilled that need now most certainly."

The Prophet said, "Go back to your community,
Tell them what you have heard, and bear witness,
Then invite them to the path of Allah continuously.
Perhaps through you, He will bring them goodness.
And when you hear that there is no more secrecy
And I have come into the open, then return to me."

Year II

Faith Spreads Secretly

The Messenger of Mercy

"In the Name of Allah, Most Gracious and Merciful,
All Praise is due to Allah, the Lord of Everything.
(He who is) the Most Gracious and Merciful,
The Sovereign-Master of the Day of Reckoning.
To You alone, ourselves do we all enslave,
And from You alone, help do we all crave.

Guide us to and upon The Straight Path,
The path of those whom You have favoured,
Not of those who have earned Your Wrath,
Nor of those who from Your Way have erred."[4]

Islam appealed to the downtrodden of society,
The impoverished, powerless and the enslaved,
For it offered them hope, equality and dignity,
And most of all, the Guidance that they craved.

A Religion that was to make all men brothers,
Where slaves and kings could stand side by side,
Where no tribe or clan was better than others,
And neither wealth, nor rank, nor ancestral pride,
Would give to anyone any precedence or immunity,
If they did not perform good actions with piety.

And Divine Guidance was by 'Amir ibn Fuhayrah found,
Though he was considered of no importance by anyone.
And Bilal's soul became free while his body was bound,
Testifying that he was in truth, a slave to only One.

'Abdullah ibn Mas'ud was a young shepherd
Who came across Allah's Messenger one day,
And when the beauty of the Qur'an he heard,
He too became a firm follower of his way.

But not all were poor and of no consequence,
Even some from noble houses heeded the call.
There was the youthful Mus'ab, raised in affluence,
Yet he became among the wisest and humblest of all.
And then the son of 'Utbah, the proud Makkan chief:
Abu Hudhayfah's heart too opened up to belief.

---

[4] (Surah Al-Fatiha (1): 1-7)

'Abdullah ibn Jahsh, Abu Salamah, Ja'far and 'Ubaydah;
Each were men possessing conviction and certainty.
And Zaynab bint Jahsh, Umm Salamah and Sawdah;
Virtuous women known for patience and purity.

With their numbers growing steadily day by day,
The Believers began to long for a place to congregate:
A place where they could recite Revelation and pray.
And so the Prophet with the Believers did deliberate,
Until they had selected the house of Al-Arqam finally.
It was at the northern base of Mount Safa situated;
A place where people could come and go secretly.

To help the needy, the traveller and the orphaned youth,
To respect parents' rights and act well with neighbours,
To be just and kind in deeds and to only speak the truth:
Such were the lessons the Prophet taught his followers.

He spoke to them about past Prophets and Scripture,
And he encouraged each of them to use their intellect,
To cast aside all superstitions, vanity and conjecture,
Then to look towards the signs in nature and reflect,
To strive to develop fortitude, courage and temperance,
And to constantly purify their hearts with remembrance.

They were reminded whenever they would meet,
"Begin each action you perform with Allah's Name,"
"And with the salutations of peace, each other greet,"
"What you wish for yourself wish for others the same."

And he would speak against all forms of ignorance,
Misplaced pride in themselves, their tribe or ancestry,
And that all people were equal despite their differences,
That Allah did not look at their forms but at their piety.
He told them women should honoured and respected,
And that their infant daughters should be protected.

And he spoke of the coming Day of Judgement,
When all their deeds would be put on measure,
Warning them of the Great Fire and its torment,
And inviting them to the Garden and its pleasure.

'Uthman ibn Maz'un, a humble man of piety,
Would come along with Khawlah, his wife.
Together their hearts found true certainty,
And worship became the centre of their life.
Then Qudama and 'Abdullah, his brothers too:
Both of them testified the Message was true.

Then came Khunays, Tulayb and Abu Sabrah,
And there was Miqdad, the brave hearted youth,
Then Nu'aym, Abu Fukhayah, 'Amir ibn Rabi'ah,
And Khabbab - each one submitted to the Truth.

And the Messenger recited when he would pray,
"When the sun is wound, and stars fall down,
And the mountains are made to pass away,
And the pregnant camels are left unattended,
And the wild beasts are together mustered,
And the seas are seething, and souls are paired,
And the female infant buried alive is questioned,
Because of which sin had she been murdered?

And when scrolls are spread, and sky is bared,
And when the Blazing Fire has been set ablaze,
And when the Garden has been brought nigh,
Every soul shall know what it has prepared."[5]

So when Suhayb and 'Ammar arrived one day,
They each listened to the Revelation in awe.
It was nightfall when they finally crept away.
'Ammar found his parents waiting by the door;
They both looked at him with a worried glance,
Afraid he had fallen under the wrong influence.

"O my parents, these idols we have adored,
Cannot cause harm, nor help us in any way,
So I testify that none but Allah is my Lord,
And from now on, to Him alone will I pray."

---

[5] (Surah At-Takwir (81): 1-14)

Seeing the profound changes in their son,
And the passion with which he would speak,
Yasir and Sumayyah would ask about his Religion,
Until an audience themselves they went to seek.
So they set out to meet the Messenger in secrecy,
And left his presence with complete certainty.

Households like that of Yasir's were still a rarity:
At a time when belief was scarce and unpopular,
The family of Yasir had submitted in its entirety,
Dedicating themselves to Allah and His Messenger.

Sa'eed had been raised by a firm monotheist:
His father Zayd had spent his entire existence
Searching for the Truth that his people missed,
But had been killed while still seeking Guidance.
So when Sa'eed learnt of the Messenger's mission,
He entered it with complete heartfelt submission.

Sa'eed's wife was Fatima, one of Al-Khattab's daughters,
And her family were all polytheists of the sternest kind,
But Fatima did not wish to blindly follow her ancestors,
And instead accepted Islam with a clear heart and mind.

'Umar, her brother, was still not aware of this yet:
Of imposing physique, broad-shouldered and tall,
He was the kind of man who'd get angry not upset,
And his fiery temperament was feared by almost all;
While 'Amr, their uncle, a man of notable influence,
Was already displaying his disdain and arrogance.

'Amr ibn Hisham was to Muhammad very near in age,
And yet they could not be further apart in personality.
Though the Quraysh considered him to be a wise sage,
As *'Abu Jahl'* instead he'd soon be known for his infamy.

Year III

Inviting the Clan

The Messenger of Mercy

And news began to gradually spread throughout Makkah,
Though the Messenger had not yet announced it openly.
Some people ignored it, while others found it wondrous,
Some felt it was revolutionary, others thought it dangerous.

Abu Lahab and his wife, Umm Jameel bint Harb, lived next door,
And had been monitoring their nephew's activities suspiciously,
Hearing words softly recited that they had never heard before,
Seeing strange guests visiting his home, more and more frequently.
Morning and night he would rise, bow and fall into prostration,
While 'Ali and Zayd would stand behind, following in imitation.

And there were those whispered rumours now in circulation:
That Muhammad, who was known for always speaking truthfully,
Was now claiming that he had received some Divine Revelation,
And that some youth and destitutes were following him obediently.

Umm Jameel would spread reports to Abu Sufyan, her brother,
"Do you know Muhammad has come with something new?"
And the chiefs of Quraysh began to discuss with one another:
What was happening in Makkah and what should they do?
Muhammad had always lived among them all so peacefully,
Would he really now come with a call to end all idolatry?

If not for its annual pilgrimage, where would Makkah be?
And where would the pilgrimage be if not for its trade?
But so far Muhammad had not called for anything openly,
So they preferred that no extra attention to him be paid.

He would not be the first in any case to have such views,
Waraqah had been a Christian and spoke of a coming Prophet,
And similar claims had been echoed in Yathrib by the Jews.
The late Zayd ibn 'Amr of Banu Makhzum had believed in it,
And he had made a scene in rejecting the gods of his family,
So he was exiled from Makkah by Al-Khattab, his uncle finally.

And like that Zayd, they knew Muhammad and some of his clan,
Did not bow before idols, and from certain meat and wine refrained,
But they did not denounce any religion, nor did they wrong any man,
And good ties with all their kith and kin they had always maintained.

"When the sky is cleft asunder,
And when the stars fall and scatter,
And when the seas are made to burst,
And when the graves are overturned,
A soul will know what it has put forth,
And all that which it has left behind."[6]

Divine Revelations would descend upon his heart:
Sometimes they felt like the constant ringing of a bell,
And that was the way that the Prophet found most hard,
And sometimes he heard a voice or saw Jibreel as well.

The Prophet for months continued to preach secretly,
Inviting only those whom he knew would be inclined
To abandon the worship of all idols, and embrace Unity,
Without revealing to anyone what was in their mind.
The Believers felt connected with one another even so,
And day by day, the movement continued to grow.

Until there came a period of time when all turned silent,
No Verses came down, and there was no new instruction;
When the heart of Muhammad was almost despondent,
As it kept longing for the cooling breeze of Revelation.

So the Prophet continued to wait patiently day after day,
Until he fell sick with grief and was confined to his bed,
Then for some days he was not seen coming out to pray.
"His Lord is angry and abandoned him!" the pagans said.
And one day even Umm Jameel passed by him mockingly,
"So now it seems that your devil has left you finally!"

These words of hers were as sharp as a sword,
And in his heart, Muhammad now began to ask
Whether he had done anything to offend his Lord,
Or how he might have been negligent in his task.

"By the early day full of brightness,
And the night when it reaches stillness!
Your Lord has not forsaken you,
Nor has He at all detested you.

---

[6] (Surah Al-Infitar (82): 1-5)

96

And surely for you what is to be,
Is better than what has already gone,
And your Lord shall give you freely,
So that you may find satisfaction.
Did He not find you as an orphan
So then He gave you accommodation?

And He had found you in confusion,
So then He gave to you direction?
And He had found you in poverty,
So then He gave you self-sufficiency?"[7]

Thus did Muhammad receive word again,
Bringing with it, coolness and tranquillity.
And no pain or uncertainty could remain,
As his Lord had spoken to him personally.

"Have We not expanded for you your chest?
And removed for you the great burden
Which upon your back heavily pressed?
And have We not raised you in mention?
So indeed with hardship comes relief,
Indeed with hardship comes relief..."[8]

Then began the next phase of his mission,
When a Verse of great weight descended,
"And to your nearest kin give admonition."[9]
And with it the era of secrecy had ended.

"O Ali! Our Lord Most High issued command
That I should warn my near of kin at once,
So bring some grain, meat and milk to hand,
And to the sons of 'Abdul Muttalib announce,
That I have invited them all to a feast today,
Let them come to hear what I have to say."

---

[7] (Surah Ad-Duha (93): 1-8)
[8] (Surah Al-Inshirah (94): 1-6)
[9] (Surah As-Shu'ara (26): 214)

Forty men arrived from Banu Hashim's nobility.
The Prophet seated them honourably upon a rug,
Then he brought out the food of small quantity:
A single leg of meat, a bowl of grain and a jug.

And so they glanced at one another with surprise,
How could even one man by this be fed sufficiently?
But then witnessed miraculously before their eyes,
How Muhammad divided between them all equally,
Till each and every one ate and drank to their fill,
And yet there was plenty of food remaining still.

But when to stand and speak the Prophet tried,
His uncle, Abu Lahab, his intention already knew.
"Your companion has bewitched you!" he cried,
And the men dispersed amidst the noise and hue.

The next morning, the Prophet rose and said,
"O Ali! Make arrangements as you did yesterday,
And invite the sons of 'Abdul Muttalib to be fed,
So that they may again listen to what I have to say."
Then when 'Ali had done what he was instructed,
The Prophet stood up to speak, unobstructed.

"Praise belongs to Allah for His Mercy,
I seek His guidance and in Him I believe,
And truly worthy of worship alone is He.
I now proclaim to you what I did receive.

O 'Abdul Muttalib sons! I say only what is true,
For never did anyone before to his people bring
Anything better than that which I now offer you:
The good of this world, and the Hereafter's blessings.
For certainly, I have been appointed as Allah's Apostle,
To call you to Him, and guide you - a task most colossal.

Which of you will help make this burden lesser?
Which of you will be the one to answer my call?
To be my brother, vicegerent and my successor,
Upon whom is this responsibility going to fall?"

But their answer came in the form of silence,
Till 'Ali stood up, though the youngest in years,
"I will, O Messenger of Allah!" was his response.
The Prophet placed his hands upon his shoulders,
"My brother, vicegerent and successor among you,
So listen to him, and obey that which he tells you."

Abu Lahab scoffed and fell down laughing,
"Ha! O Abu Talib! You did well to listen,
Now you must obey and begin following,
The commands and guidance of your son!"

While Abu Lahab had disrupted each attendance,
In the days that followed by in swift succession,
Now the members of Hashim's descendants,
In private kept pondering over his invitation.
They all knew that Muhammad had never lied,
But could they against all Arabs now take a side?

For one thing even then, to all was a certainty,
If Muhammad would now make an open claim,
There would be divisions, strife and disunity,
And Makkah would never again be the same.

Yet even so, some declared their belief openly,
Like his aunts Fatima, Safiyyah, Arwa and 'Aatikah,
While Abu Talib and Hamza both watched silently.
His uncle 'Abbas turned away, but he did not go far.
Then Al-Mughirah announced he would not accept,
And Abu Lahab had made it clear he would reject.

The Messenger of Mercy

Year IV

The Open Declaration

The Messenger of Mercy

With the light of the dawn ere the sun had risen,
The Words of Allah's Revelation now descended,
"Then proclaim openly what you are bidden!"[10]
Upon Mount Safa, the Messenger quickly ascended,
"Ya Sabaha!" his voice resounded through the city,
And people began rushing from their homes fearfully.

"O sons of Fihr!" he called, "O sons of 'Adiyy!
O sons of 'Abd Manaf and O 'Abdul Muttalib sons!"
To each tribe and clan the Prophet made his plea,
Until a huge crowd had gathered in response.

Then the Messenger addressed all the assembled groups,
"O people of Quraysh! If I were to proclaim unto you
That the valley behind me is filled with enemy troops,
Would you not then believe what I have said is true?"
"Yes of course!" the Quraysh cried one and all in unison,
"And why not, for you, Muhammad, are the truest one!"

"Then hear my warning of a thing more severe,
For I am like one who sees a danger approaching you:
The Blazing Fire! Will you then your Lord not fear?
For I have indeed, O my people, been sent unto you!"

While all of Quraysh stood by, in silence stunned,
Abu Lahab turned red of cheek as his anger flared,
"May you perish! Is it for this that you summoned?"
And left raging at what his nephew had declared.

From above, Jibreel with an answer suddenly came,
"May Abu Lahab's hands perish and may he perish!
His wealth will not avail him nor what he earned,
He will soon be made to burn in a fire of blazing flame,
And his wife, she who is the carrier of firewood,
On her neck, shall be a halter of palm-fibre turned."[11]

---

[10] (Surah Al-Hijr (15): 94)
[11] (Surah Al-Lahab (111): 1-5)

A raging Umm Jameel came carrying a heavy stone,
"Abu Bakr!" she said, "Where is he who ridiculed me?
If he were here now, a due response would be shown.
By God! How I would break his mouth certainly!
'Indeed, we reject him, *Mudhammam*, that reprobate,
His words we refuse and his religion we hate.'"

As she kept on reciting those words so vile,
Abu Bakr was shocked and gave no reply,
For the Prophet was next to him all the while,
Being protected by his Lord miraculously.

"Is it not wondrous," he said when she went away,
"How our Lord turns aside even their words from me?
She insults 'Mudhammam'- the reprobate - as you see,
While I am 'Muhammad'- the Most Praiseworthy."
Abu Bakr looked at his face and nodded in affirmation,
Amazed by the Prophet's optimism in every situation.

Banu Hashim, Muttalib, Nawfal, Asad and Zuhrah,
Banu 'Abd ad-Dar, 'Amir, Harith, Taym and 'Adiyy,
Banu Makhzum, 'Abd Shams, Sahm and Jumah:
These were the fourteen clans of Quraysh's family.

Some called him a liar, while others named him insane,
And denied that Allah would send a human Prophet.
The Recitation they claimed was just ancient sorcery,
Or that it was Muhammad himself who fabricated it.
Among all, he had always been loved and respected,
But now, for the first time his word was being rejected.

Yet the Prophet did not lose hope nor did he falter,
Never cowing before the harsh words of any critic,
Nor in his duty, fearing the blame of any blamer,
Proclaiming the Truth despite every doubting cynic.

"Noon! By the Pen and that which they are writing!
You, by your Lord's favour, suffer not from insanity.
For you there shall be a reward that is unending.
And you are upon a lofty standard of morality.
You will soon see, and they shall soon come to see,
Which of you has been afflicted with insanity."[12]

'Amr ibn Hisham would be the worst of them in arrogance:
He would never come to a discussion except it turned ugly,
So he became known as 'Abu Jahl' - the Father of Ignorance,
When he began to mislead and incite the entire community.

Each day, groups of men would pull the Messenger aside,
And in every gathering come to question him incessantly.
The Messenger would listen and let their anger subside,
Then with logic, respond to all their objections patiently.
And when they could neither intimidate nor defeat him,
They would raise their voices and then retreat from him.

"Mention your Lord within yourself, humble and fearing,
Without loudness in speech, morning and evening..."[13]
Thus, the Believers would each day purify their intentions,
And worship their Lord with hope and apprehension.

Since they could not yet practise their Faith openly,
And even their own homes housed its enemies,
The Believers in small groups would go out secretly,
To pray together amid the mountains' cooling breeze.
There they would call upon their Lord in humility,
And pray for the guidance of their entire community.

But one day a group of malicious pagans passed by there,
And chanced upon the Believers whom they had heard,
Reciting Verses of the Qur'an whilst engaged in prayer,
So they began provoking them through action and word.

---

[12] (Surah Al-Qalam (68): 1-6)
[13] (Surah Al-'A'raaf (7): 205)

Mutually enraged, fighting broke out over it,
And with a camel's jawbone, Sa'ad struck a pagan.
When they retreated and informed the Prophet,
He recited to them the Words of Revelation,
"Bear what they say with due patience,
And avoid them with a fair avoidance."[14]

'Abdullah ibn Mas'ud said one starlit night,
"Quraysh has not yet heard the Revelation,
So let me go before them tomorrow to recite
In front of the Kaaba, at Abraham's Station."

"The Beneficent One has taught the Recitation,
Has created man, taught him the way of expression.
The sun and moon follow a precise calculation,
And the stars and the trees fall in adoration.
And the Heaven He raised, imposing the Measure,
That you transgress not within the measure."[15]

The Quraysh in confusion looked one at the other,
Before they finally realised what was being said.
They rushed upon 'Abdullah with sudden anger,
And rained down swift blows upon his head.

"This is what we had been for you apprehending."
"Never were Allah's enemies so light as today,"
He replied, with his face swollen and bleeding,
"And I will go out tomorrow again, if you say."
"No," they exclaimed, "you have truly done a lot,
You made them listen to what they wished not."

The Messenger was with an important delegation
Of chiefs and notables of Quraysh who had gathered,
And was kept fully occupied by them in conversation,
When a blind man among the Believers was heard.

---

[14] (Surah Al-Muzzammil (73): 10)
[15] (Surah Ar-Rahman (55): 1-8)

"O Muhammad! Teach me that information
Which was taught to you by Divine Revelation!"
And when he who was among those in attendance
Had grown annoyed at the blind man's interruption,
He frowned and turned his back with impatience
At how he was diverted from the conversation.

And for that, Jibreel with Revelation appeared:
"He frowned and then he had turned aside,
Because to him the blind man had neared.
And what would make you know inside,
That perhaps he might become purified?
Or be reminded and benefit by the Reminder?"[16]

All those in attendance were completely stunned,
That this new religion would give such attention
To a poor blind man by the wealthy being shunned,
That it would even make it a point of contention.

"Indeed We sent it down on the Night of Decree.
And how can you know what is the Night of Decree?
The Night of Decree is superior to a thousand months;
Therein the Angels and the Spirit are sent down,
With the permission of their Lord for every matter.
Peace! It is until the emergence of the dawn."[17]

The Words of the Qur'an kept drawing attention,
And Makkah was changing - this much was clear.
Now the pagans knew something had to be done,
Or their ancestral ways would soon disappear.

Umm Anmar came to Khabbab with her clan angrily,
"O you slave! We heard something we cannot accept,
They say you left your religion to follow that Hashimi?"
"I believe in Allah alone. The worship of idols I reject,"
Khabbab, a blacksmith by trade, to her calmly replied,
"That Muhammad is Allah's Messenger, I have testified."

---

[16] (Surah Al-'Abasa (80): 1-4)

[17] (Surah Al-Qadr (97): 1-5)

Siba'a fell upon him when he said what he said,
And the youth of Banu Khuza'ah beat him more.
They picked up bars of iron and struck his head,
And left him bleeding, unconscious on the floor.

The chiefs of Makkah's elite were taken aback
At a mere slave's incredible daring and audacity;
He who had no clan to defend him from attack
Was nonetheless here declaring his beliefs openly.
They became fearful of uprising and revolution,
And met together to find an effective solution.

From Banu Makhzum, chiefs of Quraysh's military,
Walid ibn al-Mughirah and Abu Jahl were sent,
Along with their kin Khalid, 'Umar and 'Ikrimah:
Youth who were well-known for their strength.

From *Banu 'Abd Shams*, the next to enter inside
Was 'Utbah; his brother Shaybah; and Abu Sufyan:
Among the greatest of men in both wealth and pride.
And though they were the closest to them in relation,
No love was lost between them and Hashim's sons,
For their rivalry had been raging on for generations.

Banu 'Abd ad-Dar, custodians of the Kaaba named,
Sent Nadr ibn al-Harith, for his learning famed.
And *Banu Nawfal* was by Mut'im ibn 'Adiyy led,
While Jubayr and Tu'aymah followed in his stead.

Banu Sahm who prepared offerings for the idols,
Sent Al-'Aas ibn Wa'il along with 'Amr, his son.
Banu Jumah, the casters of lots before the idols,
And closest of all clans to Banu Sahm in relation,
Sent Umayyah ibn Khalaf, cruel and corpulent,
Along with his son Safwan, of harsh temperament.

And *Banu 'Amir ibn Lu'ayy*, the seventh of them,
Sent Suhayl, renowned for his eloquent tongue,
And 'Amr ibn 'Abdu Wadd, a stalwart and strong
Warrior considered equal to a thousand men.

"Muhammad had been a man well-liked among you,"
Now Nadr ibn al-Harith to his fellow chieftains said,
"The most truthful in speech and trustworthy in deed,
Until the time when grey hairs appeared on his head,
You claimed he is a sorcerer, poet or had lost his mind,
When we all know that he resembles not their kind.

He does not blow in knots, he does he compose poetry,
And his words are not the utterances of one delirious.
So, O Quraysh, think well how to respond appropriately,
For this is a situation for you most grave and serious."

"O Abu Talib, of your position we are aware,
And recognise your rank and age as is due,
But this situation is more than we can bear.
Our gods are being abused by your nephew!
If you do not restrain him we shall soon act,
And against his supporters will make a pact."

"Spare me and yourself," Abu Talib said,
When he visited the Prophet in privacy,
"And do not place a burden upon my head,
Greater than what I can bear to carry."

"O uncle! I swear by Allah with certainty,
Even if they would place in my right hand
The sun, and the moon in my left would be,
I am not going to swerve from where I stand,
And for this mission, I will continue to strive
Till Allah's word prevails or I lay down my life."

Abu Talib hearing this was affected deeply,
"And by Allah! I will not stop defending you!
As long as I live, say whatever you like openly,
This uncle of yours will never abandon you."

The Prophet then put forth his own suggestion,
"I request from them a word, which if they say,
It will lead them towards such a grand dominion,
With the Arabs and non-Arabs under their sway."
"We would say ten gladly! What is that word?"

109

"Say there is no god but Allah," he answered.

With pride and stubbornness they went away,
"Has he made all the gods into one God only?"
"A mere sorcerer and a liar," they began to say,
"Keep going and defend your gods patiently."

The Prophet was sitting with a group one day;
Among them 'Ammar, Suhayb, Bilal and Khabbab.
The chiefs of Quraysh passed by and began to say,
"And here are the barefoot ones in beggars' garb,"
As they drew up their cloaks with haughtiness,
"The ones to whom God has shown favour over us!"

"O Muhammad! Are you satisfied indeed
With the likes of these ones as your followers?
Should we enter after them taking the lead?
If you dismiss them we might not then be averse."

"Drive not away those who upon their Lord do call
Morning and evening, His Countenance desiring..."
Came the response by Revelation that silenced all,
"Thus do We try some by others, so they will be saying,
'Are these the ones amongst us whom Allah favoured?'
Is Allah of the grateful ones not Most Assured?"[18]

Yet the thinking of the chiefs remained primitive,
Believing if they had wealth, they had superiority,
And the poor were they to whom Allah wouldn't give;
So why should they then go and relieve their poverty?

And the Quraysh saw in them other kinds of inferiority,
Not only were some of them not originally from Makkah,
They were not even Arabs on both sides of their family.
And how could they with the sons of slaves be put on par?
Were shepherds now expecting to sit among nobles and chiefs,
Just because they followed Muhammad and his strange beliefs?

---

[18] (Surah Al-Anaam (6): part of 52, 53)

"The Striking Calamity!
What is the Striking Calamity?
And how will you comprehend
What is the Striking Calamity?

The Day when men shall be
Like moths scattered about,
And the mountains shall be
Like wool carded into tufts.

Then as for him whose deeds
In the Scales weigh heavily,
He will live a life of felicity.

Then as for him whose deeds
In the Scales weigh too light,
His abode will be the Abyss.
And how will you know what it is?
A Fire burning fiercely bright." [19]

The chiefs of Quraysh were used to luxury,
And they had lived freely without restriction.
They hated even the thought of accountability,
And thus remained the foremost in opposition.

"He is only saying this for some purpose,
And we have never heard its like before."
"To him, would it be sent from amongst us?
It is just an invention and nothing more."
So they went around with their calumny,
Claiming the Qur'an was just forged poetry.

They had known Muhammad since childhood,
And not even once had he ever spoken a lie,
Nor was seen from him anything but good.
His virtues were apparent and his morals high.

---

[19] (Surah Al-Qari'ah (101): 1-11)

111

In forty years he had never had any teacher,
And had not composed even one line of poetry.
He was not among the ones versed in Scripture,
Nor had he sought after any great rank in society.
The people of Makkah knew all of this and more,
But tongues denied while their hearts were sure.

"By the sun and her brightness,
And the moon when he follows her,
And the day when it displays it,
And the night when it covers her.

And the sky and its construction,
And the earth and its expansion,
And the soul and its proportion,
Then He inspired it with recognition
Of what is wrong and right for it:
Indeed he succeeds who purifies it,
And indeed he fails who corrupts it..."[20]

The Quraysh thought that they had mastered
The highest pinnacle in their command of Arabic,
But the Qur'an surpassed all poetry and rhetoric,
And was unlike anything they had ever heard.

Three chiefs secretly came out one night,
And hid near to the Prophet's residence,
Each in amazement listened to him recite,
And marvelled at its beauty and eloquence.
When dawn arrived, each one crept away,
And came across each other on the way.

"Abul Hakam!" "Abu Sufyan" "Al-Akhnas, you!"
Each shaming the other with words of blame,
"What if people came to know of what we do?"
But the next two nights they all did the same.

---

[20] (Surah As-Shams (91): 1-10)

Though by day they mocked and maligned,
In the quiet of the night, they felt to it drawn.
They could not put the Qur'an out of their mind,
And would be enraptured in awe each dawn,
Until shamed by each other, they finally swore
That they would never again approach his door.

"By the fig and the olive, and by Mount Sinai,
And then I swear by this very City of Security,
We have made man in the best of moulds certainly,
Then We returned him to the lowest of the low,

Except those who believe and do good continuously.
For them shall be a reward unfailing and continuous.
Then what causes you to deny the Recompense?
Is Allah not among all judges the most Judicious?"[21]

The Messenger performed ablution and began to pray,
At the Station of Ibrahim, his most noble ancestor.
Said Abu Jahl, "Did I not forbid you from this way?
Don't you see in followers and might, I am greater?"
And while the pagans started to cheer and applaud,
Jibreel descended with a Revelation from his Lord.

"Have you seen he who forbids a servant when he prays?
Have you seen if he is on Guidance, or calls to piety?
Have you seen if he denies and turns away?
Does he not know that Allah does see?

But nay! If he does not desist immediately,
Indeed him, We shall by his forehead seize:
That lying forehead that is acting sinfully.
So then let him call whomsoever he please.
We will summon the Stern Guardians here.
Nay! Obey him not. Prostrate and draw near."[22]

---

[21] (Surah At-Teen (95): 1-8)
[22] (Surah Al-'Alaq: (96): 9-19)

Fearless, audacious and full of great arrogance,
No one was safe from the evil of Abu Jahl's ways.
By his tongue, his hand and his foul influence,
He would injure, or incite people into a craze.

"Boycott that merchant!", "Ostracise that fool!"
"Your forefathers' dignity is being denigrated!"
"Will you allow slaves to revolt against your rule?
Or replace your ancestral religion with one fabricated?"
Such was the Father of Ignorance, wherever he went,
He would bar people from Guidance and spread dissent.

So some called it a lie while others declared it truth,
Father turned against son, brother against brother,
Spouse turned against spouse, elder against youth,
And even the closest of friends opposed one another.

The pagans would pass by the Messenger frequently,
Accosting him with all kinds of accusations and abuse.
He would extend words of peace, speaking cordially,
And ask them to reflect upon their irrational views.
Still they would argue with him, shouting over each other,
And when one finished, there would then come another.

Al-Aswad ibn 'Abd Yaghut was among the worst in rejection,
Abusing the Messenger and the Believers at every opportunity,
So Miqdad, his former slave who was now his adopted son,
Kept his Faith concealed and continued practising in secrecy.

Among the most bitterly divided was Abu Bakr's household:
Umm Ruman, 'Abdullah, Asma and 'A'isha followed his Religion,
But Qutaylah and 'Abdul 'Uzzah to polytheism continued to hold,
So Abu Bakr dissociated from them both after firm admonition.
And though Salma, his mother, believed through and through,
Abu Quhafah wouldn't abandon what his forefathers used to do.

"I swear by the day in decline,
Verily man is in a state of deficiency,
Except for those ones who believe
And perform righteous deeds constantly,
And upon another the Truth enjoin,
And upon one another patience enjoin."[23]

'Ammar and his entire family were made to suffer,
Subjected each day to harsh persecution and violence.
And Mus'ab ibn 'Umayr was thrown out by his mother,
So he experienced hardships after a life of affluence.

Nahdia, a slave-woman, was being tortured,
And so was Umm 'Ubays her daughter too,
Till Abu Bakr passed and saw their suffering,
And he took it upon himself to free them two.
He had freed several of the poorest in this way,
After hearing of the hardships of Judgement Day.

Abu Quhafah approached Abu Bakr and said,
"My son, you spend your wealth on the weak,
Why don't you free some strong men instead?"
"O father," he said, "Allah's pleasure is all I seek."

Al-Hakam came to 'Uthman, his brother's son,
"Have you indeed left your forefathers' creed?
You must return back from this new religion,
Or else, I swear that you shall never be freed!"
"I will not forsake this Faith," 'Uthman replied,
So Al-Hakam beat Ibn 'Affan and left him tied.

Talhah ibn 'Ubaydullah was goaded by a crowd,
While an old woman was throwing stones at him,
"That is his mother, Sa'bah," one man said aloud.
"He left his faith obeying the man of Banu Hashim."

An enraged Abu Jahl at Ibn Mas'ud clawed,
And rained down punches upon his face,
"Shepherd! Have you all our gods abhorred,
And taken one God alone in their place?"

---

[23] (Surah Al-'Asr (103): 1-3)

But Ibn Mas'ud would continue reciting,
And his Faith he made no attempt at hiding.

"Say: 'He is Allah, the only One.
Allah, who is not in need of anyone.
He begets not, nor was He begotten.
And for Him there is no comparison.'"[24]

Then Umayyah ibn Khalaf, proud and wealthy,
Discovered his slave, Bilal had become a Muslim,
So he dragged him out with harshness and cruelty,
And before the eyes of the Quraysh, he paraded him.
Then he tied him down, bare upon the burning sand,
And threatened him, brandishing a whip in his hand.

"O Bilal! Know that I will never let you be free
Until you die, or have returned back to our way,
To worship al-Lat and al-'Uzzah most dutifully!"
But the word "Oneness," Bilal continued to say.

Umayyah stood over Bilal with a sneer of disgust,
While he kept cracking his whip onto him violently,
But even as his blood began to mix with the dust,
With every breath, Bilal professed his Lord's Unity.
So Umayyah placed the heaviest rock upon his chest,
Laughing at the pain Bilal felt as it burned and pressed.

"Won't you fear Allah?" said Abu Bakr passing by,
"How long will you continue to oppress this man?"
"If you care so much, why not buy him from me?
Just ten measures of gold and he shall be free!"

"Ha! By al-Lat and al-'Uzzah!" Umayyah cried,
"To accept even one measure, I was prepared,"
"And by Allah!" Abu Bakr to him calmly replied,
"To pay even one hundred, I was prepared."
. So each one looked on with barely subdued glee,
As Bilal cast away his chains and was now free.

---

[24] (Surah Al-Ikhlaas (112): 1-4)

The name 'Muhammad' was now on everyone's lips,
Some praising him for bringing salvation and Guidance,
Others accusing him of creating trouble and hardships,
But Makkah had long been on the brink of subsidence.

Though against their foes they put up a united front,
The pagans bore between themselves much animosity,
Years would not erase the memory of a single affront,
And each clan and tribe proclaimed its own superiority,
The feuds and grudges of their ancestors they inherited,
And would claim virtues in things that were not merited.

Thus, a sudden clamour erupted in Makkah's streets,
As voices were raised and grew increasingly loud.
The notables of two tribes assembled with conceit,
And began to quarrel in front of the gathered crowd.

"We have more chiefs and members than you!"
Some of Banu 'Abd Manaf declared with pride,
And when they had counted and found it true,
Some of Banu Sahm in their stubbornness replied,
"If the dead among our tribes would also count,
We would surely outnumber you in their amount!"

The argument grew even more heated at this jibe,
Till they all rushed to the graveyards with eagerness,
And began counting the dead relatives of each tribe,
Each seeking to thereby validate their arrogance.

The Messenger felt upset at this display of ignorance,
Until Jibreel came to him with the Words of Revelation,
"You have been diverted by mutual competition,
Until even to the graves you make visitation,
Nay! Indeed, you are soon going to know.
Then nay! Indeed, you are soon going to know.

Nay if you only knew with the knowledge of certainty,
You are most certainly going to see the Blazing Fire.
Then you will surely see it with the eye of certainty,
Then that Day, you will surely be asked about delight."[25]

---

[25] (Surah At-Takathur (102): 1-8)

117

Now at the cusp of the blessed month of Dhul-Hijjah,
Their proud ones and their mighty had assembled.
Among them like Haman was Walid ibn al-Mughirah,
While Abu Jahl in conceit, Fir'aun himself resembled.
Thus, the chiefs each came out dressed in their finery,
And plotted together to put an end to Islam finally.

"O Quraysh! The pilgrims' approach is nigh,
Let us agree upon a single word, one and all,
So that no man amongst us may the other belie
When we are asked about Muhammad's call."

"Then let us say he is a soothsayer certainly,"
"No, he does not murmur or vaguely insinuate,"
"Then he is mad or possessed by an evil entity,"
"No, there are no indications at all of that state."
"Then he is a poet speaking rhythmically,"
"Or he is a magician performing sorcery."

"No, poetry of every form we have seen,
His speech does not into any metre fall,
And he does not engage in acts unclean,
Or like magicians, blow on knots at all."

"Then, O son of Mughirah, what is your view?
"His words are sweet, well-based and fruitful,
Whatever you say about him is proven untrue,
But let me think what will best find approval."
So he reflected and frowned and deliberated,
Turned, and with arrogance became inflated.

"This is naught but ancient magic handed down,
This is nothing more than a mere mortal's word!
Thereby he creates troubles and divides families,
Claiming that he is receiving Allah's decrees.

And has Allah for His Revelations selected
Muhammad over a great man of the Two Cities?
I, Walid, Quraysh's greatest chief am neglected,
While I have great wealth and sons and ease.
And there is in Ta'if, 'Urwa ibn Mas'ud at-Thaqifi,
Who might also have Revelation if it were reality!"

118

But while Walid thought of himself as great,
And an army of sycophants would stoke his vanity,
His view against the Truth could never militate,
And the response from God came with true gravity.

"Soon in Saqar I shall have him thrown.
And what is Saqar, how will you understand?
It leaves nothing, spares naught, burns to the bone!
Over it, nineteen do stand. And We have not placed,
Any other besides angels as the Fire's Keepers,
And made not their number but a trial for Disbelievers."[26]

This was just one of many descriptions of the Fire;
A terrible place of punishment for the reckless proud,
Meant to warn mankind from following low desires,
And it was this warning that was recited to a crowd.

But instead, Abu Jahl snorted, "Do you not hear?
O Quraysh! Are you folk so powerless and weak?
One Keeper to be handled by each ten of you here!"
"Nay!" retorted Abul Ashaddayn as he stood to speak,
"I myself will be taking care of the first seventeen,
And let the rest among you all be divided between."

At Abu Talib's house arrived a group waiting to be fed,
Each one of them was a chief, wealthy and famous.
And having eaten, they drew up their cloaks and said,
"Now what is it that your nephew wants from us?"

Abu Talib turned to Muhammad to answer instead,
So he stood before them and spoke clear and true,
"I am the Messenger that Allah has sent," he said,
"As a Warner, and a Bringer of glad tidings to you,
So, O my people, worship none except Allah alone,
And turn away from those idols of wood and stone."

---

[26] (Surah Al-Muddaththir (74): 26-31)

"That is enough now! This is doomed to fail!"
Exclaimed 'Uqbah, annoyed and exasperated,
"With him indeed no words shall ever avail,
It is far better he be killed and eliminated!"

Abu Talib looked at him but stayed silent.
Had it not been shameful to abuse a guest,
'Uqbah would never have found him so patient.
Still the matter upon his heart heavily pressed:
Not only were the Quraysh adamant on mockery,
But now here they were making threats openly.

And 'Uqbah was of course aware of their customs,
His clan would know to expect some retribution,
Yet if he was so brazen, it only meant one thing:
All of Quraysh had approved of such an action.

The next day, the Prophet went somewhere,
And by nightfall he still had not yet returned.
So Abu Talib searched for him everywhere,
His face grew darker and more concerned,
With every hour, after the light started to fade,
Recalling the threat that 'Uqbah had made.

With a demeanour like the coldest steel,
And a look that would brook no argument,
Abu Talib summoned his clan together,
Donning his armour and armaments.

"O sons of Hashim and of Al-Muttalib,
Sharpen your swords now and follow me,
Then sit down near a chief of every clan,
And among them by Abu Jahl especially,
For if my nephew has indeed been slain,
Ignorant of the plot he would not remain.

When you see me stand up and make the call,
'O Quraysh, we want Muhammad from you!'
Draw out your swords and strike one and all,
Until you have each killed the man next to you."

Zayd entered and found the air heavy with tension,
"No harm has come to Allah's Messenger!" he cried,
"He is in a house by As-Safa, carrying out his mission,
He became delayed, but just now I was at his side."
Abu Talib's shoulders slumped and he let out a sigh,
"Take me so that I may see him with my own eyes."

When Abu Talib saw him he became emotional,
"O my brother's son! O where have you been?"
Muhammad smiled brightly and hugged his uncle,
Assuring him that no mistreatment had he seen.

An uneasiness remained over Abu Talib even so:
Today, it was true Muhammad had not been attacked,
But hostility against him each day continued to grow,
And soon some wretch might be emboldened to act.
So the next morning, Abu Talib went to the Sanctuary,
Instructing the youth of Banu Hashim to follow closely.

"O Quraysh!" he declared in a voice that made heads turn,
"Last night Muhammad was gone and I feared for his safety,
Do you know what I intended to do if he did not return?"
"And what is that?" they asked, exchanging glances furtively.

Then every Hashimi man drew out his blade upon his call,
And the chiefs trembled seeing how far Abu Talib dared,
"I swear by God!" he said, "Had any harm come to him at all,
Not one, not a single one of you, would have been spared!"

121

Year V

Five Faiths Interact

"He has ordained for you of Religion that which He
Enjoined upon Nuh, and that which We Revealed to you,
And enjoined upon Ibrahim, and Musa and Isa - to be
Firmly established in the Religion, and not be in it divided.
Most difficult for the polytheists is what you call them to.
Allah chooses for Himself whoever He wills to be selected,
And guides to Himself the one who turns penitently. "[27]

The Messenger of Allah would come out each morning
To the Sacred Mosque through the Gate of Banu Shaybah,
Performing Tawaaf around the Kaaba whilst reciting,
Then in prayer he would turn his face towards Al-Aqsa;
His face changing colour as he beseeched his Lord,
Seeking forgiveness, Guidance and the best reward.

He would pray for his community constantly,
Singling them out by name, even his enemies,
And for the Believers of the past and posterity,
And only then for himself and his family.

Abu Jahl would approach all travellers,
"Do not hearken to Muhammad," he said,
"His own folk as fools this man considers,
He reviles our gods and maligns our dead."
"Why do you not expel him in that case?"
"The youth would follow him to any place."

Nadr ibn al-Harith would come upon each gathering,
To rudely interrupt the Recitation of the Qur'an,
Saying, "I know stories better than those he is telling,
Stories that I have heard from Rome and Isfahan!"

"And, O people! What is the difference
Between these words I say and his poetry?
He tells to you some tales of the ancients
Subjected to great destruction and fury,
And I speak of those who lived in security;
Rulers blessed with peace and prosperity!"

---

[27] (Surah As-Shura (42): 13)

The pagan Arabs admired these stories greatly,
And longed for riches like those Khosrow possessed,
Or the lands over which Heraclius held authority,
But in religion, they felt they themselves were best.

So as conflicts arose between Rome and Persia,
The pagans of Makkah found a chance to gloat,
"The Fire Worshippers are finding Divine favour,
While the Christians are now being forced out.
Thus it seems Monotheism is proven to be a lie,
And this Religion of yours will soon also die."

On the tongues of poets and upon camelback,
This claim spread around Arabia like wildfire,
And to it there was no answer ever given back,
Until the response Allah Himself did inspire.

"The Romans have been defeated,
In the nearby lowest-lying land,
But they shall after their being defeated,
Within a few years gain the upper hand.
To Allah, before and after, belongs command.
And that day the Believers will be delighted.

In the Victory of Allah. He gives victory
To whom He wills, and He is the Mighty,
The Merciful. This is Allah's Promise,
And Allah does not fail in His Promise..."[28]

Ubayy ibn Khalaf scoffed at this Revelation,
Thinking it was impossible, a mere fantasy.
The Persians were by far the stronger nation,
And the Romans had already lost much territory:
Egypt, Syria, and Iraq had all been attacked
And even Jerusalem had been brutally sacked.

With the churches razed, and their relics stolen,
Rebellions were rife, the treasury was depleted;
Now Heraclius was on the verge of abdication.
"How can the Persians by them be defeated?"

---

[28] (Surah Ar-Room (30): 2-6)

"How can the Revelation of Allah not be true?"
Abu Bakr responded with anger in his eyes,
"Prove it with a wager if you would dare to,
And let one hundred red camels be the prize!"
So between the two of them a wager was made,
Whether it would really happen within a decade.

And in this prophecy, Suhayb also took an interest.
He was an Arab who had been enslaved as a youth,
Taken and raised among the Romans of the East,
Till to Makkah he escaped and embraced the Truth.

For twenty years Suhayb had lived amongst them.
He had seen the decadence of the Roman Empire,
And had understood the reasons for their decline,
But they were not like those worshippers of fire,
And Heraclius for all his excesses was not Khosrow,
Who in arrogance was starting to resemble Pharaoh.

"So remind, if the Reminder should benefit.
He who is God-fearing will be reminded,
But the most wretched one shall avoid it:
He who will enter into the Greatest Fire.
Thereafter, in it he will neither live nor die.
He has certainly succeeded who himself purifies,
And mentions the Name of his Lord and prays.

But to the worldly life, you have given preference,
While the Hereafter is better and more enduring.
Most certainly, this is in the former Scriptures,
The Scriptures of Ibrahim and Musa."[29]

And living amid Persia's "Fire Worshippers" was Salman,
Till a desire like a flame arose from a spark within him,
To question the rites and rituals he had been raised on.
His father rejected him, like Azar had done to Ibrahim,
So he left his home and joined with those of Scripture,
And learnt the news of a Prophet expected in future.

---

[29] (Surah Al-'Aala (87): 9-19)

Many years passed until he came to Arabia finally,
But before he reached Makkah where all pointed to,
Salman was betrayed, captured and sold into slavery,
Then brought to Yathrib: a land where date palms grew.

It was a verdant city situated between two stony tracts,
Where clans fought, and people engaged in foolish acts,
But Salman did not ever give up faith and kept on hoping,
Until when while working in the service of a Jewish man,
Of a man named Muhammad, he heard people talking,
"He is a claimant of Prophethood from Hashim's clan."

Yet despite his deep heartfelt desire for meeting him,
Salman found no way to do so as he was no longer free,
So he continued praying and listening for news of him,
And he felt certain he would come to Yathrib eventually.

But nearer to home, the Prophet found less sympathy,
Experiencing each day abuse, ill-words and aggression,
Shunned in his own land and by his own community,
Though he was not calling them to any innovations,
Only that they return to their true ancestral values:
The Faith of Ibrahim and Isma'il, the upright ones.

Now, the people of Makkah were not entirely devoid of virtues,
Having been chosen over the Persians, Romans and Bani Israel
For the Final Messenger in their midst; to receive Divine news.
Though misguided, there did exist great potential in Bani Isma'il.

They would help one another in times of difficulty and grief,
And were blessed with patience, eloquence, courage and wit,
But sincerity in actions had been lost like the purity of belief,
So ulterior motives would deprive their own souls of benefit.
For they were a people driven not by thought but by emotions,
And in their worship they would merely go through the motions.

But like the Kaaba whose outside was beautified for beholders,
While its inner sanctum was polluted with much false adoration,
So did the pagans bear the weight of pride on their shoulders,
And differ between deed and intention in each act of devotion.

And the wealthy chiefs of every clan would vie in competition,
In great lavish outward demonstrations of their hospitality,
Desiring to be renowned or otherwise fearing to be outdone,
Yet when they were privately approached by the truly needy,
They would respond with only words of harshness and cruelty.

So to condemn such deeds came down Divine Revelation,
"Have you seen the one who calls the Judgement a lie,
For that indeed is the one who drives away the orphan,
And does not encourage the feeding of those most in need."[30]

One day, the Messenger came across Abu Jahl and his friend,
"Why don't you accept Islam and testify that I say what's true?"
"O Muhammad, when will your cursing of our gods end?
Had I known you were truthful I would have followed you!"
So the Messenger of Allah went away from them quietly,
While the Father of Ignorance kept glaring at him angrily.

But in private, Abu Jahl's frustration would be shown,
"We used to closely rival 'Abd Manaf's sons in dignity,
Now they have brought out a Prophet from their own,
How can we stoop so low and follow them obediently?"

And he even acknowledged that Muhammad truly
Did not bring falsehood and he had not told a lie,
But his sense of misplaced pride and tribal dignity,
Prevented him from ever admitting this publicly,
So he would deceive others and increase in rejection,
And Allah then revealed about his absurd situation.

"We know indeed what they say saddens you,
But surely it is not you that they do deny.
Rather it is the Communications of Allah
That these tyrannical ones do deny."[31]

The Prophet would pray in a middle course,
.While reciting the Qur'an in a measured tone,
Neither so loud that the pagans might disperse,
And leave him to stand, abandoned and alone,
Nor so quiet that those who listened stealthily,
Were unable to hear the Revelation with clarity.

And hoping that they might become guided aright,
The Messenger would at each and every occasion,
With deep wisdom and beautiful preaching invite
His community to reflect upon the Divine Revelation.

Yet the pagans' objections would vary from day to day,
"Why has there not been sent to us an angel instead?"
"Why does God not communicate by some other way?"
"What is the point of us returning after we are dead?"
"Why are you not greater than us in wealth and might?"
"Call on your Lord to punish us and give us no respite!"

The Messenger would listen to his people patiently,
And continue responding with gentle exhortation,
Encouraging them to overcome their own obstinacy,
And to give to the Exalted Qur'an due contemplation.

"When the Occurrence occurs,
Of its occurrence, there is no denial,
Abasing (some), raising (others),
When the Earth shakes with a shaking,
And the mountains break and crumble,
And become scattered dust particles.

And you become grouped into three kinds:
So those of the Right, how are those of the Right?
So those of the Left, how are those of the Left?
And the foremost ones are the Foremost ones,
They are the ones brought in near proximity,
In the Gardens of Pleasure and Delight.

A multitude of the former and a few among the latter,
On decorated thrones reclining, facing one another,
There wait on them youths, never altering in age,
With goblets, jugs and a drink from a pure spring.

Suffering no headache from it nor intoxication,
And fruits they choose and flesh of fowls they wish,
And wide-eyed beautiful ones like pearls hidden:
A reward for all the deeds that they used to do.
There will be no frivolity nor any cause for vice,
But the continuous greetings of words of peace."[32]

"Now if I were in your Religion to believe,"
Abu Lahab one day asked the Prophet,
"What distinction would I then receive?"
"The same reward that the Believers get."

"May this Religion perish," he replied angrily,
"Where I and all others are treated equally!"
So not only did he turn aside in arrogance,
But he increased in animosity day by day,
He did whatever he could to be a nuisance,
And made it a point to always get in his way.

Despite being so close to the Prophet in relation,
Abu Lahab was the furthest of all men from him.
He had already lived a long life of transgression,
And disbelief raged like an inferno within him.

He would contradict the Prophet constantly,
And follow him around throwing pebbles,
"My nephew is insane! O you people flee!
He is a liar, so ignore all that he peddles,
He reviles your gods and all your ancestors,
Will you really then be among his listeners?"

Many of those who would have taken heed,
Seeing Abu Lahab's insistence turned away
Saying, "If even his own blood reject his creed,
Why should we listen to what he has to say?"

---

[32] (Surah Al-Waqi'ah (56): 1-26)

Gathering together the mightiest of Quraysh's men,
Abu Jahl went forth as he boastfully began to lead:
Abul Ashaddayn whose strength was like that of ten,
'Umar among them too, and Khalid the son of Walid,
'Amr ibn 'Abdu Wadd, the great champion, battle-famed,
And Nawfal, who was by Quraysh "the Lion" named.

To oppose Islam by any means was their mission,
To awe from afar by their very numbers and might,
Or to beat down with threats and intimidation
Whichever of the Believers came into their sight.

Thus Abu Jahl along with 'Umar, his sister's son,
Would torture many of the weak Muslims frequently.
They pummelled Zunairah till she lost her vision,
But she adamantly refused to return to idolatry.

Lubaynah was by 'Umar severely whipped,
And he continued to scourge her relentlessly,
Until from his hand the whip finally slipped.
He said, "I have not stopped out of any sympathy,
But tiredness has caused my arms to turn lame,"
"Do what you like; your Lord shall do the same."

Abu Fukhayha, the freed slave, was frail and elderly,
Yet the polytheists tortured him for simply praying,
And they did not show him even the slightest mercy,
Until he could no longer know what he was saying.

Nawfal ibn Khuwaylid was Khadija's half-brother,
Yet he was the complete opposite of her in every way.
"The Devil of Quraysh" truly lived up to that moniker:
When he came across Abu Bakr and Talhah one day,
He tied them together after beating them brutally,
For no reason other than they professed Allah's Unity.

"And We destroyed how many a generation
Before them? They were in power far more mighty
So that they went and overran many a nation.
Was there (for them) any place of sanctuary?"[33]

---

[33] (Surah Qaf (50): 36)

The Prophet experienced a new loss that year,
When his son 'Abdullah in infancy passed away,
Abu Lahab at that began to laugh and sneer,
"Good news!" he said, "O what a joyous day!
First it was Al-Qasim, now 'Abdullah too is gone,
And now alas poor Muhammad has no son."

Al-'Aas ibn Wa'il too rejoiced when he heard,
"His line has now come to an end certainly,
Just like an animal whose tail is severed,
He shall perish and be forgotten totally!"
Similar taunts were heard from every chief,
Till Divine Words descended to ease his grief.

"Indeed We have given to you Abundance,
So pray to your Lord, and sacrifice patiently,
Indeed it is your enemy full of malevolence
Who will be the one who is cut off totally."[34]

The idolaters saw the Prophet sitting alone one day.
With fire in his eyes, Abu Jahl came to him running,
Spitting scathing abuse, foul words he began to say.
The Prophet looked at him and the people laughing.
He did not respond to him nor show any reaction,
But quietly walked away from their humiliation.

It was not long after this, when carrying a mighty bow,
Arrived Hamza from the hunt, to the Holy House to pray.
"O Abu 'Umarah! Had you but seen and if you did know,
How your nephew was abused and then walked away."

Abu Jahl was chuckling with his friends triumphantly,
When a bow came down forcefully upon his head.
His entire group recoiled back with fear impulsively,
"Will you insult him, O Abu Jahl?" Hamza said,
"Now that I am of his Religion, a believing man,
Why don't you strike me back now if you can?"

---

[34] (Surah Al-Kawthar (108): 1-3)

133

Abu Jahl howled, cradling his bleeding head,
Around him his clan with swords began to rise.
"Leave him alone, for I insulted his nephew," he said,
Seeing the leonine look that was in Hamza's eyes.

Quraysh for a while avoided harassing him,
With Hamza at the fore and Abu Talib behind,
It was too much to contend with Banu Hashim,
But there were many much easier victims to find.
Their oppression upon the helpless did not yield:
The ones who from their clan had no such shield.

Al-'Aas learned his son Hisham had become a Muslim,
So he subjected him to detainment and harsh torture,
And over Quraysh, this was a matter of pride of him,
That he was doing so for al-Lat and al-'Uzzah's honour.

And Khalid had seen a dream one night of a fiery pit,
Then behind him, he saw that his father, Sa'eed,
Was trying forcefully to push him straight into it.
No matter how he protested he would take no heed,
So as the searing flames came ever closer to his face,
He felt he was to be consumed by that dreadful place.

But at the very edge of it, just as he was about to fall,
A hand reached out and took hold of him suddenly.
He looked and saw the flames were becoming small,
As Muhammad pulled him to coolness and security.

He had awoken, alarmed and deeply afraid,
And went to find Muhammad with urgency.
He listened with great attention as he spoke,
And then testified to the truth of his Prophecy.
Years passed and his Faith remained concealed,
Until one day the secret somehow was revealed.

"How dare you follow Muhammad!" his father said,
"When he opposes your gods and ancestral creed!"
Then he whipped him till the whip broke on his head,
And Khalid ibn Sa'eed's entire face had begun to bleed.
"Now be gone! I will never provide for you anymore."
"Then, O father, my Lord will provide for me," he said.

Then he left his home, as Ibrahim had done before,
Peacefully, having chosen to side with Faith instead,
While Sa'eed turned to his other sons and glared,
"Whoever speaks to him again will not be spared."

The Messenger of Allah recited a warning to his folk:
"Have you not witnessed how your Lord treated
'Aad of Iram, whose pillars had been made lofty,
The likes of which were not in other cities created;
And the Thamud who hewed out rocks in the valley;
And Pharaoh, who was the owner of many stakes?

They each in the land had transgressed the limit,
And they each had made much corruption within it,
So your Lord poured on them a scourge of punishment.
Most surely your Lord is Ever-Watchful and Present."[35]

Even the most prominent of Quraysh in eloquence,
When they were placed against the Divine Revelation,
Would find themselves completely stunned to silence,
So to the Rabbis of Yathrib they turned in desperation.

"Ask him about the youth who believed secretly,
And about the one who travelled to East and West,
And ask him about the Spirit: what is its reality?
If this claimant of yours is able to pass this test,
Then he is indeed a Prophet, of that be assured,
For none other than us have the answers stored."

So Muhammad waited for Revelation patiently,
And the Believers were all thereby put to trial,
When fifteen nights had each passed by silently,
And the pagans had reached the peak of denial.

---

[35] (Surah Al-Fajr (89): 6-14)

135

Until in a tone that was sweet and melodious,
The Messenger of Allah began his Recitation:
"Or do you reckon amongst Our Signs wondrous,
The Companions of the Cave and the Inscription?
When the youth fled to the cave for sanctuary,
Saying, 'O Lord, bestow on us from Your Mercy...'"[36]

"And they ask you about Dhul-Qarnayn. Say:
'Something of his mention, I will unto you recite.
Indeed, We established him on the earth with might,
And gave him the means to access every way...'"[37]

"And about the Spirit, they question thee.
Say: 'The Spirit is from my Lord's instruction,
And you have not of knowledge been given
Anything except for a small quantity.'"[38]

When the Rabbis were informed of the answers,
They recognised what was referred to immediately,
But as they looked at their ink-stained fingers,
Pride barred them from accepting it publicly,
"How could a 'little knowledge' of us be said,
When the *Taurat* in its entirety we have read?"

And though a Prophet they had all been expecting,
They did not wish for one from their Arab cousins.
They saw them as inferior, base and undeserving,
Imagining in Allah's Mercy, their own restrictions.

But not alike were all the People of the Book.
Some were humble-hearted, not full of arrogance,
Who when they remembered God, wept and shook,
And behaved with gentle clemency and benevolence.
That group of Christians men who arrived one day,
Were among the sincerest followers of this way.

---

[36] (Surah Al-Kahf (18): 9-10)
[37] (Surah Al-Kahf (18): 83-84)
[38] (Surah Al-Israa (17): 85)

They each listened carefully to the Recitation,
And questioned the Prophet about many matters,
Then their hearts turned to their Lord in submission,
And testified, "Muhammad is among His Messengers."

Abu Jahl, hearing their words, spoke to them abusively,
"To bring information you were by your own people sent,
Instead you wretches renounced your religion in stupidity!"
"Peace," they replied at once, "We seek not the ignorant,
We have our religion and you have your religion certainly,
And we have been seeking what is best with all sincerity."

"Indeed Allah commands justice and kindness,
And the giving to those near of kin (in need);
And He forbids indecency, rebellion and wickedness;
He admonishes you so that you might take heed."[39]

The Prophet smiled as he addressed those in his company,
"You can never truly believe until you show each other mercy."
"O Messenger of Allah," they replied, "we all show mercy."
The Prophet looked at his companions and spoke soothingly,
"It is not that kindness which you show your friends or family,
It is the compassion that you extend towards all of humanity."

So he would enjoin his followers to God-consciousness,
To fulfil the rights of their relatives and the community,
To be mindful of every word and deed's consequence,
And to seek forgiveness for shortcomings frequently.

He would urge them to stop practices of ignorance:
All amulets, fortune-telling, gambling and divination,
To leave aside indecencies, and abandon intoxicants,
And all such acts of cruelty, folly and superstition;
For each of them came with a price to one's dignity,
And each of them caused damage to the community.

And to no longer brand their cattle upon their face,
Nor to cruelly set them alight in expectation of rain,
Nor to foolishly strike one animal in another's place,
And never to sacrifice them except in Allah's Name.

---

[39] (Surah An-Nahl (16): 90)

137

He would teach them to be truthful and trustworthy,
To fulfil their contracts, and to give the full measure,
To be steadfast in hardships, to give alms generously,
And to seek for it no glory, but only Allah's pleasure.

And to the Believers the Messenger would recite,
"Indeed, they were before that doers of goodness,
They used to sleep only a little of the night,
And in the hours before dawn sought forgiveness,
And from their properties was given a right,
For the petitioner and those who were deprived."[40]

And all of them were reminded by the Revelation,
"The Forgiver of sin, the Acceptor of repentance,
Severe in punishment, the Owner of Abundance.
There is no god but Him; to Him is the destination."[41]

The polytheists of Quraysh would also turn
Towards their 'gods' seeking their assistance,
Yet they remained as ever lifeless and taciturn,
Revealing nothing - not even their own existence,
And unresponsive to calls against their enemies,
So they had to take matters into their own hands.

Umm Anmar would come to Khabbab frequently,
Placing a red-hot piece of iron upon his head,
And would not stop till he had fainted from agony,
"This is for speaking to Muhammad!" she said.

Her brother, Siba'a, seized Khabbab furiously,
Then had him dragged outside by his hair.
They threw him upon the ground violently,
As though they would murder him there,
Striking him hard with measured blows,
Till blood and dirt drenched his clothes.

---

[40] (Surah Ad-Dhariyat (51): 16-19)
[41] (Surah Al-Ghafir (40): 3)

"About Muhammad, what do you say?"
"He is the slave of Allah, and His Prophet."
"About al-Lat and al-'Uzzah what do you say?"
"Two idols, deaf and dumb, with no benefit."

So they tortured him, leaving him bloody and raw,
But throughout it all, Khabbab would remember
The stories of the people who had gone before,
And recite what he had been taught by the Messenger.

"And they witnessed what they did to those who believed,
And they did not upon the Believers ever retaliate
For any other reason except that they had believed
In Allah, the All-Mighty, Most Praiseworthy and Great,
To whom belongs the Heavens' and Earth's Dominion.
And Allah is a Witness over all things in creation."[42]

Khabbab came to the Prophet, utterly dejected,
Fed up of the pagans' torture and harsh attitude.
The Prophet seeing his state felt deeply affected,
And he drew near to him with great solicitude.

"The Believers in former times suffered too,
Some were raked with iron combs side to side,
And others who endured even when sawn in two,
So be patient and endure," the Prophet replied,
"For God will establish this Faith most certainly,
Such that a Believer may travel alone in security.

Banu Makhzum were perhaps the cruellest clan
In their behaviour towards the helpless Believers,
Showing no mercy to any child, woman or man
If they had besides Allah no other protectors.

Thus, Sumayyah, Yasir, and 'Ammar, their son,
Would be subjected to the worst kind of harm,
But they each refused to bow down to oppression,
And kept declaring their unwavering faith in Islam,
So Abu Hudhayfah ibn al-Mughirah renounced them,
And took turns with Abu Jahl in tormenting them.

---

[42] (Surah Al-Buruj (85): 7-9)

Thick coats of heavy mail they were made to wear,
Then forced to stand for hours in the blazing heat.
"O Family of Yasir! Patience!" the Prophet declared,
"Indeed, Paradise is the place where you shall meet."

Abu Jahl was filled with rage, and could not tolerate
Their strength of character and resilience in every test,
So he picked up his spear, with his eyes burning with hate,
And he plunged it with great force into Sumayyah's chest.
'Ammar screamed as he saw his mother's life drain away,
And then his father too became martyred in Allah's way.

'Ammar returned to the Messenger in a state of weeping.
He consoled him, "Your parents are in Paradise certainly."
'Ammar's grief did not subside, and increased in weeping,
"Until I said some words, they would not release me!"

"And what about your heart, 'Ammar, what is its condition?"
He replied, "It is overflowing with certainty and Faith!"
"Then weep not, for indeed about you has come Revelation,
'*...except who is forced while his heart is at rest with Faith.'*[43]
Then the Messenger wiped away 'Ammar's tears and gently said,
"If they return to you, then say the same words that you said."

"Go to Abyssinia," the Prophet now started advising,
When he saw that persecution had gotten out of hand.
"They are ruled there by An-Najashi, the Just King,
And no one has to fear any oppression in his land."

The first group by 'Uthman ibn Maz'un was led,
And he was accompanied by Mus'ab ibn 'Umayr;
'Uthman ibn 'Affan; and Abu Hudhayfah at its head;
Then 'Abdur Rahman; Abu Salamah; and Zubayr;
Followed by 'Amir ibn Rabi'ah; and Abu Sabrah;
Then Sahlah; Laylah; Ruqayyah; and Umm Salamah.

---

[43] (Surah An-Nahl (16): 106)

A second group was led by Ja'far and his wife, Asma.
Among them were Sa'ad; Miqdad; Khalid; Abu 'Ubaydah;
'Abdullah ibn Mas'ud; the sons of Jahsh; Khunays; Sawdah;
'Ayyash ibn Hisham; and Ramlah, Abu Sufyan's daughter.

With the Makhzumi horsemen pursuing closely,
They came across a merchant ship at As-Shu'aybah,
And boarded it to travel to a land across the Red Sea,
Escaping from tyranny, just as the followers of Musa.
And although their pursuers had not been drowned,
Their failure had brought their egos to the ground.

In Abyssinia, the Muslims finally found security.
They were not maligned or abused in any way,
But treated with great kindness and hospitality,
And could in worship peacefully spend their days.

So their escape infuriated the pagans to no end:
If the Muslims found abroad a place of sanctuary,
Perhaps fortune would then towards them bend,
And they might grow and prosper as a community,
Then a day would come when they too, in course,
Would return to drive the Quraysh out with force.

So they sent 'Amr ibn Al-'Aas, famed for cunning,
To Axum, bearing with him great gifts and finery
To the Court of An-Najashi, the Christian King,
And he made before him an impassioned plea.

"Some foolish youth have come to your shore,
Having abandoned their ancestors' religion
For a new way that none had ever seen before;
Neither you nor us have of it any recognition,
Therefore their kin and our town's nobility,
Request that you send them back with me."

Hearing this, An-Najashi looked deep in thought,
"If you speak true, they'll be handed over to you,
But it is best I examine them first before my Court,
Since they have sought sanctuary here from you."

141

'Amr laughed as they entered into his audience,
But did not bow themselves before An-Najashi,
The King looked at them with some annoyance,
Saying, "Why do you people not bow before me?"
"We do not bow down to, besides Allah, any other,
For thus were we commanded by His Messenger."

"What is this new Religion that you have come upon,
To separate you from the faith of your community?"
To speak, Ja'far son of Abu Talib, sought permission,
And responded eloquently to an intrigued An-Najashi.

"O King! We were a people lost in ignorance,
We worshipped idols and engaged in immorality,
The weak from the strong ones had no defence,
And neither neighbour nor kinship had sanctity,
Until the time God raised a Prophet amongst us,
Known for integrity, truth and trustworthiness.

He called us to the worship of Allah alone,
To renounce all forms of falsehood and idolatry.
Our ancestors used to carve from wood and stone,
And we in their footsteps were following blindly.

He commanded us to speak truth constantly,
And to honour our promises and our pledge,
To treat neighbours and relations mercifully,
To avoid bloodshed, slander and sacrilege;
Neither to malign chaste women indecently,
Nor to take the orphan's wealth wrongfully.

He enjoined on us to uphold the prayer,
To give charity from our wealth, and fast.
We believed in him and trials had to bear,
For our people tried to return us to the past.

They inflicted upon us oppression day and night,
Torturing us with mockery, abuse and harm,
They obstructed us from our Religion and our right,
Trying to compel us to worship idols after Islam,
So we left our home so that our Faith be saved,
And came to you for the peace that we craved."

142

'Amr the son of Al-'Aas ibn Wa'il, conjured up a plan,
"O King! They only speak of Jesus to impress you,
But they believe he was nothing more than a man,
And they claim that the Trinity is falsehood too."

The King turned his eye to the Muslims again,
"Tell me now, what is your belief about Jesus?"
They were silent, till Ja'far stepped forth to explain,
"We believe only that which our Prophet has told us,
That he is indeed the slave of God and His Emissary,
His spirit, and the Word He gave to the Virgin Mary."

An-Najashi smiled and nodded in affirmation,
"Indeed about Jesus, you have said what is right,
Now I'd like to hear the Words of your Revelation,
Is there any portion from it that you can recite?"

Ja'far began with a voice, that was clear and melodious,
"In the Name of Allah, Most Gracious and Merciful."
The entire court listened, utterly overawed in silence,
For they had never heard words so brief and beautiful,
"And in the Book, the story of Mary make mention,
When to a place east, from her folk she took seclusion..."[44]

And as he continued to recite the Remembrance,
Of how the Angel Jibreel good news brought,
And how Mary gave birth to Jesus miraculously,
The King wept until his beard became wet,
And the bishops' tears made their scrolls wet.

"These words and those that were to Jesus revealed,
Are like two rays coming from the same source of light.
Not for a mountain of gold, you would I ever yield!
You may remain here as you like and enjoy every right."

---

[44] (Surah Maryam (19): 16)

143

Meanwhile in Makkah, things remained tense.
The Believers who had remained were scattered,
And the pagans too felt their homes' emptiness.
There was no family except that it had suffered
Separation from daughter, sister, brother or son,
And they wondered how long this would go on.

Between Maqam Ibrahim and the Holy Kaaba,
The Messenger of Allah would stand for prayers,
While he was watched by enemies near and far,
Trying to unnerve him with their angry stares.

And the valley echoed with the Prophet's Recitation,
"So I swear by what you see and what you do not perceive,
That verily this is the word of an Honoured Messenger,
And it is not the word of a poet; little that you believe!
Nor is it the word of a soothsayer; little that you remember!
It is from the Lord of the Worlds, a Revelation."[45]

'Umar ibn al-Khattab happened to be walking by,
And as soon as those words fell upon his ear,
They found a place in his heart involuntarily;
Never had he heard something so compellingly clear.

Yet he refused to accept it, and denied it was true:
He was not going to reject Bani 'Adiyy's traditions,
Nor was he going to go against Banu Makhzum.
This Qur'an must have some other explanation.
He had heard Walid ibn al-Mughirah call it sorcery,
And Abu Jahl said it was Banu Hashim's trickery.

'Utbah ibn Rabi'ah was among men considered great,
Chief of Banu 'Abd Shams, wealthy and respected.
"O Quraysh, I will speak to Muhammad and negotiate,
And perhaps I shall offer him what won't be rejected."

---

[45] (Surah Al-Haaqqah (69): 38-43)

"You enjoy a high station amongst us as you know,
On account of your illustrious ancestry and family,
Yet you have amongst us divisions begun to sow,
You have spoken of our religion and gods abusively,
But I have some suggestions, so please listen well,
And perhaps you will find one of them acceptable."

"Say whatever you like," the Prophet replied,
"And I will listen to whatever you have to say."
'Utbah placed his hand on his chest with pride,
"Then this can be resolved in the easiest way!"

"If you seek wealth, we will give you abundantly,
And if it's honour, then you will become our King.
If you are afflicted by some disease or an evil entity,
We will seek out physicians and continue spending
Until you have been cured. Just name your price,
I am sure that we can reach some compromise."

The Prophet listened patiently until 'Utbah ended,
Then he lifted his head, which was glistening bright,
"Just now," he said, "Divine Revelation has descended,
So, O 'Utbah, will you hear how your Lord has replied?"

"Ha-Meem! A Revelation from the Most Merciful,
A Book whose Signs are expounded, made apparent,
An Arabic Recitation, for people who are knowledgeable,
A Bringer of glad tidings and a Divine-Warner sent.
Yet most of them have turned away from it heedlessly,
Saying, 'To what you call us we are veiled certainly.'"[46]

'Utbah ibn Rabi'ah silently listened to the Recitation,
Sometimes reclining, and then leaning forward,
From afar, the Quraysh watched with anticipation,
Witnessing how he seemed to hang on every word.

"But if they turn aside now, then declare,
'I have warned you of a mighty thunderbolt,
Like the thunderbolt 'Aad and Thamud did bear.'"[47]

---

[46] (Surah Al-Fussilat (41): 1-5)
[47] (Surah Al-Fussilat (41): 13)

145

At this, 'Utbah suddenly bounded forth with a jolt,
Placing his hands upon the Prophet's mouth hastily,
"For Allah's sake, upon your people have mercy!"

He returned, flushed and shaking, full of awe,
All the chiefs around him quickly gathered,
"By God! 'Utbah's face is so unlike before,
What is it, O man! What have you heard?"

"I have heard a speech like no other before.
It is not poetry, soothsaying nor is it sorcery.
Listen well, O Quraysh! And be of this sure:
Do not interfere with this man, leave him be.
If the Arabs strike him down, it's your benefit,
But if he overcomes them, you too shall profit."

"Does the sorcery of his tongue," they cried,
"Now bewitch even you, O Abu Walid, so fast?"
"To give a wise decision, I have merely tried,
But you can act as you like," he conceded at last.

Then some time later, they came upon him again;
Four chiefs: Al-'Aas, Walid, Al-Aswad and Umayyah,
Saying, "We have a suggestion from which all shall gain.
And guidance and prosperity will be assured in Makkah
If one year we agree to worship your Lord," they said,
"Then the next you agree to worship ours instead."

The Messenger of Allah did not deign to answer;
Saying only, "Let me my Lord's command await."
The chiefs of Quraysh sat down then and were eager
To hear what the Revelation would now state.

"Say: 'O you who are Disbelievers,
I worship not what you worship,
Nor of what I serve are you servers.
I shall never worship what you worship.
Nor to He whom I serve, will you ever pray.
For you is your way and for me my way.'"[48]

---

[48] (Surah Al-Kafiroon (109): 1-6)

Year VI

Harsh Opposition

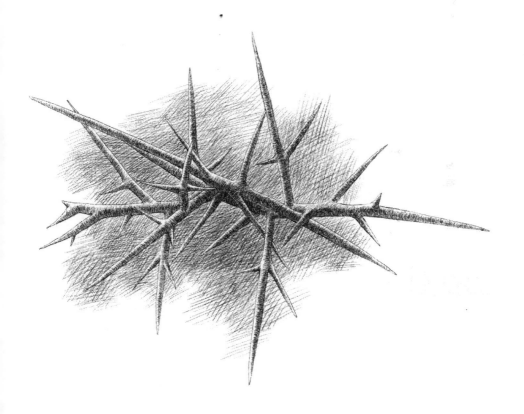

The Messenger of Mercy

"Woe to each and every slandering defamer,
Who collects wealth and counts it continuously.
He thinks his wealth will make him last forever,
Nay! Into Al-Hutamah he shall be hurled certainly..."[49]

Al-Akhnas ibn Shariq kept vilifying the Prophet,
Lying, and insulting him at every opportunity.
Nadr disturbed each gathering where he would sit,
While the two named "Aswad" mocked with impunity.
From Al-'Aas and Al-Harith there came many a test,
And Walid ibn al-Mughirah almost equalled the rest.

Walid was a man mired in his own admiration.
He considered himself among men peerless,
Worthier than any even for receiving Revelation,
And felt his wealth had made him needless.

So when his arrogance had reached its height,
The Messenger was ordered to publicly recite,
"Do not yield to every mean, frequent oath-taker,
Who slanderously goes around with calumny:
A preventer of good, a cruel, sinful transgressor,
And besides all that, marked with ignobility."[50]

The people of Makkah were at this utterly amazed:
What courage Muhammad had to say such a thing!
Yet Ibn al-Mughirah's ego by it was only raised,
And his efforts against Islam kept on increasing.

Rousing the worst of Banu Makhzum's sentiments,
Walid created a fire in the hearts of his kinsmen;
Those for whom pride and wealth took precedence.
And Abu Jahl was the most hardline among them,
For his words were the worst in their contumely,
And his actions were the harshest in their cruelty.

---

[49] (Surah Al-Hutamah (104): 1-4)
[50] (Surah Al-Qalam (68): 10-13)

And just as the Messenger would strive each day,
Abu Jahl too exerted himself with utmost exertion:
Two callers, each calling towards a different way,
One towards forgiveness, the other to destruction.

With his heart already blackened by senseless hate,
His eyes blinded by pride, and ears deaf to admonition,
The Father of Ignorance would not relent nor abate
His misguided campaign of calumny and oppression.
The arrogant, the harsh ones and the weak-minded,
All joined his ranks and vowed to oppose the Prophet.

"Nay! Indeed by this City itself I swear!
While you have been made lawful in this City.
And by the begetter and what he begot,
Man was created in distress most certainly."[51]

And Umm Jameel, Abu Lahab's aggressive wife,
Would keep inciting her husband day and night
To create further difficulties in the Prophet's life.
And she herself would with most deliberate spite,
Place thorns in his path that she had kept in store,
And would throw all sorts of filth in front of his door.

The Prophet would witness all of this and simply say,
"What kind of neighbourliness is this that you show?"
But their mistreatment would only increase day by day,
As the rancour within their chests continued to grow.

And the Quraysh would try to frighten the Messenger,
Of the wrath of their gods, and the might of their clan;
Making vague threats of reprisals that he would suffer,
And hinting there was being prepared against him a plan.
The Messenger listened to this with complete serenity,
For in his Lord he had placed his trust in its entirety.

---

[51] (Surah Al-Balad (90): 1-4)

"Indeed, the Qur'an is a decisive statement,
And it is in no way a thing for amusement.
Indeed, they are all planning a plan,
But I too have been planning a plan.
So then allow time for the Disbelievers;
Leave them gently for a short span."[52]

The plots of the pagans would each day vary,
Desperately trying to leave no stone unturned.
Through each avenue, they wandered blindly,
And from each dead end sullenly returned.

Nadr ibn al-Harith would hire several songstresses
To distract people away from the Prophet's way.
"And among the people is he who purchases
Idle talk, without knowledge, to lead astray
From the way of Allah and to take it for mockery.
For them will be a most humiliating penalty."[53]

As soothsayers called their allies from the jinn fervently,
Others hired some sorcerers to carry out their sorcery,
Along with foul men who were known for their evil eye,
So Words were revealed to counteract all they would try.

"Say: 'I seek refuge with the Lord of mankind:
Mankind's Eternal Sovereign King,
The One who is desired fervently by mankind;
From the evil of the whisperer, ever-slinking,
Who whispers into the chests of men,
From among the jinn and men.'"[54]

Then a second Surah was to him by Jibreel dictated,
"Say: 'I seek refuge with the Lord of Splitting,
From the harm of that which He has created,
And the harm of darkness as it begins spreading,
And the harm of those who carry out sorceries,
And the harm of the envier when he envies.'"[55]

---

[52] (Surah At-Tariq (86): 13-17)

[53] (Surah Luqman (31): 6)

[54] (Surah An-Naas (114): 1-6)

[55] (Surah Al-Falaq (113): 1-5)

The Messenger of Allah had until now each night,
Called on his Lord with many different invocations,
But now, these two Surahs he would simply recite,
Blow over himself, and it sufficed him for protection.

A great assembly had gathered for an occasion,
With Believers and idolaters from every clan.
The Prophet stood up, commanding attention,
And took hold of the ear and tongue of every man.
Then he began a Recitation that made them quake,
As if the Kaaba's walls themselves began to shake.

"(I swear) by the star when it fades away!
Your companion has not erred nor gone astray,
Nor has he spoken what he himself desired;
It is naught but Revelation upon him inspired..."[56]

The Quraysh listened in a state of rapt reverence.
The Recitation was melodious and full of authority,
As though the sky itself demanded their deference,
Or the earth would nearly sway due to its gravity.
It was no idle speech nor whimsical composition;
In it was certainty, dominance and admonition.

And although it was Muhammad's voice they heard,
This message was from other than him, undoubtedly.
Each sentence flowed as though it were a single word,
With the tone of one firmly established in Sovereignty.

"And have you considered al-Lat and al-'Uzzah,
And the third one, Manat, that other one?
Are the sons for you, and daughters for (Allah)?
This would then be an unreasonable division!
They are named only by you and your ancestry.
Allah has sent down for them no authority..."[57]

---

[56] (Surah An-Najm (53): 1-4)
[57] (Surah An-Najm (53): 19-23)

"Do you then at this statement marvel?
And you laugh, and are not weeping?
And engaged are you in merry-making?
So bow down before Allah and worship Him!"[58]

At that the Prophet fell into prostration,
And was followed by the entire assembly.
Such was the effect of the Divine Recitation,
Even the Disbelievers prostrated humbly,
But Walid just rubbed soil on his head,
"This much shall suffice me," he said.

Yet when news got around of that event,
The chiefs felt embarrassed and ashamed,
So together a story they decided to invent.
"He recited praise of those idols he named,
We thought he had compromised with us,
So we bowed down out of thankfulness."

This fooled the fools, all too eager anyway,
But it would not do much to stem the tide.
They each knew what had happened that day,
Even if they could not admit it out of pride.

The pagans were of varied kinds in their views:
Most of them believed in Allah as their Creator,
But still associated lesser deities with Him too,
Claiming that each one of them was an intercessor.
Three hundred and sixty at a time they venerated,
Though they had been by their own hands created.

Some of them said the angels were "Allah's daughters",
"The jinn have kinship with Allah," others would claim,
Or that, "In Ar-Rahman, we will never be believers,
For indeed we do not know or recognise that Name."

And when it came to the Day of Resurrection,
They had no certainty of belief with regards to it.
Their ideas were often riddled with contradiction,
And their minds pretended not to acknowledge it,

---

[58] (Surah An-Najm (53): 59-62)

153

As though by denial they could avoid responsibility,
And therefore no longer had to live with its reality.

And so with great hubris, conceit and arrogance,
A group of Disbelievers came to the Prophet,
"Bring the Day with which you threaten us,
And only then shall we have any faith in it."

So some powerful Verses were in response sent,
"That which you are promised will come to be,
Then when the stars turn dim, and the sky is rent,
And the mountains are dust scattered completely,
And the Messengers at their times are gathered:
For which Day have (these Signs) been deferred?"[59]

Something inside their hearts would stir at this,
Like the sudden shattering of some great illusion,
And the path they were headed on now felt amiss,
Yet they stubbornly clung on to familiar delusions.

The worst of the Quraysh would, without any shame,
Follow the Messenger, carrying dust in their hands,
And shout, "Shall I direct you to a man who claims,
When you are like *this* you will be made to stand?"
Their scepticism was stubbornness without reason,
For they all witnessed plants reborn each season.

"Nay! I swear by the Day of Resurrection,
And nay! I swear by the soul full of self-accusation.
Does man not think We can assemble his bones?
Yes indeed his fingertips, We can re-proportion."[60]

Ubayy ibn Khalaf crushed a rotten bone in his hand,
"O Muhammad!" he said as he blew it into his face,
"So you claim that the dead will rise and stand,
Tell me who will make *this* return to its place?"
The chiefs began to laugh and became jubilant,
Till the descent of Revelation made them silent.

---

[59] (Surah Al-Mursalaat (77): 7-12)
[60] (Surah Al-Qiyamah (75): 1-4)

"Does man not see We created him from a seed,
Then at once, he becomes an open adversary,
And similitudes for Us he has conceived,
While his own creation he forgets totally.
He asks 'Who will rotten bones reanimate?'

Say: 'The One who will reanimate them is He
Who in the first instance, them did create,
And He is of all creation cognizant totally.'"[61]

The sly Al-'Aas ibn Wa'il used this opportunity
To defraud Khabbab ibn al-Aratt from his due.
"Don't you claim in Paradise there will be plenty
Of gold and silver and servants for each of you?
So till the Resurrection Day you should respite me,
For I will have just as much as all of you certainly."

And despite Khabbab's demands for his payment,
Or else to return his swords back to him instead,
Al-'Aas grew ever more evasive and recalcitrant,
And so in this regard his Lord about him said,

"Have you seen him who denies Our Signs,
And says, 'I'll surely be given wealth and children?'
Has he into the Unseen looked for information,
Or from the Most Merciful taken a covenant?
Nay! We will record what he says continuously,
And extend for him the punishment extensively!"[62]

The poets would speak out against the Prophet,
Satirising him with their delirious compositions,
Yet the Qur'an was ever-sufficient a response to it,
And their ramblings were impotent by comparison.

---

[61] (Surah Ya-Seen (36): 77-79)
[62] (Surah Maryam (19): 77-79)

And to every doubtful cynic the Messenger would say,
The startling words, ***"That is the Day of the Surest Reality,***
So whoever wishes should with his Lord seek a way.
We have warned you of a near punishment certainly,
The Day when a man sees all that he has sent ahead,
And the Disbeliever says, 'Woe! If only I were dust instead.'"[63]

"O Muhammad!" said Abu Jahl, "Do you threaten me?
You know I am among the most important of men
On this earth. Indeed I am the noble, the mighty!"
Such was his arrogance, Verses were revealed then.

"Indeed, the Tree of Zaqqum is food for the sinful.
Like dregs of oil, within the bellies it will boil,
Similar to the boiling of intensely scalding water.
Seize him and drag him to the Fire's very middle,
Then pour on his head the torment of scalding water.
Taste! Indeed, you are 'the mighty, the noble!'"[64]

This did not deter him, nor did it lessen his pride.
Instead his head became puffed up and swollen,
Then a feeling of great superiority filled him inside,
As he saw himself to be the centre of all attention.

"O Quraysh!" said Abu Jahl in a gathering,
"Of the Tree of Zaqqum are you aware?
That which Muhammad keeps frightening,
Is Yathrib's buttered dates I declare by God!
If we could only of them catch a single sight,
We would gobble them down in a single bite!"

This made his audience fall over with laughter,
And this is something that he did frequently,
Recalling the Revelations some time after,
And making them the subject of his mockery.

---

[63] (Surah An-Naba (78): 39-40)
[64] (Surah Ad-Dukhaan (44): 43-49)

And Abu Jahl once rose up in a furied craze,
"I swear by Allah that tomorrow I will wait
With a stone so large that I can barely raise,
To smash his head when he is in prostration.
Banu 'Abdu Manaf can do after it as they will,
But Muhammad I myself will surely kill!"

The next morning, in front of the Kaaba,
The Prophet was found in prayer engaged.
The Quraysh watched Abu Jahl from afar,
And saw him flee like a man deranged.

"What happened?" they asked incredulously
To Abu Jahl who returned pale and petrified.
"I saw a huge camel stallion come before me
When to approach him with the stone I tried.
By Allah! I've never seen the likes of it before;
It was as though it would devour me for sure."

Abu Jahl's courage for now had all but vanished,
And with it, gone the Devil's most deadly urge,
Yet whenever one such flame was extinguished,
Another elsewhere would then quickly emerge.

'Umar ibn al-Khattab, a man of fierce temperament,
Drew out his sword and strode through the street,
"I will find Muhammad who has created dissent.
Long has he mocked the gods and spread deceit.
Now of our truth, I shall bring the surest sign,
For I will end his life with this blade of mine!"

Nu'aym replied, "How can you do such a thing?
For 'Abd Manaf's sons would never spare you.
Reform your own who are his Religion following:
Your sister Fatima, and Sa'eed her husband, too."

And at this news 'Umar became incensed,
So he ran to his sister's home furiously.
And in fear, when they his arrival sensed,
They hid Khabbab, their teacher, hastily,
But 'Umar struck his sister on her head,
And his brother-in-law too until they bled.

157

"Yes! Indeed we are Muslims," they cried,
"Do as you will, for we believe certainly!"
'Umar then felt something stir deep inside,
And he now fell still and silent regretfully.

Then when he had calmed down, 'Umar said,
"Let me see what you were reciting earlier."
They brought out an inscribed leaf and read,
Verses that made him filled with hope and fear.
'Umar began to shake and tremble to his core,
And he was overwhelmed with a sense of awe.

"In the Name of Allah, Most Gracious and Merciful.
Ta-Ha! We have not sent down to you the Recitation
So that you would become one who is unsuccessful,
But it is a Reminder for every God-fearing one..."[65]

Now 'Umar was listening to every word attentively.
"Has there come to you the story of Musa?
When he saw a fire and he said to his family,
'Wait! Indeed I have perceived a fire from afar.
A brand from it, I may bring for you perchance,
Or find by the fire perhaps some means of guidance.'

And when he came to it, he was called, 'O Musa!
Verily I am your Lord. So, take off your sandals here,
You are most certainly in the Sacred Valley of Tuwa.
And I have chosen you, so to what is revealed give careful ear.

Indeed I am Allah; there is no god whatsoever except for Me.
So serve Me and establish prayer for My remembrance continuously.
Surely the Hour is coming; I have kept it concealed purposefully,
In order that every soul's effort is to be rewarded appropriately.
So be not from it diverted by him who does not believe in it at all,
And follows his desires, for then you would into perdition fall.'"[66]

---

[65] (Surah Ta-Ha (20): 1-3)
[66] (Surah Ta-Ha (20): 9-16)

Then 'Umar came knocking at the Messenger's house stridently,
And the Believers, seeing him approach had become distraught.
"Let him enter," said Hamza. "He's welcome if his intent is Godly,
But if it be evil, he shall be slain by the very sword he's brought."

"O 'Umar!" said the Prophet, "what is your purpose?"
"To declare belief in Allah and His Messenger," he replied.
The Prophet smiled and was filled with great happiness,
As each Muslim welcomed Al-Khattab's son to their side.
And the Disbelievers became enraged when they did learn,
Of the loss of a supporter who had been so fierce and stern.

Then 'Umar went out to announce his Faith openly.
Abu Jahl's face darkened and he slammed his door
Shouting, "Your action is bad and your face is ugly!
Now do not expect any good from me anymore."

Abu Jahl incited a group of pagans against his nephew,
"Banu Makhzum withdraws from him all protection."
So 'Umar remained in his home when opposition grew,
With his family, now fearful of some violent retaliation,
Until to him came Al-'Aas ibn Wa'il, Banu Sahm's chief,
Offering protection despite 'Umar's newfound belief.

Now that everything had again been turned on its head,
The disquiet among the Quraysh continued to grow,
And one thought especially filled Abu Jahl with dread:
With even 'Umar now a Muslim, who else might follow?

Year VII

The Boycott

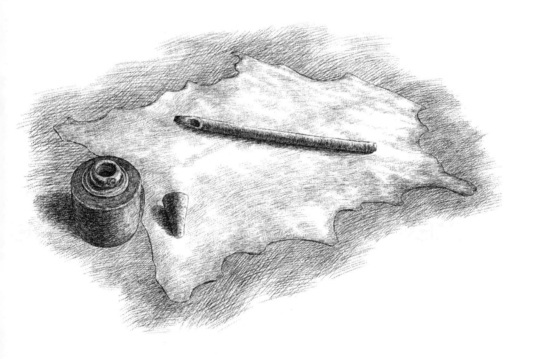

The Messenger of Mercy

"Have you not seen how your Lord
Dealt with the Companions of the Elephant?
Did He not turn their plan into discord?
And upon them birds in flocks, He had sent,
Pelting them with stones of hardened clay,
Thus He made them like consumed hay."[67]

"For the tribe of Quraysh's ongoing protection:
Their protection for the winter and summer caravan.
So let them the Lord of this House sincerely adore,
Who fed them from hunger and from fear made secure."[68]

The pagans of Quraysh were angry and exasperated,
Against their interests, Muhammad continued to preach,
So they came together, and they carefully deliberated:
Was Muhammad aught but a man with alluring speech?
Did he have any power, other than his clan's protection?
Thus they came to Abu Talib with one last suggestion.

"Without any equal in beauty, poetry, and of noble clan,
Is 'Ammarah ibn al-Walid, whom you may take as a son,
In exchange for Muhammad - a trade, man for man,
So that we may rid you of his discord and rebellion."

Abu Talib's response was one full of fury,
"This offer of yours is completely unfair,
That you should entrust your son to me,
For him to be raised and treated with care,
But that I should to your hands surrender,
The dearest of my children for his murder!

I have for you this proposal instead:
Each of you should bring his son to me,
And I shall return them all to you dead.
Now tell me which of you does agree?"

---

[67] (Surah Al-Feel (105): 1-5)
[68] (Surah Quraysh (106): 1-4)

"Your people with you have been fair,
Trying hard not to make you displeased,"
Said Mut'im ibn 'Adiyy. "But I despair,
As you are with nothing ever pleased."

"I swear by Allah!" Abu Talib replied,
"They have not at all been fair to me.
With our enemies do you take a side?
Go! Do as you will and so shall we!"
At that voices became raised angrily,
And groups separated with great enmity.

Some of the pagans would conspire together,
Whispering plots, as they would secretly gather.
"Lower your voices you fools!" one man hissed,
"Lest Muhammad's Lord should hear of this!"

So Words came to the heart of the Prophet,
Answering the foolish notions of the ignorant.
"And conceal your speech or do proclaim it;
Surely He is of what is within chests cognizant.
Does He not know - the One who has created,
While He is the Subtle, the Acquainted?"[69]

One day the Prophet wore clothes newly sown,
And was in some acts of worship deeply dutiful,
When the idolaters approached seeing him alone,
And threw upon him the entrails of an animal.

When Abu Talib of this occurrence was informed,
He mounted his swiftest camel, sword in hand,
And with tremendous wrath he quickly stormed
Through Makkah, seeking that wretched band.
And those that had mocked became terrified,
Seeing Abu Talib appear with Hamza at his side.

---

[69] (Surah Al-Mulk (67): 13-14)

"I swear if any of you moves from his place,
I will cut him down now with my sword."
They all stood frozen, with lowered face,
As the same filth over them was poured.

In a single line, the guilty ones were arraigned,
And Hamza rubbed the entrails into their faces.
Despite being humiliated they each remained
Standing motionless like statues in their places,
Until even their moustaches had been dyed red,
And not a single man dared raise his voice or head.

Not while Abu Talib's eyes still raged like fire,
"O Quraysh! By Allah, by Allah! Indeed I swear,
Whoever among you, mischief still does desire,
After knowing who I am - act now if you dare!"

Then Abu Talib turned affectionately to his nephew,
"Indeed you are Muhammad, 'Abdullah's son,
A son of the noble ones and truly noble are you.
How are you being wronged while I still live on?
And to your truthfulness we have all testified,
Since even your childhood you have never lied."

Abu Talib's courage sent a shudder in every pagan heart;
His presence, a constant obstacle to all that they sought.
And before the pagans' puffed up words could even start,
Abu Talib's tongue was ever-ready with a poetic retort.

"By the Sacred House! You lie! Leave Makkah and our lands?
You lie! Leave Muhammad, instead of fighting in his aid?
Or before we fall down dead, surrender him to your hands?
Muhammad, the one for whose sake rain clouds were made,
The one who provides for orphans and widows generously,
And to whom each and every needy one flocks eagerly?"

"He is mild in temper, just, God-fearing and astute in thought.
His deeds are noble, his inheritance fine, and his lineage pure.
The Lord of men has aided him and he has a Religion brought,
Whose truth is apparent and without doubt shall endure."

165

"Our son has never been thought by us to be a liar,
And he is not one who is inclined to falsehood at all.
So I swear, that no matter how much you should desire,
All efforts you make will fall short and weigh too small.
For I will not surrender the one whom I cared for all his life,
And rushed to protect him from all animosity and strife."

After he made this clear declaration of his intentions,
There were few men left who would dare to test him.
If every attempt would be met with swift vengeance,
No clan wanted to start a war with the Banu Hashim.

Thus to the pagans of Makkah, it was now clear as day
That Abu Talib could not be reasoned with nor bought,
The threat of force did not intimidate him in any way,
He would carry on and cared not what they thought,
So they decided that a new approach was now required
If they were serious about attaining what they desired.

"Accept no marriage with Banu Hashim anymore,
And do not buy or sell to them any commodity,
Let them all starve, ostracise them and ignore,
And let them feel cut off from our entire society!"

Once they had to these conditions agreed,
A dried goatskin parchment was brought,
Committed to ink by the hand of Bagheed,
Then each clan signed it to affirm their support,
And they chose for it a place most sacred of all:
To be suspended upon the Kaaba's inner wall.

So Banu Hashim banded together in unity,
Some for Faith, others for their familial pride,
Except Al-Mughirah, who retained enmity,
And Abu Lahab, chief among all who denied.

"Muhammad promises us that which we cannot see,
Claiming that some things will happen after we die,
But why should I suffer alongside them pointlessly?
His words I don't believe, and his prophecy I deny!"
Thus Abu Lahab chose a path for himself of his own,
Rejecting all the clear Signs that he had been shown.

Living now among the Quraysh had become impossible,
So with a heavy heart, Abu Talib announced his decision:
If the Banu Hashim were to have any hope of survival,
They would have to move into the Valley for protection.

The Valley of Banu Hashim in the centre of Makkah
Was a rocky gorge directly behind their habitations.
Its only opening was located to the east of the Kaaba,
And it was protected on three sides by tall mountains;
As-Safa and Abu Qubays stood firm on the southern side,
And Mustandhar and Khandama guarded the northern side.

The pagans having all committed to the Boycott,
Were also preventing them from leaving Makkah.
To force them into submission was Abu Jahl's plot,
But even he was surprised that it had gone so far.

As they left for the Valley in a procession of silence,
Each passed by strange faces that once were known;
Kinsman and neighbour, friend and acquaintance,
But no word was spoken and no sympathy shown.
Abu Talib looked at them and then his own family,
And began to recite some words spontaneously.

"The people exchanged friendship for separation,
Since rage has been boiling in their chests violently.
I seek refuge with the Lord of men from aggression,
And remain firm, with spear and sword ever ready.

Every great sinner, from each clan does unite,
After Sahm and Makhzum incited amongst us hate,
Driving us from our homes, forsaking us to our plight,
While we would not have left any alone in this fate.
And all relatives and friends are of no avail today,
Except a few who remain blameless in this way.

O Aba Walid, what benefit did you bring to our side,
When you came to us, and then you turned aside?
You were once known to be a man kind and wise,
So 'Utbah, listen not to slanderers and their lies.

167

Subayy and Nawfal were also not kind in behaviour,
Separating away from us with extreme opposition.
Then there is Abu 'Amir who does love to whisper,
Morning and evening, maliciously with ill intention.
And Abu Sufyan who passes by feigning sympathy,
Thinking he would conceal his long-held enmity.

O Mut'im, you of all people, are not here for us today,
While I had never abandoned you in times of need,
And against your enemies, with you stood at the fray?
I did my duty as I saw fit, so act too by your creed."

Abu Talib watched over his nephew as he slept,
And memories began to flash before his eyes,
Of how when 'Abdullah died, he had bitterly wept,
And how his death had taken them all by surprise.
But not long after that, Aminah gave birth to a boy,
And that day for him had turned their grief into joy.

And come to think of it, Abu Talib remembered too,
Even Abu Lahab that day had been full of happiness.
When Thuwaybah gave him the news of his nephew,
He had immediately freed her out of thankfulness.

And 'Abdul Muttalib held a feast of celebration.
His grandchild so fair and with eyes so bright,
Filled whoever held him with deep admiration,
And delighted whichever passer-by caught sight.
They named him Muhammad, "Most Praiseworthy,"
And never had any been named more appropriately.

That was only a few months after the great event,
"The Year of the Elephant", as it was later called,
When the proud Abraha of Yemen his army sent,
Boasting he would bring down the Kaaba's walls.

But Abraha's army was destroyed by a flock of birds,
And other strange things were later talked about:
A dazzling white light was seen headed eastwards,
Lake Sawah dried, ancient temple flames died out,
The desert swelled, pillars of Khosrow's Palace fell;
And what all of it meant, no soothsayer could tell.

It had been a year like no other, full of significance,
Momentous events seen all throughout the Earth,
Clearly betokening something of great importance:
He was now sure they heralded Muhammad's birth.

And when the plague came to Makkah in his infancy,
A disease for which there was besides God no healer,
He was sent to live with bedouins: Halimah and her family,
In the desert where air was cleaner and language clearer.
Muhammad grew quickly and he excelled in eloquence,
And Halimah returned him with the greatest reluctance.

When he was six, his mother Aminah passed away:
The second loss the young Muhammad had to bear.
And when his grandfather too reached his final day,
He had finally come into his uncle Abu Talib's care.

And when Abu Talib took him to Syria in his youth,
How they met a monk named Bahirah on the way.
Bahirah had recognised in him clear signs of truth.
And seeing the mark between his shoulders, he did say,
'This boy is the one we have been awaiting undoubtedly!
So keep him away from those who would bear enmity."

Abu Talib was reminded of the words of his own father,
"I swear by Allah that this son of mine will attain distinction."
And his affection, like how he used to show towards 'Abdullah,
Placing him on his own mat where none were given permission.

And the time that there was a drought and no rain would fall,
Till the Valley dried up and children complained they were thirsty;
But when the young Muhammad stood besides the Kaaba's wall,
And raised his hands, the Heavens immediately opened with mercy,
The Valley became full once more and joy sprung out of despair,
And ever since, Abu Talib had relied upon Muhammad's prayer.

Muhammad was even there at his side during the Fijar war,
Though he did not participate in the fighting personally.
And when it was over, he recalled the look that he saw:
A look of sadness in his eyes, for each and every casualty.

But then how his face had bloomed with such happiness,
That day they met at the house of 'Abdullah ibn Jada'an,
And founded *Hilful Fudul*, "The Alliance of the Virtuous",
When they pledged to uphold the principles of justice,
To support the oppressed ones, wherever they might be,
And to always assist the needy through means of charity.

Muhammad was truly exceptional in so many ways,
And yet his life had seemed at its most ordinary then.
He had worked as a shepherd from his earliest days,
And grew up to be the calmest, most patient of men.

Helping others was part of Muhammad's very nature,
The very first to respond in every trial and calamity,
The most loving and kind of souls to every creature.
Never was there anyone who was so full of humility,
Held higher in esteem, or with a better reputation,
Than Muhammad, the Truthful, the Trustworthy one.

True wisdom, valour, justice and great generosity,
With a presence that filled hearts with pleasure;
There was not even a single praiseworthy quality
That Muhammad did not display in ample measure.

Abu Talib could not recall a time he had not been wise,
No idle words he had ever spoken, nor any foolish deed.
He had no deficiencies in character, no association with lies.
So if ever there was any man who was destined to lead,
And to unite the Arabs and non-Arabs into a single nation,
It was Muhammad, the son of 'Abdullah, his brother's son.

And the people of Makkah had recognised it some years before,
When rebuilding the Kaaba, differences arose over the Black Stone;
When Quraysh's clans quarrelled till they were on the brink of war,
Until peace was brought through the hands of Muhammad alone.

Though they had constructed their separate walls in humility,
They reverted back to ways of ancestral pride on its completion,
Till with daggers drawn they said, "Let the first to enter the Sanctuary,
Decide which clan will get the honour to place the Stone in position."
But then they were all delighted to find the one who would arbitrate
Was none other than Muhammad, the Trustworthy, chosen by fate.

170

Muhammad, son of 'Abdullah, placed the Black Stone upon his cloak,
And said, "Let a representative from every clan take hold of a side."
And he ordered them to lift it towards the Kaaba as one united folk,
So they all shared in the honour for which they had separately vied.

And such was his love and devotion for his nephew,
Whose virtuous peak he knew he had not yet seen,
Abu Talib promised to do whatever he had to do.
Standing guard over Muhammad whenever he slept,
He would spent the majority of his nights awake,
And would willingly sacrifice all his sons for his sake.

He would command in turn, Ja'far, 'Aqeel and 'Ali,
To switch their sleeping places with the Prophet,
So that the blade or arrow of an audacious enemy
Would reach them instead of its intended target.

The ageing Abu Talib did all this with constancy,
And of his hardships never once complaining,
But he felt his bones were weakening gradually,
And that the strength of his back was waning.
Yet how ever long the Boycott would continue,
Abu Talib vowed he would protect his nephew.

Now the start of Dhil-Hijjah brought with it,
A new season as well as the birth of a new moon.
And every merchant felt sure of making a profit,
Knowing that the pilgrims would be arriving soon.

So out of storage, their gods were brought:
Mere blocks of wood carved and painted bright,
Or crudely fashioned stones, stood with support.
Meanwhile the crowds jostled to catch a sight,
Placing offerings of saffron, dates and honey,
And scenting them with musk and ambergris.

Then they began to chant as they circled round,
While flies kept settling on them one by one,
Spoiling the offerings they had placed down,
And covering those faces that they called upon.

The Hajj season offered temporary respite,
So Allah's Messenger went out from the Valley,
And with the clearest of voices began to recite,
Words that seemed to echo with their clarity.

"O mankind! A parable is struck so listen to it:
Those ones besides Allah upon whom you call,
Cannot create a fly, though they combine for it.
And should a fly take from them anything at all,
It would never from it, be by them caught:
Weak is the seeker and the sought!"[70]

The pilgrims listened to him in shock and awe:
Who was that man? What was he was reciting?
Why had they never heard the likes of it before?
And what was this way to which he was calling?

Rage was smouldering in Abu Lahab's chest,
That on this occasion he could not let out,
So he became ashen-faced with it suppressed.
Abu Sufyan looked on with disquieting doubt,
'Utbah shook his head at what he had feared,
But Abu Jahl grew prouder and simply sneered.

Who cares what he did in a few days of respite?
The last eleven months had proven one thing,
They would soon break Banu Hashim's might,
They were withering - the Boycott was working!

---

[70] (Surah Al-Hajj (22): 73)

Year VIII

Belief and Certainty

"By the night when it draws a veil,
And the day when it appears in brightness,
And by the creation of the male and the female,
Indeed your efforts for which you strive are diverse:
As for him who gives freely and is God-Fearing,
And affirms the best, We will ease him unto ease.. "[71]

Khadija would spend whatever she owned,
Till her entire wealth had been exhausted,
Then she would share whatever she had,
And give till she had nothing left to give.

Abu Jahl seized Hakim, Khadija's nephew,
"Are you taking food for Banu Hashim indeed?
Then before all of Makkah I shall humiliate you!"
Hakim's cousin, Abul Bakhtari, rushed to intercede.
"What concern is it of yours, 'Amr, if you let him be?
Are you to prevent his aunt from her own property?"

Abu Jahl was livid and kept refusing stubbornly,
And so when their quarrel had turned to violence,
Abul Bakhtari threw him to the ground forcefully,
Knocking the wind out of Abu Jahl's arrogance.

And yet occasions such as this were a rarity;
Most days, no one would dare to intervene,
So no food would be brought to the Valley,
Or those that did would fear being seen,
So they would load a camel out of sight,
And let it wander by itself into the night.

Lady Khadija sat down by her tent one day,
Watching her husband perform ablution and rise,
And following behind him as he began to pray,
Was her dear daughter Fatima, light of her eyes.

---

[71] (Surah Al-Layl (92): 1-7)

His face shone like a full moon in brightness,
And when he smiled he would light up the world.
His eyes were so deep, but full of kindness,
And his hair was black as the night, gently curled.
Sometimes striking hearts with his dignity,
And sometimes dazzling eyes with his beauty.

It seemed just yesterday when they had met,
Searching for someone to look after her caravan,
And Abu Talib had promised to bring to her the best
Among all Arabs, most honest and trustworthy man.

She had been sceptical at first but eventually agreed,
Though he was a shepherd with no experience in trade.
And honesty as Khadija had come to know first hand,
Was in such a time and place, a truly rare thing indeed,
So she asked other merchants to watch him carefully,
And to report back to her his conduct and personality.

But what happened next took her by surprise,
He came with the best returns she had ever seen,
In place of all the usual excuses, complaints and lies.
And further were the glowing words of praise so fine.

Khadija wondered what he could have done
That even those who by nature were suspicious,
And usually did not have any praise for anyone,
Had faces now blooming with such happiness
Whenever they mentioned Muhammad's name,
And spoke as though there was no one the same.

Many stories of his truthfulness were told,
Others of his cheerfulness and deep humility,
And how he was the best of all those who sold;
He did not swear, conceal or pester insistently.

So she began asking questions, first out of curiosity,
To understand what kind of man she had employed.
She found he lived a life of calmness and simplicity,
And all the ills of society Muhammad would avoid.
So it pleased Khadija, who was known for her purity,
That he indulged not in wine, gambling and indecency.

176

In mornings he would be found with the elderly,
And in afternoons with the orphans and the poor.
He would make helping the needy his priority,
And did not turn away anyone from his door.

And just like her cousin Waraqah to her had taught,
He too did not bow before the idols the pagans made,
But Allah alone was the Lord that Muhammad sought.
It was only by His Name that he vowed and prayed.
Yes, Muhammad had been a monotheist his entire life,
And though he was twenty-five, had not yet taken a wife.

At that time, Khadija was held in the utmost respect,
Well-regarded alike by both the poor and the nobility,
But whichever suitor came to her she would reject,
As she did not find in them the right sense of dignity.

Yet her regard for Muhammad was neither small,
Nor did it cease to grow with each day that passed,
Though she had barely spoken with him a word at all.
She kept on thinking, till she made up her mind at last.
And so she sent Nafisa her friend, to convey her intent:
To ask whether for marriage Muhammad would consent?

So Nafisa went and found Muhammad working outside,
"What prevents you from marriage while you are grown?"
"I have not yet the means to do so," Muhammad replied,
"Neither have I sufficient wealth nor a home of my own."

"What if this were solved and no longer an issue?
What if an honourable lady of wealth and fine family,
Had herself expressed an interest in marrying you?"
Muhammad replied, "And who might such a lady be?"
Nafisa saw he spoke with averted gaze and lowered head,
"She is Khadija, daughter of Khuwaylid," Nafisa said.

The days that followed passed by like the clouds of a dream,
And before she knew it, the arrangements had all been made.
Khadija kept on asking, could this really be it as it seems?
It felt so surreal, yet this dream of hers still would not fade.

177

And how to describe the moment she laid eyes on him?
Like a crown on his head was his turban, intensely black.
He walked with a staff, wearing the green ring of Hashim,
And bearing the mantle of 'Abdul Muttalib upon his back.
Muhammad turned every head as he entered the room,
And never had there been a more majestic groom.

Uncles took the place of the fathers for groom and bride,
As guests gathered to witness this perfect union of souls.
'Amr ibn Asad stood with Khadija, beaming with pride,
And Abu Talib was by Muhammad, pleased with his role.

"Praise be to Allah who made us from Ibrahim's progeny,
And He placed us among a blessed and secure Sanctuary,
Amidst the Sacred House and the place of Pilgrimage,
Where fruits reach us and we have been given authority.

Now, if Muhammad is with any man compared,
Then indeed he would surpass him, undoubtedly.
He is peerless among us although he is not wealthy,
And wealth is merely a passing thing in any case.
Now he and Khadija have expressed mutual interest,
The responsibility of the dowry upon myself shall rest."

Khadija could not have asked for a better man,
She could not fault him in even the slightest way,
Yet had she but known what was in Allah's plan,
And just how fortunate she had been that day.

It became clear to her, just as it was to everyone,
That greatness would be in Muhammad's destiny,
But he was interested in neither wealth nor position,
And he seemed content to live a life of simplicity.
Yet as years went by, his smile would sometimes wane,
And in private, a sombreness over him would remain.

So all too often, Muhammad would to Al-Hira retreat,
And he would turn his thoughts towards meditation.
And there, from atop the mighty mountain's lofty seat,
Would reflect upon the true purpose for all of creation.

And then he would reflect upon the state of his society:
How Makkah, founded upon Faith, virtue and hospitality,
Was being corrupted by idol worship, injustice and cruelty.
Till seven years before he first perceived Jibreel by sight,
He began to see not dreams but true visions of clarity.
His heart would remain awake throughout the night,
And his chest was gradually expanded in its capacity.

After some time, he would hear calls from the unseen,
Saying, "Peace be upon you, O the Messenger of Allah."
And hear salutations as he walked past rocks and trees,
Of all this and more, Muhammad would inform Khadija,
Matters the likes of which she had never heard before,
But never once did she doubt what he heard or saw.

In Dhil-Hijjah, pilgrims came to Makkah once more,
And the pagans felt wary of the Prophet's fame spreading,
So they began warning anyone important that they saw,
Like Tufayl, Ad-Daws' chief, who they approached saying,

"Do you see that man by the Kaaba offering prayer?
He has indeed uprooted our unity and created division,
All by means of some words that seem magical and fair.
Now you are but a traveller here, so do act with caution,
For it is far better that you do not speak with him at all,
Lest he should create discord also among your people."

So Tufayl put some cotton in his ears for security,
As he went around the Holy House in devotion,
But he soon caught the sound of a sweet melody,
And his heart turned towards it with inclination.

He sought out the Prophet later that day,
In a meeting away from the people's sight.
"About you the Quraysh say what they say,
But I would like to listen to what you recite."
So the Prophet began a stirring Recitation,
And Tufayl sat mesmerised in admiration.

Tufayl immediately accepted Islam and said,
"Among my tribe, I do carry some influence,
So I shall now do what I can to spread this call,
That they too may benefit from the Guidance."

"So remind! You are only a Reminder;
You are not over them as a controller.
But as for the one who turns and covers,
Then Allah will give the Great Punishment.
Surely to Us is their place of returning,
Then surely upon Us is their accounting."[72]

One night at Mina when the moon was at its fullness,
Quraysh called upon Muhammad to show them a Sign,
To prove that the Hour was coming in all seriousness,
And that his claim of Prophethood was truly Divine.

So the Messenger raised his hands up high,
And then he began to supplicate earnestly.
The people looked on at the cloudless sky,
And they witnessed the moon split instantly:
One part was on the near side of the Mount,
And the other on the far side of the Mount.

"Will you of this, O my people, now testify?"
Then he called the moon back and it returned,
Yet a group of them obstinately began to cry,
"It was naught but passing magic upon us turned."

Then came Trustworthy Jibreel with Divine Verses sent:
"The Hour drew near, and the moon had been rent,
And yet if they behold a portent, they turn and say,
'This was nothing but sorcery that passed away!'

They deny and follow their base inclinations,
And every matter will reach its conclusion.
There has already reached them Narrations,
In which they may find restraint and prevention."[73]

---

[72] (Surah Al-Ghaashiyah (88): 21-26)
[73] (Surah Al-Qamar (54): 1-4)

Year IX

Patience and Piety

"The Day when man shall recall what he strove for,
And the Hellfire will be exposed for all who see.
So as for him who had transgressed inordinately,
And gave preference to the life that is worldly,
Then surely the Hellfire shall be the abode.
But as for him who feared the Station of his Lord,
And had restrained his soul from low desires,
Then surely the Garden shall be the abode..."[74]

Days turned to nights, full only of hunger and fear,
While stomachs remained shrunken and empty.
Quraysh would turn their faces pretending not to hear,
As the children's cries echoed throughout the Valley.

Whatever rain came brought some relief from the heat.
Sometimes they would from animal skins make soup,
And sometimes they found nothing but leaves to eat,
Which they would still divide among the entire group.
Many had fallen sick, their faces now gaunt and pale,
And even the strongest of men were becoming frail.

The Prophet would eat the least, giving his share to others,
Tying a stone upon his stomach, patient in hunger and thirst.
Abu Talib would then refuse to eat before the son of his brother;
Remaining hungry unless the Messenger of God had eaten first.

'Ali would often be sent out to Makkah from the Valley,
And instructed to approach the merchants with caution.
Sometimes they'd offer him goods of the worst quality,
Or they would charge him rates of the greatest extortion,
Until Abu Jahl forbade them from even that little mercy,
And 'Ali would then return empty-handed to the Valley.

Yet when he looked at the face of the Prophet,
All Ali's grief and sorrow would soon depart:
That face that brought the sun's warmth with it,
And brought calmness and serenity to his heart.

---

[74] (Surah An-Nazi'aat (79): 35-41)

Even when he had been born there was that attachment.
His mother had told him that story many times before:
His first three days in the Holiest of Houses he had spent,
But Muhammad's face was the first sight that he saw;
How his smile was like the sun with all its brightness
As he took him into his arms with such happiness.

And 'Ali would neither eat nor satisfy his thirst,
With anything during the time of his weaning,
Except that which Muhammad himself took first,
And made soft and palatable for him by chewing.

'Ali throughout his youth took after his steps each day,
And how he would follow his cousin with excitement!
Following his actions, retaining each word he'd say,
Like a baby camel going wherever its mother went.

Then when he had reached five years of age,
'Ali recalled a flood, and the Kaaba being rebuilt,
And a famine which reached the severest stage
Where all stores ran short and crops would wilt.
His family bore many nights of hunger successively
But kept contenting themselves with it patiently.

Until the time when two visitors came to their door,
Saying they had come to speak to his father alone:
'Abbas, who ended up adopting his brother, Ja'far,
And Muhammad who chose 'Ali then for his own.

Those years had been the best he ever knew,
When Muhammad would each day demonstrate
To him another raised standard of a lofty virtue,
Or present some behaviour he should emulate.
He was an endless fountain of all that was good,
And 'Ali eagerly drank from it all that he could.

He recalled when he had returned late one day,
He found his beloved cousin praying anxiously,
"O Lord, let me not from this world pass away,
Until I look once more upon the face of Ali!"

When Muhammad received his first Revelation,
'Ali bore no doubt whatsoever about its veracity.
Nor in accepting it did his heart feel any hesitation,
But one question had been weighing on him heavily:
If the people denied him, and he knew some would,
Would he really be able to support him as he should?

And 'Ali had of course found his answer that very night,
When he had sought out guidance from Allah, his Lord;
Determining in any case, he would support what's right,
Instead of people's pleasure, would seek only His reward.

So then fixing his heart firmly upon the task ahead,
And to never waver, renewing his pledge each day,
'Ali would memorise each word that the Prophet said,
And he strove to emulate him in each and every way.
Three years passed before the call was made openly,
When in front of his clan, 'Ali declared his intention.

But at thirteen years of age, he was still not yet a man,
Not old enough to be given much regard by that society
Who cared only for age, wealth and the strength of your clan.
So 'Ali knew that the times ahead would be full of difficulty.
While he resolved that nothing would him from his path deter,
His fear still remained for what might befall the Messenger.

Until Ali's father, Abu Talib, brought to his heart some ease,
When he stood up in support of Muhammad, his nephew,
To be a shield for him against the violence of his enemies.
Backed with the entire strength of the Banu Hashim too,
For as long as Abu Talib lived, fear of retribution remained,
Thus the hands of Quraysh's elders' had been restrained.

Still the pagans plotted, seeking to spread their poisonous rage,
So instead they each began to incite their children to the task,
Telling them to disrupt Muhammad from preaching his Message,
And ordering them to throw stones at him whenever he passed.

So when 'Ali ibn Abi Talib saw Walid - 'Utbah's son,
And all the rest of the misguided Qurayshi youth
Throwing stones at Muhammad and making fun,
While he was calling the people towards the Truth,
'Ali with swift anger, rushed out in front of them all,
And fought the throwers till every last one did fall.

"And those who when tyranny strikes, themselves they defend,
And for an evil act is one similar to it the due recompense,
But whoever forgives and reconciles, with Allah is his recompense,
Indeed, He does not like those who are the tyrannical ones.

And indeed, whoever defends himself after suffering oppression,
Then there is no way of blame upon them. The blame is upon only
They who oppress men and transgress the earth without right or reason;
They shall have a painful torment. And whoever is patient and forgives,
Then that is indeed among the matters requiring determination."[75]
So then, 'Ali had firmly resolved to remain patient after this Revelation.

He knew that the Prophet did not want to dominate by force,
Though his enemies did not shrink away from acts of tyranny,
But he wished to transform the hearts and minds in due course,
And he continued to encourage the Believers to forbear graciously.

Thus for years, 'Ali watched as the Quraysh increased their tyranny,
And he held back his tongue and hand as he had been instructed,
The Prophet was preparing him for a purpose requiring clemency,
While the pagans continued their campaign seemingly unobstructed,
Only occasionally being checked by the likes of Abu Talib or Hamza,
When they would become a little too daring and cross a line too far.

---

[75] (Surah Shura (42): 39-43)

Meanwhile in Makkah, resentment had been brewing,
They had been hearing the children's cries in the Valley,
And had all seen their emaciated bodies slowly withering,
So some began to feel this was too far: a crime, an enormity.

"O People of Makkah!" Zuhayr ibn Abi Umayyah cried,
"Are we to eat and clothe ourselves here obliviously,
While we ignore our kin from Banu Hashim's plight,
Left to die alone, unable to trade or buy necessities?
I will now not take my seat, by Allah, I have sworn,
Till that unjust parchment we hung up has been torn!"

Abu Jahl and his cruel followers began to shout,
"No, we swear by Allah, torn up it shall never be!"
While Mut'im ibn 'Adiyy and others were calling out,
"We free ourselves from it," and, "we did not agree."

Abu Talib arrived from the Valley that very moment.
"I bring to you news from Muhammad, so now listen,
He has said Divine Revelation to him has been sent:
Except for Allah's Name, your parchment was eaten.
I promise if it is not so, I will surrender him to you,
But you must end the Boycott if what he says is true."

They hastily opened the doors to enter the Kaaba,
And found with shock, ants had eaten the parchment.
All of it, except for the words, "In Thy Name, O Allah."
Silence reigned. And that was an end to the argument.

The Messenger of Mercy

Year X

The Year of Grief

"So I swear by the twilight glow,
And the night and what it drives on,
And the moon when its fullness grows,
From state to state, you will surely go. "[76]

Years of difficulties had left their mark and course,
And Abu Talib fell sick soon after the Boycott ended.
When it was clear that there was now no recourse,
And he could no longer continue as he had intended,
He called together all his nearest relatives to his side,
And his final will to them quietly began to confide.

"Cleave to Muhammad, O my kin, after I depart:
The Truthful, Trustworthy, most virtuous of our race.
The Faith he brought has been accepted by every heart,
But the tongues only deny it from fear of losing face.
Now he has brought low the mighty chiefs by his call,
And given the poor and helpless dignity to stand tall.

And, O my kin! Be firm supporters of his Faith,
For certainly whoever follows him is prosperous.
I would, had I been given more time on this earth,
Ward away from his path all that is dangerous."

The days grew darker after Abu Talib's passing,
The burden the Messenger carried grew heavier,
The pagans of Makkah increased in their mocking,
And became more daring without Abu Talib's fear,
As though Maarib's Dam had burst, letting loose a sea,
Leaving behind only bitter fruits and scattered trees.

Though faced with constant ridicule and adversity,
The Prophet continued calling people to the right way,
Demonstrating the Truth to them at every opportunity,
Yet the polytheists' excuses would change every day.

---

[76] (Surah Al-Inshiqaaq (84): 16-19)

"He eats food like us and walks in the marketplace!"
"Why weren't angels sent instead to make it clear?"
"And why is a Messenger necessary in any case?
If we were a people in any need of Guidance here,
Could our Lord not reveal Himself if He did desire?
We think you are naught but a sorcerer or a liar!"

"And We did not send before you any of the Messengers,
Except that they ate food and walked in the marketplaces.
And We have made as a trial some of you for others;
Will you endure patiently? And your Lord is Ever-Seeing.

And those who have no expectation of meeting Us
Say, 'Why weren't angels sent to us or we see our Lord?'
Indeed too much pride in themselves they have assured,
And they have rebelled with the greatest of insolence.
The Day they see the Angels, no joy that Day for the guilty,
And they will cry, 'A barrier forbidding all totally.'"[77]

In the month of Ramadhan came a second trial:
Khadija who had in the Valley suffered greatly,
Remaining sleepless and hungry all the while,
Her body weakened, succumbed to illness finally.

She who had been Arabia's most wealthy lady,
Had spent every last dirham in the way of her Lord,
Providing to all those who were in need unreservedly.
Not even for her own shroud, she had anything saved,
So Muhammad wrapped Khadija up in his own cloak,
And with loving care, placed his beloved into her grave.

"She believed in me when no one else believed.
She was the one who would help and comfort me.
She embraced Islam when others disbelieved,
And she gave me Fatima who is a part of me."

---

[77] (Surah Al-Furqaan (25): 20-22)

The next forty days were as the darkest night;
The Messenger now found himself left all alone,
Each day facing hardships with no end in sight.
The worst treatment that he had ever been shown
Was now a daily occurrence. And he did not know
From which side would antagonism next overflow.

"And the Day the Unjust one will bite his hands and say,
'Oh how I wish I had taken with the Messenger a way.
Oh woe to me! I wish I had not taken that one as a friend.
He led me away from the Reminder when it came to me.'"[78]

And thus 'Uqbah ibn Abi Mu'ayt was to sin incited
By his vicious friend Ubayy ibn Khalaf one day.
"You sat to listen to what Muhammad recited?
Never again will I associate with you in any way,
Unless you do rid yourself of this great disgrace,
By going forth and spitting in Muhammad's face!"

And so he went out following Ubayy's command,
Yet like the one who in his rage spat at the sun,
Only upon his own face would Uqbah's spittle land,
And thus was he requited for his evil intention.

'Uqbah's son, Walid, approached 'Ali boastfully,
"I am tougher than you and far more eloquent,
And I even possess better leadership abilities."
"Is he who is Believer like him who is Defiant?[79]
Nay they are not equals!" - a sufficient answer,
Directly from the tongue of Allah's Messenger.

---

[78] (Surah Al-Furqaan (25): 27-29)
[79] (Surah As-Sajdah (32): 18)

"Say: 'I ask for it from you no reward,
Nor am I one of those who are pretentious.
It is naught but a Reminder for the worlds,
And of its truth you shall soon be conscious.'"[80]

When the Messenger announced at Dhil-Majaz's fair,
"Say there is no god but Allah: you will be successful."
Abu Jahl caught sight of him and ran after him there.
He threw dust onto him, screaming handful by handful,
"O people, ignore Muhammad and pay him no heed,
Away from al-Lat and al-'Uzza, he is trying to mislead."

When he returned home with dust on his head,
Fatima quickly rose up with tears in her eyes,
"Weep not, my dear daughter," he gently said,
"The Lord as your father's Helper will suffice."

Fatima like her namesakes had been named well:
Wise and intelligent like her maternal grandmother,
And like her aunt, bint Asad, was pious and dutiful;
That one whom the Prophet called his "Second Mother"
And so too did this Fatima, act in a such a manner,
That she was named as "The Mother of her Father."

Though he would smile just as often as he had done before,
The Believers had noticed a change in the Prophet recently.
Brief flashes of sadness in his eyes, they sometimes saw,
And despite his calmness, his footsteps would grow heavy.

And so one day, 'Uthman ibn Maz'un's wife, Khawlah,
Had decided to put forth to the Prophet a suggestion:
Asking for him to consider marrying her friend Sawdah,
A kind-hearted lady, who would be an ideal companion.
She was a widow whose smile would hide her sorrow,
And was far too generous to ever save for tomorrow.

The Messenger waited for his Lord's command,
Just as he did for every matter of importance.
And when he was told to ask for Sawdah's hand,
He obeyed His Lord with complete obedience.

---

[80] (Surah As-Saad (38): 86-88)

And yet his love for his beloved Khadija never waned.
At every occasion, he would remember her kindness,
How constant despite every hardship she had remained,
And had supported him whenever he had felt anxious.
Sawdah knew this and was not one prone to jealousy,
As she was not trying to replace Khadija in any capacity.

The Messenger recited to those in idol adoration,
"Indeed, those besides Allah upon whom you call,
Are slaves like you. So now make invocation
And let them respond to you, if you are truthful.

Do they have feet by which they walk?
Or do they have hands by which they hold?
Or do they have eyes by which they behold?
Or do they have ears by which they hear?
Say: 'Call your partners, and conspire here
Against me and give me no respite at all.'"[81]

The pagans to these Words had no real answer,
Yet they continued what they were doing even so.
And while they were not wronged by the Messenger,
Their hatred for him each day continued to grow.

Sitting in Hijr Isma'il was a group of Disbelievers,
"Never before the likes of this have we tolerated.
That man derided our values, abused our ancestors,
Reviled our traditions and our gods humiliated!"
And no sooner had these words been verbalised,
But Muhammad himself appeared before their eyes.

And he began circumambulating the Kaaba,
While being observed by his bitterest enemies.
Among them was Abu Jahl, 'Uqbah, and Umayyah,
Each time he passed they would shout obscenities.

---

[81] (Surah Al-'A'raaf (7): 194-195)

The Prophet behaved as though he had not heard,
Bearing their ignorance as he always did patiently,
But they kept increasing in the filth of their words,
Until, "By Allah!" the Prophet said to them finally,
"Listen to what I say, O people of Quraysh, carefully,
For I swear I have brought to you slaughter certainly."

At these words their faces quickly lost their colour,
Their swift tongues fell motionless immediately,
And each one of them with fear began to quiver,
Knowing that Muhammad would never speak idly.

They recalled when 'Utaybah, Abu Lahab's vicious son,
Came to Muhammad without cause and assaulted him.
He tore his shirt, spat at his face, and denied Revelation.
Muhammad said, "O Lord, set one of your beasts on him."
And it was not long before Utaybah set out on a journey,
And was pounced on by a lion who killed him viciously.

So they spoke to him with lowered voices and respect,
"Return, O Abul Qasim, for you were never ignorant."
But then after having had a restless night to reflect,
The next day their hearts had become no different.

To incite a mob against him is what they did decide,
Shouting, "Are you the one who denies our deities!"
"Yes I am the one who says that," the Messenger replied,
Standing firm against a hundred or more of his enemies.
Among them was 'Uqbah, who grabbed hold of his cloak,
And tried to strangle the Messenger with it as he spoke.

The Messenger was surrounded from every side,
Accosted and abused by that senseless horde,
"What! Would you kill a man," Abu Bakr cried,
"Just because he says, 'Allah is my Lord?'"

As Makkah's atmosphere increased in harshness,
The Messenger was ordered to take his call further out.
The nearby city of Ta'if had great wealth and influence,
But its people had fallen into confusion and idolatry.
Instead of Allah, besides whom there is no other Lord,
They made temples for al-Lat, and mere images adored.

So he travelled to Ta'if, accompanied only by Zayd,
Hoping that there the Message of Islam might spread,
But to his invitation, by the chiefs was no attention paid,
For they preferred the extravagant lives that they led.

"If you are indeed the Apostle of Allah, as you claim,
Then to listen to you and then reject would be unwise,
And if," they said, "you are not that which you claim,
Why should we speak with one who deals in lies?"

Instead of offering due warmth and hospitality,
Rudeness and ill-treatment was what was served
By all of the Banu Thaqif's heads and their nobility.
And so that all future preaching might be deterred,
They then urged the common folk to the street,
As the Prophet and Zayd quickly began to retreat.

A volley of stones was thrown at the Prophet,
And the crowds screamed, swore and abused.
Again and again, the Prophet was repeatedly hit,
Until he was left standing bleeding and bruised.

"O Allah, to You alone my complaint I express,
Of the insignificance that people see in me,
Of my lack of resources and my weakness.
O the Most Merciful of those who show mercy!
You are indeed the Lord of the downtrodden.
Your Lordship over me, I have not forgotten.

To whom would you entrust my fate?
To some stranger with a scornful stare,
Or to an enemy, who is filled with hate,
Would you give control over my affair?
It matters not to me with what I am tried,
As long as You are not at all angry with me.

And if You should remain with me satisfied,
In the light of Your Face I seek sanctuary.
I submit to You, and to You is my resort,
There is no power but by Your support."

Then he perceived over him a sudden shade,
And he heard a voice call out from on high,
"O Muhammad! We have come to your aid,
For your Lord has indeed heard your cry!"

And Jibreel, the Trustworthy, full of might,
Wings spread out wide made his descent.
"O Messenger, you are now given the right,
To invoke upon them Divine Punishment.
One word, and the mountains of this town,
Will fall upon them and turn it upside down."

The Messenger raised his hands to the sky,
Even as a pool of blood filled each shoe.
"O Lord! Forgive my people," was his cry,
"For they know not," he said, "what they do."

Zayd ibn al-Haritha was also bleeding profusely,
Having tried his utmost to shield the Messenger.
The two left the streets in search of some sanctuary.
Finding a garden owned by 'Utbah and his brother,
They began to rest there under the shade of a tree,
And wiped away the blood from their faces silently.

Suddenly within 'Utbah and Shaybah shame took root,
As they now looked upon their near relative's state,
So they sent to him their slave 'Addas with some fruit.
"In the Name of Allah," said Muhammad as he ate.

And 'Addas glanced up at him with confusion,
For years he had never heard that expression.
"I am a Christian," he said, "from Ninawa."
"You mean the town of Yunus the son of Matta?"
"How did you come to know of that name?"
"He is my brother, a Prophet, and I am the same."

"Why did you show him such love and affection?"
'Utbah asked his slave 'Addas when he returned.
"He is a Prophet and the very best of creation."
"Beware! Be not from your religion turned!"

After Banu Thaqif had rejected him harshly,
The Messenger and Zayd left Ta'if that day,
And journeyed until he came to Nakhlah Valley.
There all alone, that night he continued to pray,
When some Jinn from Nasibin heard his Recitation,
And in silence, they kept listening with admiration.

"O our community! A Scripture we have heard,
That has been revealed after Moses in truth.
Whatever came before is by it confirmed.
It guides to Truth and the way of rectitude."

"O our community! Respond to the Divine caller,
And believe in Him. He will your sins forgive,
And from a punishment most painful deliver.
Whoever does not respond to the Divine caller,
Can neither escape in the earth nor find succour;
They are the ones who are in manifest error."

Thus at Nakhlah, a whole community of Jinn believed,
While he remained unaware of his audience that night.
He proceeded to where his first Revelation was received,
Under the shade of Al-Hira, the blessed Mountain of Light.

He was now with good reason wary to enter Makkah.
With people baying for blood, and Abu Talib no more,
For him to return now would be fraught with danger,
Unless a powerful clan would his safe passage assure.
Only Mut'im ibn 'Adiyy, Chief of Banu Nawfal, agreed,
Though he remained as ever an opponent of his creed.

The Makkans were rightly astonished by the sight,
When at dawn, Mut'im called for his sons and clan;
They, who were known for great audacity and might,
Wearing their full battle dress, marched to the street.

"O Mut'im!" said Abu Jahl, "What is your intention?
When he saw the dazzling assembly of men outside.
"Is this a call to arms, or are you offering protection?"
"I am only extending my protection," Mut'im replied.
"Then we will protect whoever you protect certainly."
And with that, the crowds of men dispersed peacefully.

Accompanied by Mut'im, the Prophet entered the city,
And around the Kaaba he began to circumambulate.
The hearts of the pagans boiled with anger silently,
While their eyes revealed the depth of their hate.

The mockery and abuse did not cease for long.
Wherever he would go he would be harassed,
Yet Muhammad's heart remained firm and strong.
Each day, filth was thrown on him as he passed,
And he was ostracised from many a gathering,
Till it seemed his folk would never stop rejecting.

"O 'Abd Manaf's sons, here is your Prophet!"
Said Abu Jahl in his usual manner of mocking.
But 'Utbah replied indignantly, "And what of it?
Can there not come from us a prophet or king?"

The Messenger of God came to them and replied,
"Now as for you 'Utbah, you did not become angry
For the sake of God, but on account of your pride.
O Abu Jahl, soon you'll laugh little and weep plenty,
And as for you, O Council of Quraysh, your fate
Is that you'll enter unwillingly into what you hate."

And when the Prophet performed his morning prayer,
A group of Jinn heard his Recitation from a distance.
So they descended in Makkah and finding him there,
In a dense crowd around him they listened in silence.

Then the Angels descended with Jibreel at their head,
With the words, *"Say: 'It has been revealed unto me,*
That a company of Jinn listened and then they said,
"We have heard a most amazing Recitation certainly,
It guides to the Straight Path, and we believe therein,
So we shall never associate with our Lord anything.

And that He - Exalted is the Majesty of our Lord,
Has not taken for Himself a consort nor a son.
And that the foolish one among us has uttered
Against Allah a most extravagant transgression.'"[82]

Dhamad the exorcist came to Makkah one day,
Thinking that Muhammad was in need of a cure.
The Prophet told him to listen to what he had to say,
And began reciting a Recitation most wise and pure.
He listened to him in confusion and then surprise,
Until the point when tears nearly filled his eyes.

"I have seen many a soothsayer and sorcerer,
And listened to plenty a poet's compositions,
Yet *this* - I have never witnessed anything similar.
Give me your hand, and let me swear allegiance!"

The Messenger of Allah smiled and began to say,
"Praise be to Allah, we praise Him and seek His aid.
One whom Allah guides aright none can send astray,
And one whom Allah sends astray none can guide.
I bear witness none except Allah is of worship worthy,
He is unique without partner or equal, most certainly."

[82] (Surah Al-Jinn (72): 1-4)

Suwayd ibn as-Samit came to the Prophet saying,
"I have the Book of Luqman's wisdom with me,
Perhaps you have come with a similar thing?"
The Prophet let him read, listening attentively.

"These are some words of goodness certainly,
But a better Narration to you I shall now recite:
A Divine Recitation which was revealed to me,
Where, found within it is Guidance and Light."
Suwayd was amazed at the Words of Revelation,
And his heart became filled with admiration.

But when Suwayd returned home from his 'Umrah,
He found the city of Yathrib burning in violence
Between Al-Aws and Khazraj, two clans of Qaylah,
And Ibn as-Samit was killed in an act of vengeance.

Each day the Prophet would rise and warn his folk,
Yet the hearts of the Quraysh had long hardened,
They would hurl foul words whenever he spoke,
And uglier deeds. Still, he overlooked and pardoned,
Beseeching Allah to forgive him and his community,
And to send Guidance and Mercy for all of humanity.

Then came the month of Dhil-Hijjah and pilgrimage,
Merchants eagerly stocked up on wares in preparation,
Every corner of Makkah was filled with idols and images;
And their worship naught but whistling and celebration.

"Welcome O pilgrims! And to your gods be generous!"
Meaning those crudely-carved stones and wooden blocks.
Wadd and Suwa both towered tall, Nasr was vulturous
Yaghut resembled a lion, while Awal looked like an ox,
Then Ya'uq, the horse-headed rock that they had named,
And besides this, many other 'deities' that they claimed.

"And the words of Ibrahim (do recall),
'My Lord! Make this a city of security,
And keep me and my progeny all,
Far from any service to idolatry.'"[83]

The Messenger made full use of the opportunity,
And spoke to the pilgrims of the House of God.
He told them about Ibrahim's Religion of purity,
And the exemplary way upon which he had trod
When he rejected the worship of every false deity
Besides Allah, who created all things peerlessly.

The Quraysh hated these words more than anything,
Since idols were their greatest source of revenue,
But as long as every Arabian tribe was witnessing,
No physical harm in this month to him they could do.

So adamant on denial, they spread a new kind of claim.
"He fabricated it, or was taught by some personality!"
Yet not one candidate among Quraysh they could name,
For it was clear that none of them had such a capability,
But they continued firing blunt arrows in desperation,
Until even a Roman slave was not safe from accusation.

"And We are aware of what they say certainly,
'It is only a human being who teaches him in reality.'
The tongue is foreign of the one that they blame,
While this is an Arabic tongue, clear and plain."[84]

The Prophet went out at each and every opportunity,
And rarely would he ever be seen without a smile.
He treated all creatures with kindness and courtesy,
Spreading around Truth and goodness all the while.
And then his Lord revealed about him exclusively,
"We sent you not but to the worlds as a Mercy."[85]

---

[83] (Surah Ibrahim (14): 35)
[84] (Surah An-Nahl (16): 103)
[85] (Surah Al-Anbiyaa (21): 107)

"O Allah, give us more and do not take from us.
Grant honour to us and do not humiliate us.
Grant to us liberally and do not deprive us.
Make us pleased and be pleased with us."
And so his Lord sent upon him ten Verses,
Through which Paradise could be attained:

"Successful indeed are the Believers:
Those who offer prayers with humility,
And they turn aside from what is vain,
And they are active in giving charity,

And they who guard their chastity,
Except from those joined in matrimony,
Or those that their right hands possess,
For then they are not blameworthy,
But who seeks beyond that does transgress.

And who are attentive to trust and covenant,
And who guard their prayers carefully,
They are the heirs inheriting Paradise.
Therein they shall abide for eternity."[86]

Six men from the clan of Khazraj listened carefully
To the Prophet's preaching and embraced Islam.
"The flames of war burn constantly in our city,
We hope through you Allah removes this harm,
We will return to Yathrib and spread your call,
If they accept, you'll be the most respected of us all."

And they went away saying to each other excitedly,
"This is the very Prophet we were told would be raised,
The one that the Jews would threaten us with incessantly.
So we should all give allegiance before them in this case."

---

[86] (Surah Al-Mu'minoon (23): 1-11)

Year XI

The Call Extends

"And We have not sent you but to all of humanity,
As a Bearer of good tidings and as a Warner too.
But most of mankind do not know, and they say,
'When will this promise be, if you have spoken true?'
For all of you there shall be the appointment of a Day.
You will not delay it an hour, nor can you bring it on."[87]

And such was the evocation of the Day of Resurrection,
The Quraysh would sometimes lessen in their contumacy,
Vacillating between internal belief and habitual rejection.
Till some of them would be on the verge of testimony.

"Bear witness now to the Oneness of your Lord,
O my people, so that deliverance you may attain.
And with true Faith you will have the best reward:
Paradise, and the command of this world also gain."
The Prophet kept preaching in the markets of Ukaz,
Each season calling men at Majannah and Dhil-Majaz.

"Then make the mountains move by your supplication,
Or cause rivers to spring forth now in this barren land,
And bring back to life the great ancestors of our nation,
So that the truth of your claim we might understand."

He said, "By Him in whose hand my soul does reside,
My Lord has indeed before me a choice presented:
The request granted, your case today He shall decide;
For the Disbelievers, a chastisement unprecedented,
Or the Gate of Mercy, which I have instead preferred,
Such that you might come to believe if it is deferred."

And the Messenger did not miss a single opportunity
To help his people despite their mockery and rejection.
He would visit them in times of happiness and calamity,
Offering them assistance, advice and clear admonition.

And when he witnessed in the markets the traders' treachery,
The Prophet recited, *"Woe to the ones who are fraudulent,*
Who when they take measure from men, take it in its entirety,
And when they measure or weigh for them, they are deficient.

---

[87] (Surah Sabaa (34): 28-30)

Do they not think they will be raised on a Tremendous Day:
The Day when man will stand before the Lord of the worlds?"[88]

The pagans cried, "Instead of visiting the marketplaces as we do,
Why do you not ask for palaces and riches to fulfil your need,
Or call your Lord to send a company of angels to support you,
And demand for the Heavens to fall upon us now be decreed!"

"As for me I will never believe what you say,
Unless a ladder to Heaven comes down for you,
And I watch you as you ascend there all the way,
Then you return with a book and four angels too,
And in support of your claim they each testify.
Ah, even then I think I would not believe your lie!"

Such were the demands the pagans kept making,
Each one surpassing the other in their mockery.
When will be the exact hour of the Reckoning?
What will be for each and everything the finality?

The Messenger would bear with all of this patiently,
And whenever he was questioned would recite anew,
"Say: 'I am not among the Messengers a novelty,
Nor do I know what will be done with me or you.
I only follow that which has been revealed to me,
And I am nothing but a Warner, clear as can be.'"[89]

Walid ibn al-Mughirah and his companions said,
"Then bring a Qur'an that does not make us leave
The worship of al-Lat and al-'Uzzah instead."
And they all received their answer that very day.

"And when Our clear Verses unto them are recited,
Those who do not hope for Our meeting say,
'Bring a Qur'an other than this or change it,'
Say: 'It is not for me to change it of my own accord;
I only follow what's revealed unto me. Indeed I fear,
The punishment of a Great Day, if I disobey my Lord.'"[90]

---

[88] (Surah Al-Mutaffifeen (83): 1-6)

[89] (Surah Al-Ahqaf (46): 9)

[90] (Surah Yunus (10): 15)

The pagans and the Believers were now opposites:
In their personalities and pastimes they differed,
In dress and speech, and in thoughts and habits,
Even though the same Message they had all heard.

The Quraysh would often gather near the Kaaba,
And there they heard the Recitation of the Prophet,
"Indeed you and what you worship besides Allah,
Are the firewood of Hell. You will all come to it.
Were these gods, they would not have come to it,
But they shall all abide therein for eternity."[91]

These words had greatly distressed the pagans,
Until Ibn az-Ziba'ra shouted an objection loudly,
"Then Jesus is worshipped by the Christians!
What say you? Are our gods better or is he?"

So at once the Quraysh cheered in jubilation,
And laughed with faces blooming with mockery,
Thinking they had finally overcome the Revelation,
And had finally against Ar-Rahman gained a victory.
And when the crowd had become less raucous,
The response came from the lips of the Prophet.

"Those for whom the good has gone forth from Us,
Will be removed far therefrom most certainly.
They shall not hear even the faintest sound of it,
And in what their souls desire will abide eternally."[92]

Whenever their stratagems ended in futility,
The Quraysh would go to their Jewish allies;
They who had studied the Scriptures thoroughly,
To see if there was any solution they could advise.
Muhammad seemed to always have a response,
Yet all they needed was to frustrate him once.

---

[91] (Surah Al-Anbiya (21): 98-99)
[92] (Surah Al-Anbiya (21): 101-102)

The Rabbis advised the pagans self-assuredly,
"Pose to this Prophet of yours this question:
'Why did the Israelites go to Egypt initially?'
For none but us would know this information."

So when Quraysh did question their Messenger,
He immediately recited, ***"In Yusuf and his brothers,***
Certainly there were Signs for the inquirers..."[93]
And told a story that would amaze every listener;
Of hardship and hope, Faith, patience and piety,
An example of true forgiveness and generosity.

"I have been commanded to offer worship only
To the Lord of this City, Who has sanctified it,
And unto Whom belongs all things in their entirely,
And I am commanded to be of those who submit."[94]

There were five mockers most adverse to the Truth,
Al-Harith ibn at-Tulatilah, foul of tongue and mind;
The harsh and gluttonous Al-Aswad ibn 'Abd Yaghut;
And Al-Aswad ibn Muttalib, the spiritually blind;
Then Al-'Aas ibn Wa'il, the boastful and asinine;
And Walid ibn al-Mughirah, stiff-necked in pride.

These five tongues ceaselessly continued abusing;
Their hearts dripping with hatred for the Messenger.
Ugly words, taunts, ridicule, slander and lampooning.
Each and every day, this mistreatment would recur.

Until Jibreel descended by his Lord's permission,
"Indeed against the Scoffers We shall suffice you,"[95]
He pointed at the first whose head became swollen,
Then to the second one - and with fluid his belly grew,
The third lost his sight when he threw a leaf in his face,
And Al-'Aas and Walid were soon to also meet disgrace.

---

[93] (Surah Yusuf (12): 7)
[94] (Surah An-Naml (27): 91)
[95] (Surah Al-Hijr (15): 95)

"So remind, for you are not, by your Lord's grace,
A soothsayer or one who is suffering from insanity.
Or do they say, 'a poet, for which we do await
Him to be afflicted in time with some calamity?'

Say: 'Wait! For indeed I am with you waiting.'
Or do their intellects command them to this?
Or are they a people who are transgressing?
Or they say 'he forged it?' Nay, they believe not.
Then let them produce a discourse matching
This, if they should be truthful in what they say.

Or have they been created by nothing at all?
Or were they themselves their own creators?
Or did they create the Heavens and the Earth?
Nay they are lacking every kind of certainty.

Or have they with them your Lord's depositories?
Or are they the ones who are in control of them?
Or do they have a stairway on which they listen?
Then let their listener bring out a clear authority.
Or does He have daughters while you have sons?
Or do you ask a fee, so they are burdened by debt?

Or do they have (knowledge of) the Unseen,
So that they then continue to write it down?
Or are they intending on executing a plan?
But the Disbelievers are the objects of a plan.

Or do they have any deity other than Allah?
Above what they associate, Allah is Exalted Far!"[96]
And when the Messenger had finished reciting,
There was no man of Quraysh who was not shaking.

And among them was Jubayr the son of Mut'im,
A young man who hated Islam with great passion,
But that evening those Words had an effect on him,
And for a brief moment they caused him to question
What proof he had for what his forefathers claimed,
Yet he remained upon it so he would not be blamed.

---

[96] (Surah At-Tur (52): 29-43)

Makkah had very little formal law at this time,
So rights could only be obtained through might,
And the influence of a tribe could negate any crime,
While the poor and powerless would find no respite.

"I am a traveller," announced a man one day,
"And that 'Amr ibn Hisham has defrauded me.
He has taken my camels but now refuses to pay.
Who will help me get what is mine rightfully?"
Perhaps that man had expected justice to rule,
Or he had heard of the famous *'Hilf-ul-Fudul.'*

But the assembly of Quraysh did not care,
Instead they saw a chance for mischief.
"Do you see that man sitting over there?
He is the one who will help you certainly!"

The pagans of Quraysh followed behind excitedly,
For they knew Abu Jahl despised no one more,
And had for no one else a greater animosity,
Than the very man sent knocking on his door.
"Who is it?" Abu Jahl asked gruff and impatiently,
"It is Muhammad!" he replied, "Come out to me."

Abu Jahl opened the door, pale and terrified.
"O 'Amr, give to this man his rightful due."
Without arguing, Abu Jahl quickly complied,
"I'll give his money, right now in front of you!"

When the pagans heard what had happened,
They could hardly believe that it was really true,
"O Abul Hakam! Indeed we are all stunned!"
Abu Jahl turned aside saying, "Woe to all of you!
I was filled with terror just by hearing that voice,
And after seeing what I saw, I really had no choice."

And Nadr ibn al-Harith rose one day with smugness,
"O Allah!" he said, "If it is really the Truth from You,
Then do rain down stones from the skies upon us,
Or inflict us with any other painful torment due."

Immediately, Jibreel to the Messenger was sent,
"A supplicant demanded a punishment to befall.
For the Disbelievers, there is none to prevent
From Allah, the Lord of the Ways of Ascent.
To Him ascend the Angels and the Spirit in a day,
The measure of which is fifty thousand years.

So be patient with gracious patience. Indeed
They see it as distant, And We see it as near.
On the Day when the sky will be like murky oil,
And the mountains will become like wool.

And no friend will ask anything of a friend,
Though they will be shown each other,
And the criminal will wish he could be
Ransomed from the punishment of that Day

By his children, and his wife and his brother,
And his nearest kin who had sheltered him,
And all who are on earth in their entirety,
Just so that it might then rescue him.
No indeed! It is the Flame burning intensely,
Snatching away the scalps completely..."[97]

---

[97] (Surah Al-Ma'arij (70): 1-16)

In the heat of sun and in the depths of night,
The Messenger of Allah would raise his hands,
Praying his community would be guided aright,
And that his call would spread to distant lands.

Despite every setback he continued striving,
And he arranged meetings with those near and far.
Every major tribe, the Messenger kept on inviting;
Meeting the chiefs of Kalb, Kindah and Banu Hanifah.
Though each one refused and gave him an ugly reaction,
The Messenger of God would not relent from his mission.

The burdens were many and the carriers were few,
Yet the Messenger spoke with passion undeterred.
He went out to others and proclaimed what was true,
So that the Word of God could be by all people heard.

"If we swear allegiance and you are victorious,"
Asked Banu 'Amir's chief when they met privately,
"Will you promise to give your succession to us?"
"That is Allah's affair, no decision comes from me."
"What! Should we stand against Arabs for your sake,
Then later, someone else would the benefits take?"

So when to their own land, they had gone back,
They informed a respected elder of that event,
"A Qurayshi asked us to defend him from attack,
Claiming that he was a Prophet Divinely-sent."

The elder placed his hand upon his head,
"O my people! What a lost opportunity!
He was indeed truthful in what he said!
I swear that none from Isma'il's progeny,
Has ever a claim to Prophethood falsified,
Where then was your sense?" he cried.

214

And that year when pilgrims arrived from near and far,
The Messenger would finally witness some acceptance,
When twelve men from Yathrib met him at Al-'Aqabah
With hearts abounding with Faith to pay their allegiance.

They said, "We shall not worship besides Allah any other,
And we pledge to refrain from every form of indecency.
We shall neither falsely accuse nor backbite one another,
Nor shall we steal property, nor ever kill a soul unjustly.
We will obey you, O Prophet, in the good you command,
Shall support your truth, and with you in hardship stand."

He replied, "If to these promises you fully comply,
You will certainly be to Paradise admitted in the end,
But if you should swerve, or these commands belie,
Then it shall be Allah's decision where you are sent."

And when the Pledge had reached its completion,
They requested that a representative to them be sent
In order to teach to them the Words of Revelation,
And to provide explanations of what was meant.
So Mus'ab ibn 'Umayr was appointed for this duty:
To Yathrib sent as the Messenger's first emissary.

Mus'ab continued preaching among them constantly,
Helped by As'ad ibn Zurarah in carrying out his mission.
The leaders of Al-Aws and Khazraj testified immediately,
Then their entire clans followed them in submission.

Year XII

Ascension

"He said, 'Indeed I invited my people night and day,
Yet my invitation increased them not except in flight.
And indeed, whenever I invited them so that You may
Forgive them, they put their fingers in their ears,
And covered themselves up with their garments;
Persisted, and were arrogant with great arrogance.'"[98]

Now whenever the Messenger would approach near,
The people would then all get up and walk away,
And if his words should ever fall upon their ear,
Would act as if they had not heard what he'd say.

This pained him far more than their abuse,
For with abuse, he could respond beautifully,
And good treatment no heart would refuse,
But he feared for his people's future anxiously;
If he did not with them in any measure interact,
How would they learn wisdom and how to act?

So he continued on praying for them day by day,
Though they made him a stranger in his own land.
"O Lord, grant them Guidance, show them the way,
And open their hearts so they might understand."

So in every district of Makkah, the Prophet went
To spread the word in every road and marketplace;
That as a Bringer of glad tidings he had been sent,
That they could each in Paradise gain their place,
And that even if they had committed sins ignorantly,
Their Lord was still inviting them towards His Mercy.

"Say: 'O my servants who have acted extravagantly
Against themselves, do not despair of Allah's Mercy!
Indeed, Allah is He who forgives sins in their entirety.
Indeed, it is He who is the Forgiving and Merciful.'"[99]

---

[98] (Surah Nuh (71): 5-7)

[99] (Surah Az-Zumar (39): 53)

219

When the Messenger each day went out for worship,
Some would insult him or throw rubbish on his head,
Others would stare at him as though to make him trip,
And there were a few who averted their gaze instead,
Who if they heard from the Messenger any Recitation,
They would flee from it like wild donkeys from a lion.

"Behold! They fold up their chests to hide from Him!
Behold! Even when wrapped up with what they wear,
He knows what they conceal and what they reveal;
Verily, of what is in the chests, He is the All-Aware."[100]

One day, Abu Jahl and his retinue approached the Prophet,
"O Muhammad! Are you a prophet while here alone you sit?
Look at my supporters, for that rank I am more worthy.
For all of your preaching, you have no helpers, no army,
Had a prophet been needed, it would have surely been me!"

And as if to demonstrate, Abu Jahl each day
Would gather dozens of men in his company,
Hanging on every word that he would say,
As he would slaughter camels frequently.

"Do you see this?" Abu Jahl said with disgust,
Pointing to the Messenger engaged in prayer
By the Kaaba, lowering his face to the dust.
"Which of you will take those entrails there,
And throw them upon Muhammad as he prays,
So that we may dissuade him from his ways?"

So when he saw the Prophet was about to prostrate,
'Uqbah placed the intestines of a camel upon his back.
And the Prophet remained motionless in that state,
Till Fatima came to remove the weight from his back.

He gazed at his dear daughter with great affection,
The one he had rightfully named *"Umm Abeeha"*
On account of her motherly concern and devotion.
Each day she increased in resemblance to Khadija,

And was truly the fulfilment of his Lord's assurance:
"Indeed, We have given to you Great Abundance."[101]

Abu Jahl, Shaybah, 'Utbah, Walid, 'Uqbah and Umayyah,
Against these men the Messenger then made his plea,
For their evil had transgressed the limits and gone so far,
And his Lord promised that their end he would soon see.

"And they say, 'There is not but our worldly existence;
We die and we live, and naught but time destroys us,'
And they have of that no knowledge, only assumptions.
When Our clear Verses are recited to them as evidence,
They possess no argument at all with which to dispute,
Only, 'Bring back our forefathers if you tell the truth!'

Say: 'Allah causes you to live and then causes you to die,
Then He will assemble you for the Day of Resurrection,
There is no doubt about it, but most people do not know,
And Allah's is the Heavens' and the Earth's Dominion.'"[102]

The Disbelievers would turn everything into a great mockery,
The Qur'an, the Messenger, and even their Lord Most High,
In their gatherings they would all jest and ridicule constantly,
And the Resurrection, Heaven and Hell they would each deny,
Demanding clear Signs as if they had not already been shown,
Yet evidence for their forefathers' claims they had never known.

They were a people who did not wish to progress in any way,
Pride had created an impenetrable barrier in front of their eyes,
And their ears had turned deaf to all the Messenger would say,
So their hearts had now become completely devoid of all light.

"....and He guides to Himself whoever does turn;
Those who believe and whose hearts are at rest,
By the Remembrance of Allah. Unquestionably,
By the Remembrance of Allah do hearts find rest.
Those who believed and performed deeds of piety,
A good state is for them and a goodly return."[103]

---

[101] (Surah Al-Kawthar (108): 1)
[102] (Surah Al-Jathiyah (45): 24-27)
[103] (Surah Ra'ad (13): 27-29)

On a clear night in Rajab, piercingly solemn,
The Prophet was woken by Jibreel's visitation.
"Rise, O Muhammad! The time has now come
For you to respond to your Lord's invitation!"

And from Masjid-ul-Haram he began his mission,
When He mounted Buraaq, that most noble steed,
Whose every step went to the extent of its vision.
They journeyed across the earth at lightning speed,
Halting at Taybah, Madyan, Sinai, and Bethlehem,
Then they finally alighted at Al-Aqsa in Jerusalem.

He tied Buraaq to a ring upon the Western Wall,
And then came to the Masjid of the blessed land.
There he led the Prophets in prayer, one and all,
When they each came down by Allah's command.

Then he was given the means of ascent,
And guided by Jibreel, he ascended high,
Upon steps of gold and silver that went
Beyond the firmament of the Nearest Sky.
At each Heaven, he was given salutation,
And greeted with great joy and celebration.

Some of the Greatest Signs he did witness,
As he looked upon the wonders of creation;
Seeing the entire Universe and its vastness,
He perceived things beyond comprehension.

He saw *Bayt-ul-Mamur* and its magnificence,
And saw the wonder of each angelic delegation.
He was taught blessed Words of Remembrance,
And was made to see the reality of every action.
He saw the great beauty of the Believers' reward,
And saw what awaited the sinful from their Lord.

He was offered a choice between milk and wine,
And he chose the purer, more natural of the two.
"O Muhammad!" said Jibreel, "This was a Sign,
And your Nation shall remain guided after you."

He met with Adam and Nuh, the two fathers of humanity,
And spoke with Musa: he who had spoken directly to Allah.
There was Idris and Yahya, Harun, Yusuf, and 'Isa, son of Mary,
At the Seventh Heaven was Ibrahim, "the intimate friend of Allah".
"O Ahmad! My son, tonight you will meet your Lord privately,
So do what you can to help the needs of your Community."

Then Jibreel towards *Sidratul Muntaha* began to lead;
To the Furthest Lote tree, and the utmost boundary,
Beyond which, no other creature was able to proceed,
Muhammad went to converse with his Lord in privacy.

And with three excellent gifts, he eventually emerged.
First, he was given two sublime Verses of Revelation,
Then a promise that all would have their sins purged,
Except those who remain polytheist among his Nation,
And finally he was awarded five prayers, each day due,
So that each and every Believer could meet his Lord too.

And then when he descended back to Jerusalem,
He remounted onto Buraaq and to Makkah returned.
Jibreel bade him farewell as the dawn had now come,
And he prayed with his face towards Al-Aqsa turned.

The Messenger sat by the Sacred Mosque in silence.
Abu Jahl passed by him noticing that sombre sight,
And asked, "Has there been some kind of occurrence?"
He replied, "I was taken to Jerusalem this very night."
And Abu Jahl's face then turned from surprise to glee,
"If I call others will you repeat what you said to me?"

Abu Jahl summoned Quraysh excitedly,
To embarrass him publicly was his aim.
"Now tell your people what you told me!
Come, O people! Come listen to his claim!"

"All was bearable until what you said today.
By al-Lat and al-'Uzza! Of lies this is your worst.
Al-Aqsa is for us a month's journey each way,
Which you claim in a single night you traversed!"
Mut'im ibn 'Adiyy avowed in a disapproving tone,
"Now your falsehood to all has been shown."

"O Mut'im, what an evil word," Abu Bakr cried,
"You said to the son of your brother certainly,
When you faced him and claimed that he lied,
But I bear witness that he speaks truthfully."

Then the Messenger upon the Makkans' request,
Began to describe Al-Aqsa and its environs pure,
In such a manner that even the sceptics confessed
Was only possible for him who had visited it before;
Answering every question with detail and precision,
While those who knew confirmed the description.

But even this was not enough for the Disbelievers,
So they turned it into a great mockery and joke.
They would wink when they passed the Believers,
And would laugh whenever the Messenger spoke.

"Then should We turn the Reminder away and ignore
You, because you are a people of great extravagance?
And how many a Prophet had been sent by Us,
Among those communities that had gone before,
But there would not come to them a Bearer of Prophecy,
Except that they would make of him continuous mockery."[104]

On a bright moonlit night of the month of Dhil-Hijjah,
Seventy-five helpers met with the Prophet secretly,
In a rocky valley close to Mina named Al-'Aqabah,
To renew their pledge of allegiance and sincerity.

"In all states and conditions to hear and obey,
And to spend in both times of ease and scarcity,
To promote goodness, and repel every evil way,
Fearing no blame in this from those who disagree,
And to defend the Messenger with lives and property.
If you do all this, your reward will be Paradise certainly."

---

[104] (Surah Az-Zukhruf (43): 5-7)

"O people of Khazraj!" 'Abbas, his uncle began to say,
"Muhammad is the most honourable of Banu Hashim,
Do you pledge that you will never deceive nor betray?
You invite him to your land and say you will support him,
But are you willing to fight all the Arab tribes to this end?
If you cannot, know we, his kin, are prepared to defend."

"Besides all that which we have already expressed,
If there was anything else in our hearts," Bara' replied,
"It would not remain now concealed in our chests.
Nay! We intend only to obey and sacrifice at his side!
We are ready, O Messenger, so our pledge do accept,
And each generation of us in combat has been adept."

Abul Haytham looked at the Prophet and said quietly,
"O Messenger, we have previously made peace by a pact
With the Jews, which now we will dissolve immediately."
"Let agreements of peace," he replied, "remain intact."

"And then when this matter will be concluded finally,
Will you leave us, and return to your own folk and city?"
The Messenger of Allah replied as he smiled graciously,
"No, blood is blood; I am with you, and you are with me."
Abul Haytham stretched his hand to pledge allegiance,
And every man after him soon followed in obedience.

The Prophet placed twelve representatives in his stead,
"Just as the disciples were chosen for Jesus son of Mary,
You shall, for your people, indeed be a surety." he said,
"And as for my own people, I myself will be the surety."

From Khazraj: As'ad ibn Zurarah, famed for nobility;
Al-Bara' ibn Marur; and high-spirited Sa'ad ibn 'Ubadah;
Rafi ibn Malik, 'Abdullah ibn Rawaha, Sa'ad ibn Rabi,
Al-Mundhir; 'Abdallah ibn 'Amr; As-Samit's son, 'Ubadah;
And from Aws: Usayd ibn Hudayr, pre-eminent in person;
Sa'ad ibn Khaythamah; and Rifa'a, 'Abdul Mundhir's son.

Then from atop Al-'Aqabah a piercing cry was heard,
"Beware O people of Mina! Take heed of Mudhammam,
He and all of the apostates have now secretly gathered,
And are right now preparing against you a stratagem!"

"By Him who sent you with Truth!" one Ansari cried,
"If you wish, we will raise up our swords tomorrow."
"We were not ordered to do this," the Prophet replied.
"Rather, back to your camps you should quietly go."

The delegates of Quraysh came out the next dawn,
While the air hung over them heavy and forlorn.
"It seems last night you made a pact with that man,
And offered to him against us arms and sanctuary,
But by God, we have had no quarrel with your clan,
And would not fight against you, except unwillingly."

'Abdullah ibn 'Ubayy was the very loudest in denial,
"This is clear falsehood!" he vehemently exclaimed,
"My people never do anything without consulting me,
And never would they do what you have claimed."

The chiefs of Quraysh considered the matter carefully,
And concluded that the meeting had indeed occurred.
So they sent after the people of Yathrib a hunting party,
Yet none except for Sa'ad ibn 'Ubadah could be captured.
They dragged him to Makkah on a rope pulling his hair;
Sa'ad would not reveal anything and continued to bear.

Suhayl ibn 'Amr slapped him while he was mockingly paraded,
But he was helped by Harith ibn Harb and Jubayr ibn Mut'im.
Sa'ad was a generous man with whom they had often traded,
So they drew their swords at the Kaaba and interceded for him.

Now, among the people of Ansar great anger had been felt,
And they were considering declaring war on Quraysh over it,
For such an insult to their most respected chief had been dealt.
Though Sa'ad returned to them unharmed and put an end to it,
Still there remained an uneasiness among Al-Aws and Khazraj,
For much blood had been spilt before over many a smaller grudge.

226

Year XIII

The Hijrah

"Alif. Laam. Meem. Do the people think they will be
Left alone to simply say 'we believe' and not be tried?
And We have tried those before them most certainly;
So Allah will know the truthful and know those who lied."[105]

The dark flames of oppression raged on fuelled by hate.
Now the pagans spared no expense in their campaign.
If the Muslims would not cease, they too would not abate.
Hubal, or the Lord of Muhammad: both could not remain.

And to each cause, followers began to rally,
Coming to 'Utbah, Abu Jahl, and Umayyah,
To Nadr, Al-Akhnas, and Al-Aswad al-Asadi,
To Abu Lahab, Abu Sufyan, and Tu'aymah,
As these were the nine heads of disbelief,
And each one of them, a proud pagan chief.

Then they set out in groups like wolves in a pack,
While their prey fled from the coming onslaught,
For this day they were all too ready to attack,
And tear apart any of the Believers they caught.

Makkah was becoming a shadow of itself now,
A far cry from a place of peace and security.
Ignorance was being raised and Truth made low,
Becoming the very centre of denying Allah's Unity.
And all they who would remain now to challenge it
Were oppressed, and none more so than the Prophet.

The Prophet told the Believers when they were alone,
"I have been shown the land to which you shall emigrate:
A land of palm trees between two black tracts of stone;
That is the land of Yathrib where your brethren await."

So when the order was given to perform *Hijrah*,
Under cover of darkness and in complete secrecy,
The *Muhajiroon* began leaving the city of Makkah.
In small groups at a time, they travelled cautiously,
And while leaving most of their possessions behind,
Were hopeful for what they would in Yathrib find.

---

[105] (Surah Al-Ankabut (29): 1-3)

"And say: 'O Lord, let my entry be a goodly entry,
And let my departure be a goodly emergence,
And do grant for me some help and authority,
From that which is with You in Your presence.'"[106]

The Prophet himself had not yet attempted emigration,
Not until almost every last Believer had succeeded,
Even though he himself faced the most oppression.
The news of this reached the Believers in Abyssinia;
They had long dreamt of the day they could return,
So towards Yathrib in groups they started to turn.

Suhayb ar-Rumi had been intending to leave the city,
And had managed to hide most of his wealth out of sight,
So he bade his time waiting for the right opportunity.
While the pagans placed him under watch day and night.

'Umar put on his sword and brought out his bow for all to see,
Then he circumambulated seven times around the Holy Kaaba,
Before announcing that to leave for Yathrib was his intention,
And said with the loudest and clearest voice that he could muster,
"Whoever wants his wife widowed and his children made orphan,
Then let him come now and meet me over there in that valley!"

No challenger came, so along with 'Ayyash, to Yathrib he did proceed,
But when Abu Jahl learned that his half-brother had also left Makkah,
Wasting no time, on his swiftest camel he raced after them with speed,
And then several days later, the tyrant intercepted them at Quba.

"Your mother vowed to never comb her hair, nor enter shade,
Until and unless she does see you, O 'Ayyash, once more."
"Do not listen!" said 'Umar, "It is but a trick he has played."
But he replied, "Let me relieve her of what she swore."
So when 'Ayyash, trusting his brother, had turned back,
Abu Jahl tied him up and subjected him to a vicious attack.

---

[106] (Surah Al-Isra (17): 80)

The Quraysh gathered in Dar an-Nadwah,
To now make a decision of great importance.
News of the Prophet had spread near and far,
And day by day, Islam was growing in influence.

'Abd Shams took precedence at the proceedings,
'Utbah, Shaybah, and Abu Sufyan took their seats,
Their kinsman, Al-Hakam, proudly sat at their side.
Abu Jahl and Walid of Makhzum, of warlike fame,
Entered too, dressed up in all their pomp and pride,
Along with Abu Lahab, Banu Hashim's chief in name.

Then entered one after the other, notables from every clan:
Nadr spoke for 'Abd ad-Dar; Umayyah and Ubayy for Jumah;
With Al-'Aas gone, Nabih and Munabbih spoke for Banu Sahm;
From Nawfal: Mut'im's son Jubayr, with Al-Harith, and Tu'aymah;
Banu Asad was represented by Zama'a, the nearest in sympathy,
Along with Hisham's son Hakim, and a reluctant Abul Bakhtari.

"Imprison him!" said one, "Exile him" another cried,
"Chase him to where harsh desert dwellers reside!"
An old man from Najd had been listening carefully,
He sighed loudly and shook his head impatiently,
"No! From wherever he lives, he will draw support,
A decisive act is needed! So give it more thought."

At those words, Abu Jahl jumped to his feet,
"Let each and every clan, a sword unsheathe,
And let each and every man strike in unison,
With that then, the problem shall disappear,
And 'Abd Manaf's sons cannot fight everyone,
So of their retribution we need no longer fear."

For now that Abu Talib was no longer present,
Nor was there Mut'im left to hold them back,
The chiefs of each clan all gave their consent,
And set about plotting how they would attack.

And to strike at midnight they did decide,
But from this, Abu Lahab began to dissuade,
"Some women and children may still be inside,
And if they should get caught up in your raid,
What then to embarrass us will the Arabs say?
But if we wait, he will surely come out to pray."

So with faces covered and swords at the ready,
Their heart bubbling with murderous intent,
That night a group of assassins waited silently,
Expecting that they would strike at any moment.

The Prophet gave his green Hadhrami cloak to 'Ali,
And asked him whether he would sleep in his bed.
"O Prophet, will you be safe?" 'Ali asked immediately,
"For if so, then I gladly volunteer to stay in your stead."
Then the Prophet of his own safety did firmly assure,
And that 'Ali too by Divine protection would be secure.

Then he enjoined unto him a further task,
"Return every trust to its owner faithfully."
For it was none but Muhammad all would ask
To take care of their goods and their property.

Abu Jahl was waiting outside with his men.
"Muhammad claims if you follow his Religion,
That you shall rule Arabs and non-Arabs then,
And after death, vast gardens you shall be given,
But if you refuse, fire is all that you shall earn,
And in it, the lot of you shall be left to burn!"

"Yes, I do say that," the Prophet replied,
"And you are one of those with that end."
Then with a handful of dust he came outside,
Reciting the Verses that his Lord did send.

"And We have set upon them a barrier
In front of them, and behind them a barrier,
Then We have covered them completely,
So that they are no longer able to see."[107]

---

[107] (Surah Ya-Seen (36): 9)

When they snapped out of their stupor finally,
Each of them shook off the dust from his head,
And from a hole, peered into the house silently,
Seeing a cloaked figure there, asleep on the bed.
"Dawn approaches, has he his prayer forgotten?
Indeed he never used to sleep this long!" they said.

They burst in, drawing out their swords in unison,
And swiftly pulled off the green cloak from the bed.
But it was only 'Ali who sat up in complete serenity.
"Where is Muhammad?" they exclaimed furiously.

"Did you leave him in my care," 'Ali replied,
"That you are making such demands of me?"
When they realised Muhammad was not inside,
The pagans began to rush around frantically.

The city came alive then with great clamour,
As Abu Jahl instigated a thousand men to action.
With reddened faces, they hurried door by door,
Searching every peak, ditch, and alley in desperation.
"Find Muhammad! Strike him with spear and sword,
And I guarantee a hundred camels as your reward!"

But the Prophet by now had already left Makkah,
With only Abu Bakr accompanying him on the way.
Asma had provided them with camels and supplies,
And the Prophet promised for his own share to pay.

And as they journeyed off into the night silently,
He looked with sadness at the city of his birth.
"You are the most beloved place to Allah and to me
From among all the various places on this earth.
And had not my people expelled me forcefully,
I would never have chosen to leave you willingly."

Reaching Mount Thawr from a southern road,
They ascended till they reached a cave opening.
For three days they kept that cave as their abode,
To shelter them from the forces that were pursuing.

And each evening, fresh milk to them was offered
By 'Amir ibn Fuhayrah, the slave that Abu Bakr freed,
Who ensured using his sheep, their tracks were covered,
Then would return to Makkah before anyone took heed.
He would observe all of Quraysh's movements carefully,
So he could report back news to the Prophet faithfully.

Most pursuers were scouring every northern road,
Just as the Messenger himself had already anticipated.
And they were exhausting every horse that they rode,
In longing for the hundred camel reward that awaited.

And then finally, on the morning of the third day,
Came a group of fierce men searching the south.
A bedouin skilled in the art of tracking led the way,
And followed the trail to Thawr, right up to the mouth.
"Camel prints obscured by a herd of sheep," he said,
"But no doubt, into that cave their tracks have led."

And Abu Bakr's heart began to quicken in its beat,
When he saw that their enemies were drawing near.
He said, "If even one of them glances at his feet,
They would surely see the two of us hiding here!"

"And what do you think," the Messenger replied,
"Of two, the third of whom is Allah at their side?"
Abu Bakr looked at the Prophet with stifled grief,
And saw that his face was bright with tranquillity.
The Prophet's words were calm and full of belief,
"Grieve not," he said, "for Allah is with us certainly."

Then the pagans noticed a spider's web had been spun,
Covering over the entrance of their cave completely.
"How can anyone enter here without it being broken?"
And noticed some wild doves nested in an adjacent tree.

So at that, the pagans stopped and were deterred
From entering the cave, and went off confounded,
Mutually exchanging blame, believing they had erred.
Abu Bakr, seeing this, was now completely astounded.
He praised Allah for saving them from their enemy,
And testified Muhammad was His Messenger certainly.

So when they had both proceeded from that place,
They hired the help of Ibn Urayqit, a desert guide,
And towards the city of Yathrib turned their face,
Aiming to approach it from the obscurest side.

And on the first of Rabi' al-Awwal they set out,
Travelling west across the Valley of Ibrahim,
Then north along the Bushaymat mountains,
Headed on a rocky tract towards Al-Ghamim,
Going past Al-Hudaybiyyah from the right,
And the pass of Al-Murar, verdant and bright.

On the second day, they travelled west to avoid
The busy trade route of the town of 'Usfan;
And crossed through the yellow hills of sand
Until they came to the great Mount Jumdan.

They went west of the village of Amj cautiously;
Near Al-Khulaysah's speckled tract they prayed,
Then they traversed along the uneven path tirelessly,
Till the western edge of the golden Valley of Qudayd,
Where they then came upon two tents standing erect,
And Umm Ma'bad came out to them with respect.

"I have no milk to offer; this goat's udders have dried,
And my husband has the whole flock out in the Valley."
"In Allah's Name," said the Prophet as he wiped its side,
And the bucket began to overflow with milk immediately.

When Abu Ma'bad returned after the group had gone ahead,
"Where did all this milk come from?" he asked with incredulity.
"A blessed man passed by here," the elderly Umm Ma'bad said,
Describing a man surpassing all in appearance and personality.
"By Allah, this is the man of Quraysh!" He replied excitedly,
"And if I get the chance I will now go to see him personally."

235

Meanwhile, the Prophet had gone north through the Valley,
Along the tract of Al-Mushallal, which was a well-known way.
And after a while, they reached the spacious Kulayyah Valley,
Carefully avoiding any caravans heading to Syria that day.

Suddenly the sound of hooves was heard, approaching fast;
A pagan named Suraqah ibn Malik came brandishing his sword.
He had guessed the route upon which the Prophet passed,
And now had his eyes set upon claiming the entire reward.
The Messenger turned to face him with composure and calm;
His face shining bright with belief, showing no fear of harm.

While Suraqah stared at them with a resolute look in his eye,
Like that of an angry lion, just about to strike for the kill.
The Messenger spoke, as he raised both his hands to the sky,
"O Allah, save us from his mischief in any manner You will."

Then Suraqah and his horse began to sink into the sand,
So he drew out his bow, intending to let loose an arrow,
But a paralysis overtook him and it fell from his hand.
"O Muhammad!" he cried, "Ask your Lord to let me go,
And I swear that you shall see no more trouble from me;
I will even dissuade others from pursuing you certainly!"

He raised his hands again, and Suraqah's horse became free.
"O Muhammad! I swear your Religion will prevail one day!"
Then Suraqah went back and told whoever he would see,
That there were no signs that anyone had passed this way.

The Prophet had promised Suraqah a wondrous thing:
That a day would come when Islam would gain victory,
And Suraqah will be given the bracelets of Persia's King.
Abu Bakr thought about those words during the journey;
Whatever Muhammad said would, no doubt, come to be,
And it gave him hope in the future, despite the difficulty.

They went on with the declining sun at a steady pace,
Reaching the Valley of Kharrar, and then on to Juhfah;
The Prophet had many a time passed through this place,
And seen its white dust upon the pilgrims to Makkah.

And it was here Revelation by the Prophet was received,
When his heart became filled with a sense of longing.
"He who ordained the Qur'an for you, indeed
Will bring you back to the Place of Returning."[108]
And so he turned away from Makkah now resolute,
And continued his journey along the winding route.

Then they passed Ghadir Khumm on the third day,
And filled their water skins at the Spring of Ahya.
Avoiding many snakes and scorpions along the way,
They navigated the stony course of Abu Duwaymah.

Northbound they went along the Path of Humayyah,
Reaching the foothills of Mount Mustazilat soon.
Then through the watercourse of Al-Musaydirah,
The Pass of Rijalayn full of ancient graves by afternoon,
And west of Mount Al-Mulaysa, smooth and white,
Then in the Valley of Liqf, they camped for the night.

Then they traversed along rocky rivulet creeks
All day, until they reached the Valley of Mijah,
With its black mountains of imposing peaks;
Then northeast through the famed Valley of Qaha.

But on the fifth day, they were now slowed down,
After the use of one of their mounts had been lost
As they passed through a valley near Al-Arj town
And a narrow and meandering path they crossed.
So that night, under the stars and the azure shade,
It was there, the Prophet and his companions stayed.

Then early next day, they crossed the Pass of Rakubah,
Past the noble Mount Warqan, tall and of a reddish hue,
That the Prophet remarked was a mountain of Jannah;
And seeing it, no one had any doubt his words were true.

---

[108] (Surah Al-Qasas (28): 85)

Up through the Valley of Hafr they proceeded to go,
And filled their waterskins at Al-Khatir's wells gratefully.
Then they reached the Valley of Reem, dusty and narrow,
And it was here that Abu Ma'bad caught up to them finally.
For days, he had been trailing after the tracks of their journey,
And he now came to the Prophet to offer his testimony.

On the seventh day, they were preceded by a gentle breeze;
They crossed the Valley of 'Aqeeq, known for delicious water,
And passed the Well of Shaddad under the shade of trees,
And followed the road till they stopped at Al-Jathjathah.

Northeast they went on Rabi' al-Awwal's eight day,
Going towards the red mountain of Hamra al-Asad,
And the Meadow of Khakh's green shrubs and hay;
Crossing the lava tracts on Mount Ayr's eastern side,
They continued through the neighbourhood of 'Usbah,
Until the Messenger ordered them to alight at Quba.

They were welcomed by Bani 'Amr ibn 'Awf's hospitality,
And the Prophet founded on obedience and piety there
The first Masjid established for the Muslim Community,
And for four days he waited and remained in prayer.

Till from the distance, a familiar figure came into sight;
His feet had become swollen from a lengthy journey;
The Prophet rose to greet him and held him tight:
His beloved cousin 'Ali had returned to him finally.
'Ali who had slept in his bed, expecting to be killed,
Had returned every trust, and every promise fulfilled.

And following in his footsteps, two bright lights emerged:
His mother, Fatima; and his cousin, the more radiant one.
'Ali had brought them safely with the honour they deserved,
And the Prophet now smiled with the warmth of the sun.

All of them followed as the Messenger of Mercy led;
The road had been long and they had journeyed far,
A land of palm trees and fresh dates was just ahead,
And the sound of celebration could be heard from it,
As they neared Madinah, the City of the Prophet.

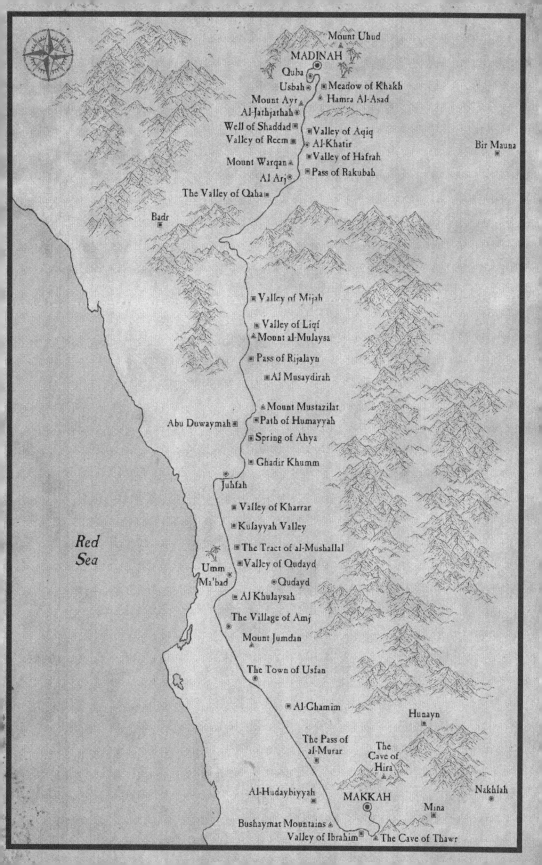

Personalities

The People of Makkah:

Banu Hashim:

Prophet Muhammad (ﷺ)

The final and greatest Messenger of God. He is known by many names and titles, the most famous of which are *Al-Mustafa* (the Chosen one), *As-Sadiq* (the Truthful), *Al-Amin* (The Trustworthy), and *Ahmad* (The Praised). His father was 'Abdullah ibn 'Abdul Muttalib and his mother was Aminah bint Wahb. He was a descendant of Prophet Ibrahim (ﷺ) through Prophet Isma'il (ﷺ). The people of his time had forgotten the true teachings of their forefathers and had instead fallen into idol worship and immorality. After twenty-three years of constant preaching, struggles and sacrifices, Prophet Muhammad (ﷺ) guided almost the entire Arabian peninsula back to monotheism.

Khadija bint al-Khuwaylid

She was from Banu Asad. She was the first and most beloved wife of Prophet Muhammad (ﷺ), as well as the mother of his daughter Fatima az-Zahra. She was well respected in the time of *Jahiliyyah*. She was referred to by the titles *"At-Tahirah"* (the Pure), and *"Ummul Yateem"* (Mother of the orphans). She did not worship idols as she had learned about monotheism from her cousin Waraqah ibn Nawfal. She was also one of the richest women in Arabia on account of her highly profitable trading business that she had inherited from her father. On the advice of Abu Talib she employed Muhammad (ﷺ) to conduct trade for her, and she soon became deeply impressed with his personality. She eventually sent a proposal for marriage, and they remained together for a period of twenty-five years. She was the first person to accept Islam at his hands. She encouraged her friend Lubabah to accept Islam too. Throughout his entire mission, she was his strongest supporter. During the three years of exile in the Valley of Banu Hashim, she expended her entire wealth in order to support Islam and the Muslims. Her life there was very difficult, and soon after the Boycott ended, she passed away. The year she died was referred to as "The Year of Grief". The Prophet (ﷺ) would always recount her goodness, even years later – and said that she was one of the four greatest women to have ever lived. She is buried in the graveyard of Mu'alla in Makkah.

Al-Qasim ibn Muhammad

The firstborn son of Prophet Muhammad (ﷺ) and Khadija. It was after his birth that the 28-year-old Muhammad (ﷺ) became known as "Abul Qasim". Qasim died of an illness in infancy, aged three.

'Abdullah ibn Muhammad

He was the second son of Muhammad (ﷺ) and Khadija. He also died in infancy. Some of the polytheists mocked the Prophet (ﷺ) and said that he would end up with no male progeny to carry forth his lineage. Surah Kawthar was revealed as a response.

Zaynab bint Muhammad

According to most historical reports, she was the eldest of the four daughters of the Prophet (ﷺ). Some sources say that she and her sisters Ruqayyah and Umm Kulthum were actually the daughters of Khadija's sister, Hala, that Khadija had adopted after the latter's death. And Allah (ﷺ) knows best. Zaynab was one of the first to accept Islam when the Prophet (ﷺ) announced his mission. However, her husband Abul 'Aas ibn ar-Rabi did not. There was a separation between them but he did not wish to divorce her. He fought on the side of the polytheists in the Battle of Badr and was captured, but was released by the Prophet (ﷺ) without ransom. A few years later, he accepted Islam and he reunited with Zaynab. She died soon after this and was buried in Madinah.

Ruqayyah bint Muhammad

She was also either one of the biological or adopted daughters of the Prophet (ﷺ). She was initially married to her cousin, 'Utbah the son of Abu Lahab, but he divorced her without touching her. Ruqayyah then married 'Uthman ibn 'Affan and accompanied him to Abyssinia. They returned at a later time and emigrated to Madinah. She died from an illness in the second year after the Hijrah shortly after the Battle of Badr.

Umm Kulthum bint Muhammad

Like her sisters Ruqayyah, Zaynab and Umm Kulthum, she was raised in the home of the Prophet (ﷺ) and Khadija. Whether she was their biological daughter or the niece of Khadija varies between sources. She was initially married to her cousin, 'Utaybah the son of Abu Lahab, but he divorced her without touching her. This was on the order of Abu Lahab who ordered his two sons to divorce the two daughters of Muhammad (ﷺ) out of hatred for the Message. After the death of her sister Ruqayyah, she was married to 'Uthman ibn 'Affan. She also died a few years later in the lifetime of the Prophet (ﷺ) and had no children.

Fatima bint Muhammad

She was the daughter of Prophet Muhammad (ﷺ) and Khadija: the youngest of four daughters according to some sources, and his only biological daughter according to others. She was the only one who outlived the Prophet (ﷺ), albeit for only six months. Her title was *Az-Zahra* (the Radiant). She has an exceptionally high status in Islam on account of her virtues and piety. She has been named by the Prophet (ﷺ) as one of the four greatest believing women, along with Khadija, Mary (the mother of Jesus), and Asiya (the wife of Pharaoh). She was the most beloved of all people to the Prophet (ﷺ). She was married to 'Ali ibn Abi Talib and gave birth to Al-Hasan, Al-Husayn, Zaynab and Umm Kulthum. She was the first member of the Prophet (ﷺ)'s household to pass away after him (ﷺ). She was buried in Madinah - the exact location is unknown as she asked had 'Ali to bury her in secret.

Abu Talib ibn 'Abdul Muttalib

He was the chief of Banu Hashim. It is said his real name was 'Imran, or 'Abd Manaf. He was a paternal uncle of Prophet Muhammad (ﷺ) and the full brother of 'Abdullah. His half-brothers included Hamza, 'Abbas and Abu Lahab. His sons were Talib, Ja'far, 'Aqeel and 'Ali. Muhammad (ﷺ) was raised in his home from the age of ten. Abu Talib performed the marriage ceremony for him and Khadija. Unlike the majority of his family, Abu Talib did not publicly declare Islam, but remained a firm protector of him and prevented the pagans of Quraysh from harming him. His poetry has been recorded and contains many lines acknowledging the truthfulness of the Messenger (ﷺ). For three years he remained in exile with the Prophet (ﷺ) in the Valley of Banu Hashim, protecting him. Abu Talib died in the tenth year of the Prophetic mission: the same year Khadija died. The Prophet (ﷺ) referred to that year as "The Year of Grief." Only after Abu Talib's passing were the Quraysh brave enough to directly target him, and from that point on the persecution only increased.

Fatima bint Asad

She was the daughter of Asad ibn Hashim ibn 'Abd Manaf. She married her cousin, Abu Talib, and became the mother of seven children: Talib, Umm Hani, 'Aqeel, Jumanah, Rayta, Ja'far and 'Ali. Prophet Muhammad (ﷺ) referred to her as his "Second mother" as it was in her home that he was raised after being orphaned. She was among the very first Believers and the foremost of them. She was an exceptionally kind woman who lived a life of utmost purity. At the time of the Prophet's (ﷺ) Hijrah, she remained in Makkah until she emigrated along with her son 'Ali ibn Abi Talib and Fatima the daughter of Muhammad (ﷺ). When she passed away in 4 AH, the Prophet (ﷺ) personally buried her in the graveyard of Al-Baqi, giving her his own shirt as a shroud. He showed her extra care when lowering her into the grave and widened her grave for her. He recalled her many kindnesses to him, prayed for her and confirmed that she was one of the women of Paradise.

'Ali ibn Abi Talib

He was the youngest son of Abu Talib and the first cousin of Muhammad (ﷺ). His mother Fatima bint Asad gave birth to him in the Kaaba itself. He was raised from childhood by Muhammad (ﷺ). 'Ali had never worshipped idols. He was the most obedient of people to the Messenger (ﷺ). He accepted Islam at the age of ten, preceded only by Khadija. He would defend the Prophet (ﷺ) from the attacks of the children of the pagans whenever they threw stones. On the Night of Hijrah, he slept in the bed of the Prophet (ﷺ) to allow him a chance to escape. In Madinah, when every Muslim was assigned a 'brother', 'Ali was chosen to be the "brother of the Prophet (ﷺ). He was also given the honour of marrying Fatima, the daughter of Muhammad (ﷺ). Their children were Al-Hasan, Al-Husayn, Zaynab, and Umm Kulthum. 'Ali carried the banner and distinguished himself in every battle in which he participated including Badr, Uhud, Khandaq, Khaybar and Hunayn. He was given a special sword named Dhul-Fiqar by the Prophet (ﷺ) and was named *Asadullah al-Ghalib*, "the Ever-Victorious Lion of God". He was also famed for his knowledge, justice, humility, generosity and eloquence. When the Prophet (ﷺ) passed away, 'Ali was the one who washed his body and made his funeral arrangements. He became the fourth caliph in 35 AH after the unrest that led to the killing of 'Uthman ibn 'Affan. The period of his caliphate was five years. Despite seeking to avoid further conflict, he faced opposition from several sides resulting in the battles of Jamal, Siffin and Nahrawan. Even so, he ruled with justice, treated his opponents with mercy and dedicated himself to helping the needy. As he led the morning prayer on the nineteenth of Ramadhan 40 AH, 'Ali was struck with a poisoned sword and succumbed to the effects of poison three days later. He was buried in a place near Kufa, now known as Najaf. His son Al-Hasan briefly succeeded him as caliph.

Ja'far ibn Abu Talib

He was the son of Abu Talib, and the elder brother of 'Ali. He was one of the earliest Believers. In physical appearance, he bore a great resemblance to his cousin, Muhammad the Messenger of Allah (ﷺ).

Ja'far was known for his generosity, bravery and powerful skills as an orator. He was the leader of the delegation sent to Abyssinia, where he made an eloquent speech which convinced the Negus to allow the Muslims to remain. He moved to Madinah a few years after the Hijrah and proceeded to meet the Prophet (ﷺ) at Khaybar just as the battle had ended. The Prophet (ﷺ) was delighted to see him and remarked that he did not know whether he was happier over the conquest of Khaybar or to see Ja'far again. He was killed in the Battle of Mutah where he lost both his arms. The Prophet (ﷺ) was grieved by his death before being informed by the Angel Jibreel (ع) that Ja'far would be given two heavenly wings as compensation for his arms. He was thereafter known as *Ja'far at-Tayyar* - the one who flies in paradise.

Hamza ibn 'Abdul Muttalib

He was the paternal uncle of the Prophet (ﷺ). On his mother's side, he was his cousin. He was a skilled hunter, powerful warrior and among the very bravest of men. He openly declared his Islam in the fifth year of the Prophetic mission in a famous event. After he found out that Abu Jahl had been abusing his nephew, Hamza struck Abu Jahl hard on his head with his bow and challenged him to return it: the latter backed down and acknowledged his fault. Hamza's protection of Muhammad (ﷺ) was such that Quraysh were terrified of angering him. He was known as, *Asadullah*, "The Lion of God". He performed Hijrah to Madinah before the Messenger (ﷺ) and was therefore not present when Quraysh were plotting to assassinate him. He was a commander at Badr and one of the first three combatants from the side of the Muslims. He was killed in the Battle of Uhud by a spear thrown by the slave Wahshi on the instructions of Hind bint 'Utbah. She then mutilated his body, and tried to chew his liver, but was unable to swallow it. He was given the title of *"Sayyid as-Shuhuda"* meaning "the Master of Martyrs" by the Messenger of Allah (ﷺ). Lady Fatima and her sons Al-Hasan and Al-Husayn used to visit his grave frequently.

Safiyyah bint 'Abdul Muttalib

She was a paternal aunt of the Prophet (ﷺ), and the full sister of Hamza ibn 'Abdul Muttalib. She married 'Awwam ibn Khuwaylid who was the brother of Khadija, and she became the mother of Zubayr ibn al-'Awwam. She was very tough with Zubayr in order to raise him as a warrior. Safiyyah was one of the earliest Believers to accept Islam. She performed Hijrah to Madinah along with her brother Hamza and her son Zubayr. She was an exceptionally brave woman who was present at several battles where she helped transport water and retrieve arrows. At Uhud, she picked up a spear and rebuked those among the Muslims who fled. She saw the mutilated body of her brother, Hamza, and composed an elegy as she wept over him. She is also said to have defended herself and killed a man with a pole during the Battle of Khandaq when Madinah was under siege. She was present at Khaybar too where she witnessed her son fighting. She reportedly died during the caliphate of 'Umar in the year 20 AH.

Arwa bint 'Abdul Muttalib

She was a paternal aunt of the Prophet (ﷺ) and one of the earliest Believers after her son Tulayb ibn 'Umayr. She outlived the Prophet (ﷺ) and some poetry in praise of him is attributed to her. She is reported to have died during the caliphate of 'Umar in the year 15 AH.

'Aatikah bint 'Abdul Muttalib

She was a paternal aunt of the Prophet (ﷺ) and one of the earliest Believers. She was the stepmother of Umm Salamah after marrying Abu Umayyah ibn al-Mughirah from the Banu Makhzum. She had a frightening dream three days before the Battle of Badr in which a rider called out that destruction would fall upon Quraysh in three days. Then a stone was hurled from the top of Mount Abu Qubays and it entered every household except for those of Banu Hashim and Banu Zuhrah. She informed her brother 'Abbas of this who told others. Abu Lahab heard of it and thus did not join the army out of fear. Abu Jahl however made it a point of mockery, suggesting that the Banu Hashim were not content with only their men claiming Prophethood but now their women were too. Details of her later life are limited and unclear. Some sources say that she eventually performed Hijrah to Madinah and is buried in Al-Baqi while others say she died in Makkah. There are some reports that she outlived the Prophet (ﷺ), and some poetry in praise of him is attributed to her. However, this is unlikely to be correct as she does not appear in any historical records, whereas her two sons 'Abdullah and Zuhayr who accepted Islam do appear.

'Abbas ibn 'Abdul Muttalib

He was the uncle of the Prophet (ﷺ) on his father's side. His wife was Lubabah, the second woman to believe. However, 'Abbas himself did not outwardly express belief in Islam until after the Hijrah. Nonetheless, he, along with the majority of Banu Hashim, protected the Prophet against his enemies. 'Abbas was among those who were exiled in the Valley of Banu Hashim. He was present at the Second Pledge of Al-'Aqabah, where he emphasised to the Ansar that they should not pledge allegiance unless they were prepared to take the responsibility for protecting Muhammad (ﷺ) upon themselves. 'Abbas was a wealthy merchant with good ties to the various clans of Quraysh. He did not emigrate when the Believers emigrated. He went along with the polytheists in the Battle of Badr and was subsequently captured. Then shortly afterwards he publicly embraced Islam. He took part in the Conquest of Makkah, defended the Prophet (ﷺ) at Hunayn and was present in the expedition to Tabuk. His son 'Abdullah ibn 'Abbas was a famous companion of the Prophet (ﷺ), and an authority on the Qur'an. From among his descendants came the 'Abbasid dynasty of caliphs. 'Abbas died in Madinah and is buried at Al-Baqi.

Umm Fadl, Lubaba

She was from Banu 'Amir. She was the wife of 'Abbas ibn 'Abdul Muttalib. She was one of the first women to accept Islam. She remained in Makkah with her husband who had not yet expressed belief. After news reached them of the Muslim victory at Badr, Abu Lahab began beating her slave.

To defend him, she struck Abu Lahab with a tent pole on his head. That wound was destined to be his end. Pustules developed from it and Abu Lahab died in a humiliating and painful manner.

'Ubaydah ibn al-Harith

He was from Banu Hashim. His father was Harith ibn 'Abdul Muttalib, an uncle of the Prophet (ﷺ). His brother was Abu Sufyan ibn al-Harith (not to be confused with Abu Sufyan ibn Harb). 'Ubaydah was one of the very first to accept Islam. He was a God-fearing and patient man. He led an expedition that is now named after him. He was among the first three Muslim combatants in the Battle of Badr and lost his leg while facing his opponent. He succumbed to his injuries soon afterwards and was thus considered the first martyr of Badr.

Abu Sabrah ibn Abi Rahm

He was the son of Bara' bint 'Abdul Muttalib and was therefore a cousin to the Prophet (ﷺ). He was among the emigrants to Abyssinia along with his wife Umm Kulthum, the daughter of Suhayl ibn 'Amr. They later returned to Makkah and performed Hijrah to Madinah. Abu Sabrah took part in various battles alongside the Prophet (ﷺ) including Badr. During the caliphate of 'Umar, he was one of the commanders in the conquest of Persia. He eventually returned to Makkah where he died during the caliphate of 'Uthman.

Zayd ibn al-Haritha

He was from Banu Kalb. He was kidnapped and enslaved as a child. Khadija presented him to Muhammad (ﷺ) who freed him, and they then raised him as an adopted son. Even after his own family found him, he was given a choice to return, but he preferred to stay with Muhammad (ﷺ) on account of his good treatment of him and lofty personality. He was one of the very first to accept Islam. He was the only person to accompany the Prophet (ﷺ) during his journey to Ta'if. He is the only companion mentioned by name in the Qur'an (in 33:37 which clarified that he was not in fact the actual son of Muhammad (ﷺ)). Zayd was a skilled archer and a capable military leader who fought at Badr, Uhud, Khandaq and Khaybar. He was killed at the Battle of Mutah in which he was a commander and the standard bearer. The Prophet (ﷺ) wept greatly at his death. He had a son named Usamah who the Prophet (ﷺ) also appointed to command, and in one of his final acts, ordered him to go with an army to the place where Zayd had been killed.

Abu Lahab ibn 'Abd al-Muttalib

His real name was 'Abd al-'Uzzah, which was probably given to him by his mother, Lubnah bint Hajar. His title of *Abu Lahab* (the Father of Flame) was said to be given to him either due to his red cheeks or his fiery temper. He kept his hair in two locks, wore expensive cloaks and was described as being handsome in appearance. Despite being a paternal uncle of Muhammad (ﷺ) and his neighbour, Abu Lahab became his worst enemy after he declared Prophethood. This was due in part to the influence of his wife Umm Jameel who also bore a deep hostility to the Prophet (ﷺ). Abu Lahab is the only person from among the Disbelievers of Makkah to be mentioned by name in the Qur'an. He had a bad character, was easily angered and often drunk. He became the apparent chief of Banu Hashim in Makkah after the death of his half-brother, Abu Talib. He was among the conspirators to murder the Prophet (ﷺ) on the night of Hijrah, and he had agreed to accept blood money. He did not take part in Badr himself but paid someone to take his place. Soon after hearing of the Muslim victory, and being struck by a tent pole following an argument, he developed pustules all over his body and died. Abu Lahab's body gave off such a foul and unbearable stench that no one wanted to be near him and even his family abandoned it in the street for three days. Then afterwards, out of a sense of shame, they dug a pit, pushed him into it with long poles and threw stones at it from a distance until he was buried. Such was his humiliating end. He is one of the confirmed inhabitants of Hellfire.

'Utaybah ibn Abu Lahab

He was the son of Abu Lahab and was therefore a cousin of Prophet Muhammad (ﷺ). He was among the most vicious and aggressive of people in his manners. He was initially married to Umm Kulthum bint Muhammad (ﷺ) but divorced her before consummation as per the instruction of Abu Lahab in order to cause harm to Muhammad (ﷺ). One day, he assaulted the Messenger of Allah (ﷺ) and expressed his disbelief of various Surahs of the Qur'an. The Messenger (ﷺ) prayed against him at that time. Not long after this, 'Utaybah had gone on a trip when he, alone among everyone, was attacked by a lion and devoured. This event filled the Quraysh with fear and they relented for a time from harassing the Messenger (ﷺ).

Thuwaybah

She was a slave owned by Abu Lahab and his wife. It is said that when she informed Abu Lahab about the birth of Muhammad (ﷺ), in a moment of happiness he freed her. She was the first wet nurse of Muhammad (ﷺ), before he was given to Halimah. She had also been the wet nurse of Hamza ibn Abdul Muttalib two years earlier. She used to visit Muhammad (ﷺ) and Khadija after they got married. When the Prophetic mission began, Thuwaybah accepted Islam. She died in the year 7 AH.

Al-Muttalib ibn 'Abd Manaf

He was the brother of Hashim ibn 'Abd Manaf. When Hashim died, Al-Muttalib brought his orphaned son, Shaybah, to Makkah. The latter had been previously living in Yathrib with his mother, so no one knew him. They assumed he was a slave Al-Muttalib had acquired and thus referred to him as 'Abd al-Muttalib. Al-Muttalib raised "'Abd al-Muttalib" and helped him to become a man of prominence in Makkah. The descendants of Al-Muttalib sided with Abu Talib in his defence of the Prophet (ﷺ), and so were also subjected to the same Boycott that was placed by the rest of Quraysh against the Banu Hashim.

Banu Asad ibn 'Abdul 'Uzzah:

Nawfal ibn Khuwaylid

He was the paternal half-brother of Khadija. He was a strongly built man of imposing physique. He was known as the "Lion of Quraysh" by the pagans, and the "Demon of Quraysh" by the Muslims. He did not hesitate to bully or intimidate those who had accepted Islam. In one famous incident, he bound Abu Bakr and Talhah together with a rope. His son, Al-Aswad ibn Nawfal, believed and emigrated to Abyssinia to escape the persecution that he faced. Nawfal ibn Khuwaylid fought in the Battle of Badr where he challenged and was killed in a duel by the "Lion of God", 'Ali ibn Abi Talib.

'Amr ibn Asad

He was the paternal uncle of Khadija and acted as her guardian after the death of her father. He was there as her representative on her marriage ceremony to Muhammad (ﷺ). He appears to have died before the Prophet's mission began.

Al-Aswad ibn Muttalib ibn Asad

He was related to Khadija, with their fathers being paternal cousins. On his mother's side he was related to the Prophet (ﷺ). Despite this, he had no insight into religion: he lived and died as a pagan. He was among the most inveterate of the Prophet's (ﷺ) enemies who persisted the most in their mockery. Finally, the Angel Jibreel (ﷺ) threw a green leaf in his face and he turned blind. He still persisted as a follower of Abu Jahl in his campaign against Islam. Al-Aswad lost three of his sons in Badr fighting against the Believers. He most likely died soon after that, before the Battle of Uhud.

Zam'ah ibn al-Aswad

He was the son of Al-Aswad ibn Muttalib. Like his father, he was one of the opponents of Islam and in its early phase was with the chiefs of Quraysh who tried to persuade Abu Talib to stop his nephew (ﷺ) from preaching. Zam'ah's son Al-Harith accepted Islam, but after Zam'ah imprisoned him, he returned back to paganism. His other son Yazid ibn Zam'ah accepted Islam and was one of the Believers who emigrated to Abyssinia in order to preserve his Faith. Even so, Zam'ah was among the polytheists of Quraysh who objected to the economic boycott against the Banu Hashim and helped end it. Zam'ah quarrelled with Abu Jahl saying that he had not been consulted about nor approved of the parchment being written. He never did accept Islam however, and remained among those who mocked and rejected it. He eventually fought in the Battle of Badr along with his son Al-Harith and was killed by 'Ali ibn Abi Talib after facing him in combat.

Zubayr ibn al-'Awwam

His father, Al-'Awwam, was the brother of Khadija bint Khuwaylid. His mother was Safiyyah bint 'Abd al-Muttalib. He had been raised by his cousin, Nawfal ibn Khuwaylid, who was tough with him but not as tough as his mother. Zubayr grew to be a tall, slender but physically strong man, with shoulder-length hair. He accepted Islam on the invitation of Abu Bakr. He took part in the Hijrah to Abyssinia. He was a courageous and proven warrior. He fought in the battles of Badr, Uhud, Khandaq, Khaybar, Hunayn and the Conquest of Makkah. After the passing of the Prophet (ﷺ) he remained a close supporter of 'Ali ibn Abi Talib for many years. He was also involved in the Ridda wars, the Battle of Yarmouk, the conquest of Persia and the conquest of Egypt. He became a politically significant figure, playing an important role in the period of tribulation surrounding the killing of the third caliph, 'Uthman ibn 'Affan. He eventually found himself as one of the commanders in the Battle of Jamal on the side fighting against 'Ali ibn Abi Talib. However, at a certain point he chose to leave the battlefield after being reminded of the forewarning of the Prophet (ﷺ) pertaining to that very situation. Later that evening, whilst praying he was killed by a man who had followed him. Despite their recent differences, 'Ali was saddened by the news of the death of his cousin Zubayr, who had supported the Messenger of Allah (ﷺ) and himself on a number of previous occasions.

'Abdullah ibn Jahsh

He was from Banu Asad on his father's side. His mother Umama bint 'Abdul Muttalib, was from Banu Hashim, making him a cousin of the Prophet (ﷺ). His sister was Zaynab bint Jahsh, who eventually became a wife of Prophet Muhammad (ﷺ). He was among the first emigrants who went to Abyssinia. 'Abdullah ibn Jahsh also took part in the Nakhlah raid, the Battle of Badr, and fought in the Battle of Uhud where he was killed by Al-Akhnas ibn Shariq.

Zaynab bint Jahsh

Her father Jahsh ibn Riyab was from Banu Asad and her mother Umama bint 'Abdul Muttalib was an aunt of Prophet Muhammad (ﷺ). Her brothers were 'Abdullah ibn Jahsh and 'Ubaydullah ibn Jahsh. Zaynab was married to Zayd ibn Haritha but this ended in divorce. Later, after the completion of the waiting period, she married her cousin, Prophet Muhammad (ﷺ). Some Verses of the Qur'an were revealed regarding this. Zaynab was known for being generous and praying a lot. She worked as a tanner and leather worker. She died in Madinah nine years after the Prophet (ﷺ) passed away.

Abul Bakhtari ibn Hisham

His real name was Al-'Aas. His father, Hisham ibn Harith ibn Asad, was the cousin of Khadija. He was a polytheist but had never caused harm to the Messenger (ﷺ) or the Believers by his hand or tongue while they had remained in Makkah. He had some honourable traits which included a sense of justice as well as courage and loyalty. He was among those who had tried to help the Banu Hashim with food supplies during the period of the economic boycott, and he even physically fought with Abu Jahl because of this on one occasion. He also played an important role in helping to end the Boycott. Nonetheless, he remained a polytheist and was present in the meeting at Dar an-Nadwa where he had suggested that the Prophet (ﷺ) should be imprisoned rather than killed. He went along with the plan to assassinate him in the end. Later, he joined the army of Abu Jahl in the Battle of Badr. Due to his earlier attitude of kindness, the

Prophet (ﷺ) forbade his killing and urged the Believers to keep away from him. Abul Bakhtari was informed of this, but when he learned that his friend was not also given a similar security he insisted on fighting alongside him even if it meant he died. He was thus killed at Badr by Al-Mujadhir ibn Ziyad whom he had attacked. The Prophet (ﷺ) was saddened by his death. His son, Al-Aswad ibn Abil Bakhtari, did end up embracing Islam however.

Hakim ibn Hizam

He was the son of Hizam ibn Khuwaylid, and thus a nephew of Khadija. When the Prophet (ﷺ) began preaching Hakim refused multiple invitations to Islam, but also had no particular animosity towards the Prophet (ﷺ) or the Believers. Even whilst remaining a polytheist, he disapproved of the actions of Abu Jahl when he had enforced an economic boycott against the Banu Hashim. He therefore took it upon himself to help them. Khadija would on occasion purchase flour from him. He would then load up a camel to send out to the Valley. He was caught doing this by Abu Jahl who quarrelled with him. Abul Bakhtari came to his aid at that time. He was among those who were present at the meeting when the Quraysh plotted to kill the Prophet (ﷺ). He reluctantly fought in the Battle of Badr on the side of the pagans. He finally accepted Islam at the time of the Conquest of Makkah and fought on the side of the Prophet (ﷺ) at the Battle of Hunayn. He was among those who the Prophet (ﷺ) gave gifts to in order to reconcile their hearts. He lived to an old age and died in Madinah.

Banu Nawfal:

Mut'im ibn 'Adiyy

He was the chief of Banu Nawfal. Mut'im had been a long-time friend of Abu Talib. However their relationship became strained after Mut'im joined the other pagans on several occasions in asking Abu Talib to stop his nephew Muhammad (ﷺ) from preaching. Mut'im remained staunch in his denial of Islam, but generally lenient in his attitude towards the

255

Prophet (ﷺ) whom he had always liked and respected. He was opposed to the three-year boycott of Banu Hashim and was among those who eventually helped end it. After Abu Talib passed away, Mut'im saw that the persecution against the Messenger (ﷺ) increased considerably and he felt obliged to render him some assistance. Upon his request, he helped him to safely return to Makkah after he had come back from Ta'if, and announced to everyone that Muhammad (ﷺ) was under his protection at that point. This did not prevent him from later denying the Mi'raaj. He also forbade his son Jubayr from marrying 'A'isha the daughter of Abu Bakr because she and her father were Muslims. He died while still a polytheist at around the age of ninety. That was before the time that the Quraysh decided to make a plot against the Prophet's (ﷺ) life. The Prophet (ﷺ) never forgot Mut'im's relative kindness to him. After the Battle of Badr, he remarked that if Mut'im had still been alive and had asked him for the release of the Makkan prisoners, he (ﷺ) would have released them all without ransom for his sake.

Jubayr ibn Mut'im

He was the son of Mut'im ibn 'Adiyy. His attitude towards Islam was decidedly a lot harsher than his father's. When Mut'im passed away, Jubayr attended the council of Quraysh and was part of those who attempted to kill the Prophet (ﷺ) on the Night of Hijrah. Later, Jubayr's uncle was killed by Hamza ibn 'Abdul Muttalib in the Battle of Badr, prompting him to seek revenge. As Jubayr was the slave owner of Wahshi, a man who was skilled at spear-throwing, he allowed Hind to hire him for the purpose of killing Hamza. Jubayr eventually accepted Islam after the Treaty of Hudaybiyyah but before the Conquest of Makkah. Despite his outward antagonism to Islam, Jubayr said that the seeds of belief had first become planted in his heart some years earlier when he heard the Messenger of Allah (ﷺ) reciting Surah Tur in his evening prayers. Jubayr lived the rest of his life as a Muslim and narrated several traditions that he heard from the Prophet (ﷺ). He died towards the end of the rule of Mu'awiyah ibn Abi Sufyan at around 57 AH.

Tu'aymah ibn 'Adiyy

He was the brother of Mut'im ibn 'Adiyy and became chief of Bani Nawfal after him. He was part of those who plotted to kill the Prophet (ﷺ) on the Night of Hijrah. He was an argumentative and arrogant man who clung to polytheism and rejection of the Truth. He reportedly killed Sa'ad ibn Khaythamah in the Battle of Badr and was then himself killed by either 'Ali ibn Abi Talib or Hamza ibn 'Abdul Muttalib.

Banu 'Abd Shams:

'Utbah ibn Rabi'ah

He was a prominent chief of Quraysh, noted for his sagacity and extensive knowledge of poetry. He opposed the Prophet (ﷺ) and the Message of Islam, but like many of the other pagans, was deeply impressed with the expressive power and inimitable eloquence of the Qur'an. He was with the chiefs of Quraysh during their different attempts to bribe or coerce the Messenger (ﷺ) collectively as a group. On one occasion, he tried to personally negotiate with the Messenger (ﷺ), thinking he could convince him to stop preaching. Some Verses from Surah Fussilat were revealed in response to that. The awe of that experience left him initially attempting to get Quraysh to back down, but following their refusal, he joined with them in fighting against Islam. He used to be a friend of Abu Talib, who had held him previously in high regard. However, his obstinate attitude and lack of support for Muhammad (ﷺ) created a huge rift between them. He gradually became more and more harsh in his attitude - beginning with slander and mockery and then with assault. He was eventually among those who agreed to the plot to assassinate the Prophet (ﷺ) on the Night of Hijrah. Then, despite his initial reluctance for battle, he was one of the first three pagan combatants in the Battle of Badr after being provoked by Abu Jahl. Reports vary on this, but it appears Utbah initially faced and struck down 'Ubaydah ibn al-Harith who was martyred a short while later. Utbah was then himself killed by either Hamza or 'Ali, after they had dispatched his brother Shaybah and his son Walid, respectively. His other son, Abu Hudhayfah, witnessed that and said with regret that he wished

257

his father had accepted Islam. 'Utbah also had a daughter called Hind who married Abu Sufyan and instigated the Battle of Uhud as revenge for the death of her father, uncle and brother at Badr.

Shaybah ibn Rabi'ah

He was the brother of 'Utbah and an important chief of Quraysh. He was a cruel-hearted individual and was found taking pleasure in every gathering in which the Messenger (ﷺ) was harmed. He used to mock the Qur'an and oppress the Believers. Shaybah was one of the men who the Messenger (ﷺ) prayed against when they had crossed all limits. He was among the first three pagan combatants in the Battle of Badr, and he was reportedly killed by Hamza ibn 'Abdul Muttalib.

Walid ibn Utbah

He was the son of 'Utbah ibn Rabi'ah. He was a fierce warrior who hated Islam with a passion and constantly opposed the Prophet (ﷺ) and the Believers. He had shown great animosity to his brother Abu Hudhayfah in particular after he accepted Islam. Walid was among the first three pagan combatants in the Battle of Badr, and he was killed with a single strike by 'Ali ibn Abi Talib who was of a similar age to him.

Abu Sufyan ibn Harb

His real name was Sakhr, but he was better known by the title Abu Sufyan. He was from the clan of Banu Umayyah. He was the brother of Umm Jameel, and the husband of Hind bint 'Utbah. He also had a son named Mu'awiyah who later became the founder of the Umayyad dynasty of caliphs. Abu Sufyan remained an active enemy to the Messenger of Allah (ﷺ) throughout the entire period of his mission in Makkah and most of his time in Madinah. He was among those who plotted to assassinate him on the Night of Hijrah. When the plot was unsuccessful, he filled up his caravan with the goods left behind by the Believers with the aim of selling them. It was this caravan that the Believers were pursuing that led to the Battle of Badr taking place. After the Battle of Badr and the deaths of most of the pagan chiefs, Abu Sufyan became the leader of the Quraysh.

He instigated the Battle of Uhud and the Battle of Khandaq. His daughter Ramlah became a Muslim and married Prophet Muhammad (ﷺ). Abu Sufyan only accepted Islam along with his wife at the time of the Conquest of Makkah when they saw that they no longer had the means to oppose the spread of Islam. The Prophet (ﷺ) treated him with kindness and gave to him and his other former enemies generously in order to reconcile their hearts. Abu Sufyan participated in later campaigns along with the Believers. He later lost one eye in the Siege of Ta'if, and the other in the Battle of Yarmouk. He died at the age of ninety in Madinah.

Ramlah bint Abi Sufyan

Better known as Umm Habiba, she was the daughter of Abu Sufyan and Safiyyah bint Abi al-'Aas. She was among the early Believers along with her husband, 'Ubaydullah ibn Jahsh. They had one daughter - Habiba - together. Ramlah and her husband undertook Hijrah to Abyssinia and remained there for many years. After 'Ubaydullah died there, and she had completed the waiting period, Ramlah married the Prophet (ﷺ). Their wedding ceremony took place in Abyssinia although the Prophet (ﷺ) was not physically present. The King of Abyssinia, An-Najashi, who is reported to have accepted Islam by this point, performed the wedding ceremony. Ramlah later moved to Madinah after the Hijrah to live in a chamber the Prophet (ﷺ) had built for her. At one point after the Treaty of Hudaybiyyah but before the Conquest of Makkah, Abu Sufyan visited her at her home in Madinah. Ramlah did not allow her father to sit on the mat of the Prophet (ﷺ), while he still remained a polytheist, much to his surprise. Ramlah died during the caliphate of her brother Mu'awiyah and is buried in Madinah.

Umm Jameel bint Harb

She was the wife of Abu Lahab and the sister of Abu Sufyan. Her real name was Arwa. She was a vicious, foul-mouthed and inveterate enemy to Islam and the Messenger (ﷺ). Her house was neighbouring his in Makkah and she would go out of her way to cause him difficulty and pain. In Surah Lahab, the Qur'an describes her as "the carrier of firewood", which is either a reference to her activity of collecting thorny branches to place in the path of the Prophet (ﷺ), or it is a reference to her frequent spreading of gossip and slander, or it may indicate that she is responsible for her husband burning in the fire as she used to constantly incite him. The Qur'an also says that she will have a twisted rope of fibre placed upon her neck. In this regard, it has been narrated that Umm Jameel was in a forest carrying firewood one day, when the rope she had with her, slipped got caught between her necklace and a tree and ended up strangling her to death.

Harith ibn Harb

He was the older brother of Abu Sufyan. He was among the pagans of Makkah. He had at one point been married to Safiyyah bint 'Abdul Muttalib prior to her marriage to Al-'Awwam. He had good trade relations with Sa'ad ibn 'Ubadah of Yathrib and the two would offer hospitality to one another. Therefore, when Sa'ad ibn 'Ubadah had been captured by the Quraysh and dragged along on a rope after the Second Pledge of Al-'Aqabah, Al-Harith responded to his call for help and interceded for him. Further details of his life are limited and it is not clear if he ever embraced Islam, although the likelihood is that he died before this.

'Uqbah ibn Abi Mu'ayt

He was from the clan of Banu 'Abd Shams. He, like Abu Lahab, was a neighbour of the Prophet (ﷺ) in Makkah. Both were among the most ruthless antagonists of the Prophet (ﷺ). On one occasion he spat on the face of Prophet Muhammad (ﷺ) when encouraged to do so by his vicious friend Ubayy ibn Khalaf. Another time, he flung the waste from a slaughtered camel onto the Prophet (ﷺ) while he was in prostration. 'Uqbah's daughter Umm Kulthum became a Muslim before the Hijrah and travelled to Madinah after the Treaty of Hudaybiyyah. 'Uqbah fought in the Battle of Badr and was reportedly one of only two prisoners who were executed for their crimes. He was beheaded by a single sword strike from 'Ali.

Al-Walid ibn 'Uqbah

Not to be confused with the similar sounding Al-Walid ibn 'Utbah. He was the son of 'Uqbah ibn Abi Mu'ayt and 'Urwa bint Kurayz ibn Rabi'ah. He was thus the maternal half-brother of 'Uthman ibn 'Affan. He was among the poets and was known for both his liberality and his fondness for wine. He displayed a great deal of open hostility to the Prophet (ﷺ), until he accepted Islam after the Conquest of Makkah. The Prophet (ﷺ) at one point asked him to collect the *zakat* (alms) from the Banu Mustaliq. However, he failed to do so and fled with the claim that they had tried to attack him. According to many commentators, a Verse of the Qur'an (49:6) was revealed about this, which refers to him as a *Fasiq* meaning a "transgressor". Similarly, they have said that another Verse (32:18) was revealed regarding a dispute he had with 'Ali ibn Abi Talib. Walid was later given positions of governorship during the caliphates of 'Umar and 'Uthman. However, it has been reported that 'Uthman was forced to dismiss him from his post in Kufa and punish him when he was found guilty of consuming alcohol and leading the prayers in a drunken state. 'Ali was reportedly the one who had administered the punishment of seventy lashes on him. Walid later fought against 'Ali ibn Abi Talib in the Battle of Jamal, but was like everyone else forgiven by him after the battle. He later held positions under Mu'awiyah ibn Abi Sufyan, his cousin. And he was the governor of Madinah who Yazid ibn Mu'awiyah commanded to try and secure the allegiance of Al-Husayn ibn 'Ali, the grandson of the Prophet (ﷺ). Walid did show Husayn some respect at that time and rejected the advice of Marwan ibn al-Hakam to kill him immediately if he did not give allegiance to Yazid. Walid died in Raqqa and was buried there some months after the Martyrdom of Husayn at Karbala.

Hind bint 'Utbah

She was the daughter of 'Utbah ibn Rabi'ah, and the wife of Abu Sufyan ibn Harb. For a long time, she remained a notorious enemy of Islam and the Believers. Her father, brother and uncle were killed in the Battle of Badr by 'Ali and Hamza, and she vowed to never forgive or forget that. She was a key force inciting Abu Sufyan towards waging wars against the

Prophet (ﷺ). She composed inflammatory poetry and personally led a group of women in urging the pagans to fight during the Battle of Uhud. She also hired Wahshi, an Abyssinian slave belonging to Jubayr ibn Mut'im, to take revenge on her behalf: he managed to kill Hamza by throwing a spear at him during the battle. Then she mutilated Hamza's body, made pendants out of his body parts and began chewing his liver. She continued her efforts against Islam until the Conquest of Makkah when it was clear that further resistance was impossible. The Prophet (ﷺ) pardoned her and she accepted Islam. She then broke the idols in her home. During the caliphate of Abu Bakr, she and other women played a role in urging the Muslim men to fight in the Battle of Yarmouk. She died during the caliphate of 'Umar.

Her son Mu'awiyah and her grandson Yazid both ended up becoming caliphs.

Abu Hudhayfah ibn 'Utbah

He was the son of 'Utbah ibn Rabi'ah, and the brother of Walid and Hind. Despite being raised in the household of one of the bitterest enemies of the Prophet (ﷺ), he was among the first to accept Islam. He fought in the Battle of Badr and witnessed the death of his father, uncle and grandfather. He remained on the right path and obeyed the Messenger(ﷺ). He was killed fighting against Musaylimah the Liar's forces in the Battle of Al-Yamama during the caliphate of Abu Bakr.

Sa'eed ibn Al-'Aas

He was the son of Al-'Aas ibn Umayyah. He was a harsh-tempered polytheist who was respected on account of his wealth and sons. He was deeply involved in the trade and veneration of idols. He had an extreme hatred of Islam and tortured his son Khalid when he found out he had become a Muslim. He told his other sons 'Amr, Ubaydah, Al-'Aas and Aban to oppose him. However, 'Amr became a Muslim and emigrated to Abyssinia along with Khalid. Ubaydah and Al-'Aas fought at Badr on the side of the pagans and were killed. Aban survived the battle and eventually became a Muslim after the Battle of Khaybar. Sa'eed himself died a few months from sickness after Badr as a Disbeliever. Until his last moments he was hoping to end Islam if he recovered.

Khalid ibn Sa'eed

He was one of the very first to accept Islam. He became a Believer after seeing a vivid dream where he saw Muhammad (ﷺ) rescuing him from a raging fire that his father, Sa'eed ibn Al-'Aas, was pushing him into. He kept his faith hidden for a long time because he knew his father was an enemy of Islam. When he eventually discovered Khalid, praying in a desolate area in Makkah, his father whipped him severely then disowned him. Khalid and his wife eventually emigrated to Abyssinia after the situation became unbearable. He was chosen to act as the representative of the Umm Habiba in Abyssinia when she married the Prophet (ﷺ). Khalid emigrated to Madinah in 7 AH. He was present at the Conquest of Makkah, Hunayn, and Tabuk. He was among the most faithful of men in obeying the Prophet (ﷺ)., was one of his scribes, and was appointed by him to collect the Zakat in Yemen. He was killed in a battle against the Romans in Syria during the caliphate of Abu Bakr.

Al-Hakam ibn Abil 'Aas

He was the grandson of Umayyah ibn 'Abd Shams. Al-Hakam was among the inveterate enemies of the Prophet (ﷺ). He was a man of such repugnant character and crimes that after the Conquest of Makkah, the Prophet (ﷺ) exiled him from Makkah to Ta'if and warned him and his son Marwan never to return to the same town as himself. However, both did manage to return to Madinah during the caliphate of his nephew 'Uthman ibn 'Affan. 'Uthman showed them generosity and kindness and gave them important positions. Al-Hakam died in the year 56 AH. His son Marwan played a key role in various events including the situation surrounding the killing of 'Uthman; the Battle of Jamal; he was a supporter of the governments of Mu'awiyah and Yazid; called for the killing of Al-Husayn ibn 'Ali, and eventually he became a caliph and the father of the subsequent Umayyad caliphs.

'Uthman ibn 'Affan

He was a merchant from the clan of Banu Umayyah, born around five years after the Year of the Elephant. Abu Sufyan was his uncle, 'Uqbah ibn Abi Mu'ayt was his stepfather and Walid ibn 'Uqbah was his half-brother. 'Uthman was however one of the earliest to accept Islam, having accepted it on the invitation of Abu Bakr. Following the harsh treatment he received from his family, 'Uthman and his wife Ruqayyah were among those who took part in the first Hijrah to Abyssinia. Afterwards, he emigrated to Madinah and became wealthy through trade. He was unable to take part in the Battle of Badr as he was looking after his wife, who died soon after that. After Ruqayyah's death, he married Umm Kulthum. He was present at Uhud and Khandaq. He provided provisions for Tabuk. He was present at the Farewell pilgrimage and Ghadir. He was one of the first people to give allegiance to Abu Bakr as caliph, and it was he who wrote down Abu Bakr's will on his deathbed confirming 'Umar ibn al-Khattab as his successor. 'Uthman succeeded 'Umar as caliph. The duration of his caliphate was twelve years; the latter half of which was marked by considerable instability. 'Uthman was ultimately killed in the year 35 AH in a brutal manner by a group of rebels who entered his house, following widespread protests and a siege. He was buried in a graveyard in Madinah, now part of Al-Baqi. His killing triggered a period of further unrest which was only temporarily controlled by 'Ali ibn Abi Talib who the people of Madinah elected as caliph after him. Eventually, the dispute regarding his killing led to the Battle of Jamal and thereafter the Battle of Siffin.

Hamnah bint Sufyan

She was the daughter of Sufyan ibn Umayyah ibn 'Abd Shams. She was a polytheist who was opposed to Islam. She tried to force her sons Sa'ad ibn Abi Waqqas and 'Amir ibn Abi Waqqas to recant from their faith by means of undertaking a hunger strike herself. However, this did not work and she reluctantly began to eat and drink again when they urged her. It is not clear if she ever accepted Islam.

Banu Makhzum:

Al-Walid ibn al-Mughirah

He was an elder from the clan of Banu Makhzum who were responsible for matters related to warfare. He was among the very richest and most influential of the chiefs in Arabia - so much so that he was regarded as one of the "two great men", along with 'Urwa ibn Mas'ud at-Thaqifi of Ta'if. On account of his wealth, sons and position in society, he became very arrogant. His views held a great deal of sway over the rest of Quraysh and they would frequently consult with him about what to do about the spread of Islam. Abu Jahl was his nephew, the son of his brother Hisham. On one occasion Walid offered his son 'Ammarah to Abu Talib as a replacement, if he would hand over Muhammad (ﷺ). Walid is criticised in several places in the Qur'an including 74:11-26, 6:10 and according to some commentators 68:10-14, where nine negative traits of his are enumerated, one after the other. Walid died in the year 1 AH from an infection of an old wound that he had received on his foot, many years before. That wound itself had been caused by his arrogance. He is one of the confirmed inhabitants of Hellfire, specifically in the level known as Saqar.

Abu Hudhayfah ibn al-Mughirah

Not to be confused with Abu Hudhayfah ibn 'Utbah who was a Believer from Banu Abd Shams. This Abu Hudhayfah was the brother of Walid ibn al-Mughirah. He was the former slave master of Sumayyah bint Khayyat. He was a wealthy man who was very happy with the social order that had allowed his family to prosper at the expense of others. He was therefore antagonistic towards Islam which threatened to disrupt that. He participated in torturing Sumayyah, Yasir and 'Ammar. However, he did not have it in his mind to kill them - that was done by Abu Jahl, whose enmity and tyranny exceeded all others. Abu Hudhayfah is said to have eventually accepted Islam at the time of the Conquest of Makkah.

Khalid ibn al-Walid

He was the son of Walid ibn al-Mughirah. He was a skilled rider with a sturdy physique. He was placed in command of a unit of horsemen who were sent after the first emigrants but was unable to prevent them from escaping to Abyssinia. He later led the cavalry charge against the Prophet (ﷺ) at Uhud, and remained hostile to him until he finally converted to Islam after the treaty of Hudaybiyyah. He went on to become a famous Muslim general, regarded by many as being among the most capable in history due to his leadership in the Ridda wars, the Battle of Yarmouk, the conquests of Persia, Iraq, and Syria. Following certain controversies, he was relieved of overall command by 'Umar ibn al-Khattab, in favour of Abu 'Ubaydah ibn al-Jarrah. He died of sickness during the caliphate of 'Umar ibn al-Khattab.

'Ammarah ibn al-Walid

He was one of the many sons of Walid ibn al-Mughirah. He was well-regarded among the Quraysh for his intelligence and handsome features. At one point, Walid ibn al-Mughirah offered him to Abu Talib to take as an adopted son in exchange for handing over Muhammad (ﷺ) to them: an offer that Abu Talib angrily refused. Although further details about his life are limited, some reports have characterised him as a shameless womaniser who died as a polytheist. It is said that he accompanied 'Amr ibn al-'Aas on his journey to Abyssinia when he attempted to convince An-Najashi to hand over the Muslims to them. Due to his spreading of corruption, 'Ammarah was allegedly detained, castrated and exiled to live in a forest, where he was found many years later having lost his sanity.

Abu Jahl, 'Amr ibn Hisham

He was a prominent man of Quraysh who was born in the same year as Prophet Muhammad (ﷺ). On his father's side he was from the clan of Banu Makhzum, and on his mother's side he was from Banu Tamim. He used to be known among the pagans by the title "Abul Hakam," meaning "the Father of Wisdom," due to the cunning and strategic aptitude he displayed. Such was the high regard they held him in, he was even admitted at the age of thirty to be a member of the council of Dar an-Nadwa which normally required a minimum age of forty. However, after his opposition to Islam surfaced, the Messenger of Allah (ﷺ) referred to 'Amr as "Abu Jahl", meaning "the Father of Ignorance" and this is the name that stuck to him. He was also referred to as "the Pharaoh of this nation" on account of his extreme arrogance and oppression towards the Believers. Another title was *"Asadul Ahlaf"* – "the Lion of the Opposing Groups" that had sworn to fight against Islam. He actually admitted on one occasion that he knew Muhammad (ﷺ) was truly a Prophet, bur he was opposing him out of a sense of tribal pride and envy. Abu Jahl was a cruel tyrant who used to torture the Believers and attempted to kill the Prophet (ﷺ) more than once. He was the killer of Sumayyah bint al-Khayyat, the first martyr in Islam and he had tortured Yasir and their son Ammar too. He was one of the main architects of the Boycott against Banu Hashim and also the person who came up with the plan to assassinate the Prophet (ﷺ) on the Night of Hijrah. It was on account of his obsession and instigation towards violence that the Battle of Badr took place. He was killed in that battle: first he was wounded by two youth from Ansar (Mu'adh ibn 'Amr and Mu'awwidh), then he was later found by 'Abdullah ibn Mas'ud who finished him. He was arrogant to the very end. Many Verses of the Qur'an have been revealed criticising him. He was buried in a well in Badr, along with the other pagan chiefs. He is one of the confirmed inhabitants of the Hellfire.

'Ikrimah ibn Abi Jahl

He was the son of Abu Jahl. He was among the harshest of enemies of the Muslims for a very long time. He was the commander of the left wing of the pagan army in the Battle of Uhud. Eventually, after the Conquest of Makkah, he became a Muslim. He had initially fled to Yemen, but returned when he had been informed that the Messenger of Allah (ﷺ) had pardoned him. During the caliphate of Abu Bakr, he was part of the Muslim conquest of Syria. He was killed in the Battle of Ajnadayn fighting the Romans.

'Ayyash ibn Hisham

He was the maternal half brother of Abu Jahl. He had become Muslim before the Hijrah. He left Makkah with 'Umar ibn al-Khattab, but Abu Jahl caught up to them and tricked him into returning to Makkah by making him worry about his mother. He was then captured and tortured by Abu Jahl, but refused to give up his faith. The Prophet (ﷺ) prayed for his safety. He eventually managed to make it to Madinah, reportedly along with Hisham ibn al—'Aas. During the caliphate of 'Umar, 'Ayyash participated in the Battle of Yarmouk where he was killed fighting the Romans.

Sumayyah bint al-Khayyat

She was a dark-skinned woman of Abyssinian origin. She was born around twenty years before the Year of the Elephant and spent several years of her life as slave owned by Abu Hudhayfah ibn al-Mughirah of Banu Makhzum. Later, she was freed and allowed to marry Yasir ibn Malik, a Yemeni man who had come to Makkah under the protection of Abu Hudhayfah. Sumayyah and her husband both followed the pagan religion of Banu Makhzum, but after their son 'Ammar introduced them to Islam, they became among the earliest Believers. Sumayyah underwent great hardships and was tortured severely by Abu Hudhayfah and Abu Jahl. She kept refusing to worship idols, or to disavow Prophet Muhammad (ﷺ), so the tyrannical Abu Jahl stuck a spear into her chest. The Messenger of Allah (ﷺ) gave her the distinction of being "the first martyr in Islam" and confirmed that she is in Paradise.

Yasir ibn 'Amir

He was originally from Banu Madhij, a Yemeni tribe. He came to Makkah along with two of his brothers, in search of their lost brother, but unlike them chose to remain. He was given protection by Abu Hudhayfah, a chief of Banu Makhzum, which indentured him to them. Around four years before the Year of the Elephant, Yasir was given permission to marry Sumayyah, a slave woman who was then freed. Years later, when the Messenger of Allah (ﷺ) began his Mission, Yasir and Sumayyah both embraced Islam after being introduced to it by their son, 'Ammar. Although he had no real position in society and was not physically imposing, Yasir was among the foremost of Believers and the firmest of men. He was martyred after extensive torture was inflicted on him by Abu Jahl. His wife had already been martyred at that point. The Messenger of Allah (ﷺ) confirmed that he and his family will meet in Paradise.

'Ammar ibn Yasir

He was the son of Yasir and Sumayyah and was around the same age as the Prophet (ﷺ). He learnt about Islam in its earliest days and went in secret to hear the Prophet (ﷺ) in the house of Al-Arqam. Then he invited his parents to Islam also. He was tortured severely for his Faith and witnessed the martyrdom of both his parents, so with his tongue he uttered words of disbelief in order to protect his life, then went to the Prophet (ﷺ) in a state of weeping, believing that he had become a Disbeliever. The Prophet (ﷺ) received Revelation at that moment, affirming the Faith of 'Ammar. He performed Hijrah to Madinah, helped construct *Masjid an-Nabawi* and participated in all the battles at the side of Allah's Messenger (ﷺ). On a number of occasions, the Messenger (ﷺ) informed 'Ammar that he would be killed by the "rebellious group". This was so well-known among the Muslims that during the Battle of Jamal, in which 'Ammar fought on the side of 'Ali ibn Abi Talib, his mere presence there caused Zubayr ibn al-'Awwam to leave the battlefield. 'Ammar was eventually martyred in the Battle of Siffin fighting as a commander on the side of 'Ali ibn Abi Talib, against the forces of Mu'awiyah ibn Abi Sufyan.

Abu Salamah ibn Abil Asad

He was from Banu Makhzum on his father's side. On his mother's side he was from Banu Hashim. His mother was Bara', the sister of 'Abdullah ibn 'Abdul Muttalib - so he was a cousin of Prophet Muhammad (ﷺ). Abu Salamah was the first husband of Umm Salamah. They emigrated to Abyssinia together, Then after several years, they returned to Makkah. However she was unable to perform Hijrah alongside him; so he went first, then she went at a later time. Abu Salamah fought at Badr. He was injured by an arrow in the Battle of Uhud. A few months later in the expedition of Qatan, which he led, that wound opened up again and became inflamed and he died from it. He was a man who always saw the best in people and situations. Even on his deathbed, he exhibited extraordinary Faith, encouraged his wife to be patient and he prayed that she would be given a husband better than himself.

Umm Salamah

She and her husband, Abu Salamah, were among the earliest Believers. She performed Hijrah to Madinah after him. Later, after Abu Salamah was martyred, and she completed the period of waiting, she was married to the Prophet (ﷺ). She was the last of his wives to pass away, living past the time of the martyrdom of Prophet Muhammad's (ﷺ) grandson Husayn ibn 'Ali. She was eventually buried in Al-Baqi in Madinah.

Zuhayr ibn Abi Umayyah

He was the son of Abi Umayyah bin al-Mughirah, and 'Aatikah bint 'Abdul Muttalib. He was the brother of Umm Salamah. He was noted to be one of the pagans of Makkah who opposed the Pact of Boycott against the Banu Hashim. It is unclear whether he ever accepted Islam as various sources report different things.

Sawdah bint Zam'ah

She was among the earliest of Believers, along with her husband Sakhran ibn Amr. They were persecuted and so emigrated to Abyssinia. After some time, they returned and Sakhran fell ill and died. Some time after she was widowed, the Prophet (ﷺ) who had also recently become a widower, married her. She was the first woman he married after Khadija. She was in her fifties at that time. She was a kindly woman with a good sense of humour and a caring personality. She would often lighten the mood and she helped the Prophet (ﷺ) look after his children. She outlived the Prophet (ﷺ) and was eventually buried in Al-Baqi in Madinah.

Al-Arqam ibn Abil Arqam

He was a teenager from the clan of Banu Makhzum and was among the early believers. He was the son of 'Abd Manaf ibn Asad, also known as Abil Arqam. He had inherited from his late father a house at the foot of Mount Safa, which he granted to the Prophet (ﷺ) to use as the first meeting place for the Believers. He emigrated to Madinah. He fought in Badr, Uhud, Khandaq and other battles alongside the Prophet (ﷺ). He lived until the time of the caliphate of Mu'awiyah.

Banu Taym:

Abu Quhafah

His real name is said to have been 'Uthman ibn 'Amir. He was the chief of Banu Taym and the father of Abu Bakr. He rebuked his family when they accepted Islam. On several occasions, he advised Abu Bakr not to spend his wealth freeing weak slaves when he could free strong ones instead. Abu Bakr informed him he was only doing so to seek the pleasure of Allah (ﷺ). He lived to an advanced age and lost his sight. He finally accepted Islam after the Conquest of Makkah. At that time, he had white hair so the Prophet (ﷺ) instructed him to dye it. Abu Quhafah passed away a few months after his son, having witnessed three generations of his family become Muslims.

Salma bint Sakhr

She was also known as Umm al-Khayr. She was the mother of Abu Bakr. She accepted Islam at an early stage in the house of Al-Arqam. She performed Hijrah to Madinah. She is said to have outlived Abu Bakr by a few months.

Abu Bakr ibn Abi Quhafah

He was a merchant from the clan of Banu Taym. He was nicknamed *Abu Bakr* (Father of the young camel) due to his fondness for camels as a youth. It is said his real name was 'Abdullah. He was two years younger than the Messenger of Allah (ﷺ). Abu Bakr has been described as being

271

of slender build, of medium height, light skin, sunken eyes, protruding forehead and a thin beard. He was one of the very first to accept Islam and among the most influential of Muslims. He invited several people to accept Islam. He had a reputation for generosity, and freed a number of Believing slaves such as Bilal through his wealth. However, his clan was not powerful and he was not able to offer protection to the Prophet (ﷺ), or to render assistance to him during the economic boycott of Banu Hashim. He performed Hijrah alongside the Messenger of Allah (ﷺ) and was his companion in the Cave of Thawr. His daughter 'A'isha became one of the wives of the Prophet (ﷺ). There are some Verses of the Qur'an which relate to him. He was present in all the battles the Prophet (ﷺ) participated in. He was chosen to be the first caliph by a group of Muhajiroon and Ansar who had gathered in the *Saqifah* (hut) of Banu Sa'ida after the Prophet (ﷺ) passed away in 11 AH. The period of his caliphate was two years. He initiated a series of battles that became known as the Ridda wars. Among them the Battle of Al-Yamama is most famous as it resulted in the end of the false prophet Musaylimah the Liar. He also began the conquest of the Persian and Roman Empires. Abu Bakr died after a short illness and appointed 'Umar to be his successor, witnessed by 'Uthman ibn 'Affan and 'Abdur Rahman ibn 'Awf. He was buried next to the grave of Prophet Muhammad (ﷺ) in Madinah.

Umm Ruman

She was the wife of Abu Bakr and the mother of his children, Aisha and 'Abdur Rahman. She accepted Islam along with her household. She performed Hijrah to Madinah, and died there at the end of the lifetime of the Messenger of Allah (ﷺ).

'Abdullah Ibn Abi Bakr

He was the son of Abu Bakr and Qutaylah. He was among the early Believers. He stayed among the Quraysh and reported news of their conversations to his father while he was hiding in the Cave of Thawr with the Prophet (ﷺ) at the time of Hijrah. He himself emigrated to Madinah some months later along with his sisters. He was shot by an arrow during the Siege of Ta'if and died of a flare up of his injury three years later, about eighteen months before the death of Abu Bakr.

Asma bint Abi Bakr

She was the daughter of Abu Bakr and Qutaylah, and was among the first to accept Islam. She was the elder half-sister of Aisha. She was married to Zubayr ibn al-'Awwam, who she later divorced after having eight children with him. She assisted the Prophet (ﷺ) and her father on the Night of Hijrah by providing them with food. She famously tore her belt in half and used it to secure the goods together. She was thereafter known as "*Dhat an-Nitaqayn*", or "she of the two belts" due to this. She remained in Makkah for a few months afterwards before performing Hijrah herself. She is reported to have lived to the age of 100 years and witnessed many events throughout her life including the Battle of Yarmouk, the Martyrdom of Husayn ibn 'Ali, and the subsequent opposition to Yazid by her son 'Abdullah ibn Zubayr. Asma died in the year 73 AH, ten days after her son was killed. She was buried in Al-Baqi.

'A'isha bint Abi Bakr

She was the daughter of Abu Bakr and Umm Ruman. She was already a young girl at the time that the Prophet (ﷺ) began preaching. She was at least sixteen years of age at the time she married the Prophet (ﷺ), in contrast to what the more sensationalised, contradictory and unproven reports say. Several Verses of the Qur'an were revealed about situations relating to her. These include the Event of *Ifk* (the Great Slander of which she was exonerated in 24:11-20) and Surah Tahrim. She narrated a great number of traditions from the Prophet (ﷺ) and was considered an important source of knowledge for the community. The Prophet (ﷺ) showed her a great deal of kindness and affection. She, like all the wives of the Prophet (ﷺ) was known by the title, "*Ummul Mu'mineen*", or "Mother of the Believers", which indicated that they were expected to adhere to a higher standard than other women, were subjected to certain limitations and that no one would be permitted to marry them after the Prophet (ﷺ). The Messenger of Allah (ﷺ) passed away in the home he

273

built for her and is now buried there alongside Abu Bakr and 'Umar. She was at times politically active and played a significant role at the time of the caliphates of 'Uthman and 'Ali. She was one of the commanders at the Battle of Jamal, which was in fact so-named because of her presence on a camel; but she was pardoned for her role by 'Ali ibn Abi Talib, the fourth caliph, who sent her back to Madinah with respect and honour. Her brother Muhammad ibn Abi Bakr who had fought on the side of 'Ali, escorted her back to her home. 'A'isha remained mostly out of the political sphere for the rest of her life, and would weep whenever she recalled the tribulations surrounding the Battle of Jamal. She died in Madinah in 58 AH and is buried in Al-Baqi alongside the other wives of the Prophet (ﷺ).

Qutaylah bint 'Abdil 'Uzzah

She was one of the wives of Abu Bakr and the mother of Asma. She belonged to the Banu 'Amir ibn Lu'ayy clan. When the Prophet (ﷺ) began preaching, she did not accept Islam but chose to remain as a polytheist, so Abu Bakr divorced her (although some sources say he had already divorced her beforehand). Seven years after the Hijrah, Qutaylah went to Madinah to visit her daughter. However Asma did not want to accept her gifts or company, until some Verses of the Qur'an (60:8-9) were revealed about this situation and the Prophet (ﷺ) had commanded Asma to be good to her mother despite her disbelief as she was not among those who fought against or caused harm to the Believers. There is no definite record of her accepting Islam, but some sources have suggested she may have become a Muslim after this event or after the Conquest of Makkah.

'Abdul 'Uzzah ibn Abi Bakr

He was the eldest son of Abu Bakr and Umm Ruman. He did not accept Islam initially, unlike the rest of his household, and he remained with the polytheists for a long duration. He fought in the Battle of Badr against the Muslims. At one point he had a chance to kill his father, but avoided him and went in a different direction. He also fought alongside the pagans at Uhud. Eventually he accepted Islam after the Treaty of Hudaybiyyah, and thereafter became known as 'Abdur Rahman ibn Abi Bakr. He then fought on the side of the Muslims and distinguished himself in many battles by his skill. During the caliphate of Abu Bakr, he fought in the Battle of Al-Yamama where he killed the general of the false prophet Musaylimah. He also killed many of his opponents in the Battle of Yarmouk. He was involved in the conquests of Syria and Egypt in the caliphate of 'Umar ibn al-Khattab. He was opposed to Mu'awiyah ibn Abi Sufyan's appointment of Yazid as his successor but did not take up arms against him. He died in Makkah and was buried there.

'Abdullah ibn Urayqit

He was a servant of Abu Bakr. He was originally from a clan called Banu Du'il. He was a trustworthy man who possessed knowledge of various travel routes and helped guide Abu Bakr and the Prophet (ﷺ) to Madinah during the Hijrah. He was still a polytheist at that time, but he eventually accepted Islam. He had a son called Qarib who was martyred alongside Al-Husayn ibn Ali at Karbala.

'Amir ibn Fuhayrah

He was a slave of African origin, who was one of the earliest Believers. He was severely tortured. Eventually, he was freed by Abu Bakr. Thereafter he continued served Abu Bakr by milking his sheep. During the Hijrah he assisted and accompanied the Messenger of Allah (ﷺ) and Abu Bakr. He fought at Badr and Uhud. He was one of seventy missionaries killed at Bir Ma'una.

Talhah ibn 'Ubaydullah

He was from Banu Taym and was a relative of Abu Bakr. He has been described as being dark-skinned, with a narrow nose and wavy hair. He was a wealthy cloth merchant who had heard from a Christian monk in Syria that according to Scripture, the Final Prophet would soon appear in Arabia. Talhah was among the first that Abu Bakr approached, inviting him to accept Islam at the Prophet's (ﷺ) hands. He faced frequent abuse from his own mother. He and Abu Bakr were on one occasion beaten and tied up together by Nawfal ibn Khuwaylid. He emigrated to Abyssinia and thereafter to Madinah. He became very successful in trade and his generosity towards the poor was well-known. Talhah did not fight in Badr as he and Sa'eed ibn Zayd were sent ahead as scouts. Even so, he was awarded a share of the spoils as if he had been present. Talhah was a brave warrior who sustained several injuries at Uhud including his left arm becoming paralysed. He was present in other battles alongside the Messenger (ﷺ). He participated in the Ridda wars during the caliphate of Abu Bakr, and he was a close confidant of 'Umar, when he became the second caliph. He played a significant role in both the election of the third caliph, 'Uthman ibn 'Affan, and the period of tribulations surrounding his killing. This ultimately led to him becoming one of the commanders in the Battle of Jamal against 'Ali ibn Abi Talib. He was killed by an arrow said by some sources to have been fired by Marwan ibn al-Hakam – who was a commander on his own side - although this event has been disputed by others. Talhah was buried in Basra, Iraq close to the site of the Battle of Jamal.

As-Sa'bah al-Hadhrami

She was the mother of Talhah ibn Ubaydullah. She originally belonged to the tribe of Sadif from Hadhramaut in Yemen, but was allied to Banu Umayyah in Makkah. She opposed Islam at the outset and persecuted her son when she found out he had become a Muslim. Her brother, Al-'Aala al-Hadhrami, accepted Islam prior to the Conquest of Makkah, was sent as an envoy by the Messenger to eastern Arabia, and played an important role as a commander during the caliphates of Abu Bakr and Umar. It is said that As-Sa'bah eventually accepted Islam and died during the lifetime of the Messenger. It has also been said she lived until the time 'Uthman was killed. And Allah (ﷺ) knows best.

'Abdullah ibn Jada'an

He was the cousin of Abu Quhafah. 'Abdullah ibn Jada'an was a man who had lived the first part of his life as a hardened criminal, possessing neither wealth nor esteem from people. In fact, most people detested him. One day however, he came across a small cave opening and seeing what he thought was a snake, in a state of despair entered it. Within it, he found a great deal of valuable treasure that had been hidden by the kings of Banu Jurhum. He used his newly-found wealth to generously feed people, entertain guests and relieve the poverty of those in need, even as far as Syria. He soon became a person who was loved by everyone. Muhammad (ﷺ) and Abu Jahl had been sat together at one of these feasts in their childhood. It was there that Abu Jahl sustained an injury on his knee that left a scar by which his body was later recognised after the Battle of Badr. It was also at the house of 'Abdullah ibn Jada'an that *Hilful Fudul,* "the Alliance of the Virtuous", was established. He did not give importance to the Day of Judgement however and he died as polytheist about eighteen years before the first Revelation of the Qur'an.

Banu Zuhrah:

Aminah bint Wahb

She was the daughter of Wahb ibn 'Abd Manaf, who was a chief of Banu Zuhrah. It has been narrated that she was a monotheist. She had a pure character and lived a blameless life. She married 'Abdullah ibn 'Abdul Muttalib and became the mother of Prophet Muhammad (ﷺ). She found the pregnancy very easy. 'Abdullah died before she delivered. She was heartbroken and never remarried. Her grief only subsided in the presence of their son Muhammad (ﷺ). Although she was reluctant to do so, she sent the infant Muhammad (ﷺ) to live with Halimah and her bedouin family in the desert for the sake of his health and upbringing. He was returned to her when he was five or six years old. She took him on a visit to Yathrib where they visited the grave of 'Abdullah, but Lady Aminah fell ill soon after and died during the return journey. She was buried in the village of Al-Abwa.

Al-Akhnas ibn Shariq

He was a wealthy man originally from Banu Thaqif who was closely linked to Banu Zuhrah in Makkah. He was among those who used to mock and harass the Messenger of Allah (ﷺ). However, he greatly admired the

Qur'an and would at times leave his home to stealthily listen to its Recitation in the night. When the Messenger (ﷺ) returned from Ta'if, he sought protection, but Al-Akhnas refused claiming that Banu Zuhrah would not accept it. Al-Akhnas did not take part in the Battle of Badr. He fought at Uhud on the side of Quraysh and killed 'Abdullah ibn Jahsh, the cousin of Muhammad (ﷺ). Several Verses of the Qur'an are said to be revealed in criticism of him (including 104:1 and 2:204). Al-Akhnas ibn Shariq died as a Disbeliever.

Al-Aswad ibn 'Abd Yaghut al-Kindi

Although of Yemeni origin, he was associated with the Banu Zuhrah. He was one of those who would constantly mock the Messenger of Allah (ﷺ). He rejected Faith and was one of the followers of Abu Jahl, bearing the greatest of animosity towards the Believers. Eventually, the Angel Jibreel (ﷺ) pointed to his belly, and it became swollen up with fluid. He died as a Disbeliever.

Miqdad ibn 'Amr

He was the son of a man named 'Amr al-Bahrani. He was a man with incredible strength, courage and intelligence. He was originally from Yemen but fled his homeland as a fugitive and came to Makkah. He became the servant of Al-Aswad ibn 'Abd Yaghut, and impressed him so much that the latter ended up adopting him as a son. Miqdad thereafter became known as Miqdad ibn Al-Aswad. When the Messenger of Allah (ﷺ) began preaching, Miqdad became among the early Believers. He kept his faith secret for years from Al-Aswad, as the latter was among the most hostile of men towards Islam. During the expedition of Abu Ubaydah in the first year of Hijrah, Miqdad pretended to be pursuing after the Believers who had emigrated from Makkah to Madinah, but instead went to join them. He participated in the Battle of Badr and was one of only two Muslims who fought on horseback. He is reported to have captured Nadr ibn al-Harith. He fought at Uhud as an archer and was one of the few who did not flee. After the lifetime of the Prophet (ﷺ), he remained a close associate of 'Ali ibn Abi Talib. He is said to have been present at the burial of Lady Fatima az-Zahra. Miqdad also took part in the conquests of Syria, Egypt and Cyprus. He was famed for his recitation of the Qur'an which he taught to the people of Syria. He died in 33 AH during the caliphate of 'Uthman. He left behind a considerable amount of wealth, some of which he bequeathed to Al-Hasan and Al-Husayn, the two beloved grandsons of the Messenger of Allah (ﷺ).

Sa'ad ibn Abi Waqqas

His father Malik ibn Uhayb (better known as Abi Waqqas) was from Banu Zuhrah, and his mother Hamnah bint Sufyan ibn Umayyah was from Banu Umayyah. Sa'ad was described as being tall, with a strong physique and curly hair. He accepted Islam at the age of seventeen. When his mother found out about this, she tried to compel him to recant by all possible means, even by refusing to eat. However, he gently told her that he could not leave his Faith for anything. One day, when a group of Muslims were praying, some pagans abused them, and a fight ensued. Sa'ad ended up striking one of them with the jawbone of a camel. This has been said by various sources to be the first bloodshed in Islam. A Revelation descended urging the Believers to remain patient and overlook the provocations of the polytheists. Sa'ad performed Hijrah to Madinah. He was a skilled archer who took part in the Battles of Badr and Uhud. His brother 'Umayr ibn Abi Waqqas also accepted Islam and was killed at Badr. After the Prophet (ﷺ) passed away, Sa'ad played a pivotal role in the conquest of Persia and Iraq. He was made the governor of the newly founded city of Kufa by the caliph 'Umar, which he himself had helped to design. He eventually became very wealthy and lived till the age of eighty. He was involved in the selection process that resulted in 'Uthman ibn 'Affan becoming chosen as caliph. He remained neutral at the time of 'Uthman's killing. He did not pledge allegiance to 'Ali ibn Abi Talib as caliph but did not oppose him either. In his later life he had some interactions with Mu'awiyah who was now caliph, but refused when asked to curse 'Ali ibn Abi Talib, citing his many virtues. However, Sa'ad had a son called 'Umar ibn Sa'ad who later became the leader of the army that killed Al-Husayn ibn 'Ali at Karbala on the orders of Yazid ibn Mu'awiyah

- and in a twisted irony, given his father's achievements, boasted that he fired the first arrow against him.

'Abdur Rahman ibn 'Awf

He was a successful merchant from Banu Zuhrah who accepted Islam on the invitation of Abu Bakr. His original name was 'Abdu 'Amr, but after he became a Muslim, the Prophet (ﷺ) renamed him as 'Abdur Rahman. He was a close friend of 'Uthman ibn 'Affan as their fathers had also been close friends and business partners. He emigrated to Abyssinia and then Madinah. During the Battle of Badr, he wished to take his friend Umayyah ibn Khalaf captive and sustained a scar protecting him but was unable to prevent him from being killed. He took part in many other battles and led the expedition of Dumat al-Jandal. On several occasions he gave from his wealth generously. After the Prophet (ﷺ) passed away, 'Abdur Rahman became a close advisor of Abu Bakr who was now the caliph. He was one of two witnesses to the appointment of 'Umar as the successor of Abu Bakr. He participated in various battles in the conquest of Persia. He was also instrumental in the selection process that resulted in 'Uthman ibn 'Affan becoming the third caliph. He eventually became extremely wealthy through various kinds of trade. He had more than thirty children. He died in Madinah in the year 33 AH.

Banu 'Adiyy:

Al-Khattab ibn Nufayl

He was the chief of Bani 'Adiyy. He died shortly after the Prophet (ﷺ) openly declared his mission. He was a staunch polytheist who did not accept Islam. He had a few years earlier exiled his nephew Zayd ibn 'Amr out of hatred for his monotheistic views. Although he did not live to see it, he could never have imagined that his children, 'Umar, Zayd and Fatima, would all eventually abandon the idol worship he had taught them and accept Islam instead.

'Umar ibn al-Khattab

He was the son of Al-Khattab ibn Nawfal from Banu 'Adiyy, and Hanthamah bint Hisham of Banu Makhzum. Abu Jahl was his maternal uncle. 'Umar was described as being very tall, well-built and bald-headed, with a reddish complexion and a long moustache. He used to be among the staunch supporters of polytheism, and would torture the early Muslims alongside his uncle. Then one day, in the sixth year of the Prophetic mission, 'Umar himself embraced Islam. He left his home, intending to kill the Messenger of Allah (ﷺ) but discovered that his own sister and her husband had become Muslims. He went to their home and beat them, but then when he became calm, allowed them to recite something from the Qur'an. Then when 'Umar heard the Verses of Surah Ta-Ha, he was deeply affected and went to the Prophet (ﷺ) to also become a Muslim. After this he faced a great deal of opposition from his clan, especially from Abu Jahl who disowned him. 'Umar became a prominent and vocal supporter of the Prophet (ﷺ). After the Hijrah, he was present in all the battles with the Messenger of Allah (ﷺ). His daughter, Hafsah, became one of the wives of the Prophet (ﷺ) after her previous husband was martyred at Uhud. Umar was present at the Treaty of Hudaybiyyah which was a particularly difficult time for him. 'Umar became the second caliph after his close friend, Abu Bakr passed away in 13 AH. The period of his caliphate was ten years and was marked by internal stability and external expansion. He oversaw large scale military campaigns to conquer the regions of Persia, Iraq, Syria and Palestine. Finally, he was stabbed by a Persian slave named Abu Lu'lu'a as he led the morning prayers, and he succumbed to his injuries three days later. Before he passed away, he initiated a six-man selection process which resulted in 'Uthman being appointed as the third caliph. 'Umar was buried next to the graves of Prophet Muhammad (ﷺ) and Abu Bakr in Madinah.

Fatima bint al-Khattab

She was one of the early Believers who became a Muslim in the house of Al-Arqam. She was the sister of 'Umar, and the wife of Sa'eed ibn Zayd. She also had a brother called Zayd ibn al-Khattab who became a Muslim before 'Umar did. Fatima was a brave and God-fearing woman whose heart was deeply attached to the Qur'an. It was through Fatima that 'Umar ibn al-Khattab eventually accepted Islam. She performed Hijrah to Madinah along with the rest of the Believers and lived a good life. She died during the caliphate of her brother 'Umar.

Zayd ibn 'Amr

He was a sincere man from the clan of Banu 'Adiyy. He was close friends with both the monk Waraqah and 'Abdul Muttalib. He began to dislike and speak out against the idolatry and ignorant practices of his people. He was often rebuked for this by his paternal uncle, Al-Khattab ibn Nufayl who eventually drove him out of Makkah. Zayd went in search of the truth and travelled extensively throughout Syria but did not feel satisfied with what was being practised by the Jews or the Christians. Therefore he decided to follow what he knew of the pure Faith of Ibrahim, which was belief in Allah (ﷻ) without any partner. Zayd came to believe that there would be a prophet that would soon appear in Makkah. Five years before the Prophet (ﷺ)'s first Revelation, Zayd was attacked by a group of bedouins on his way back to Makkah and he was killed. With his final breaths he prayed for the guidance of his son, Sa'eed, who ended up becoming a Muslim. Prophet Muhammad (ﷺ) later confirmed that Zayd ibn 'Amr was one of the people of Paradise, and would like Ibrahim (ع) be "raised as a Nation unto himself."

Sa'eed ibn Zayd

He was the son of Zayd ibn Amr, the *Hanif*. Due to his father's influence, Sa'eed grew up with a disdain for idols. He was quickly attracted to the Message of Prophet Muhammad (ﷺ) and accepted Islam along with his wife, Fatima bint al-Khattab. Sa'eed was beaten by his brother-in-law, 'Umar when he discovered this fact, but the latter soon become a Muslim himself. Sa'eed emigrated to Madinah and was made the brother of Rifaa ibn Malik. Both Sa'eed and Talhah were sent by the Prophet (ﷺ) as scouts to monitor the movements of the caravan of Abu Sufyan, and as a result they did not participate in the Battle of Badr. However, they were both given a share of the spoils as if they had been present. Sa'eed fought in all the other battles including Uhud, Khandaq, Khaybar and the Conquest of Makkah. He lived up until the time of the caliphate of Mu'awiyah and was buried in Madinah.

Nu'aym ibn Abdullah

He was an early Believer who concealed his Faith. He was close to 'Umar ibn al-Khattab and when he learned of his plan to kill the Prophet (ﷺ), out of desperation he informed 'Umar that his sister and brother-in-law were Muslims, hoping that he could thereby prevent him from reaching the Prophet (ﷺ). This ended up working better than he could have imagined. He performed Hijrah, was present at Hudaybiyyah and was killed in the Battle of Yarmouk during the caliphate of 'Umar.

Zunairah ar-Rumiyyah

A slave girl of Roman origin, belonging to the Banu Makhzum. She was one of the earliest Believers. She lost her vision as a result of torture inflicted on her by Abu Jahl and 'Umar ibn al-Khattab. The pagans ascribed this to the "power of al-Lat and al-'Uzzah" but Zunairah countered that their idols were powerless and all things came from Allah. Later, her vision returned - and the ever-obstinate Abu Jahl claimed this was due to "Muhammad's magic." Zunairah remained firm on the path of Islam, and was eventually freed by Abu Bakr.

Lubaynah

A slave girl who was one of the earliest Believers. She was tortured by 'Umar ibn Al-Khattab, who only stopped whipping her when his arms felt tired. However she would not recant her Faith.

'Amir ibn Rabi'ah

He had been adopted by Al-Khattab, the father of 'Umar, and used to be known as 'Amir ibn al-Khattab until the Qur'an commanded for people to be called by their actual fathers' names. He was among the early Believers. He and his wife, Laylah bint Abi Hathmah, emigrated to Abyssinia, and then were among the first to emigrate to Yathrib, where they lived simple lives of piety. 'Amir participated in Badr and other battles. 'Amir narrated many hadith from the Prophet (ﷺ) whom he loved dearly. He lived until the end of the caliphate of 'Uthman.

Laylah bint Abi Hathmah

She was the wife of 'Amir ibn Rabi'ah and among the early Believers. She was one of the first to emigrate to Abyssinia due to the persecution they faced. After returning she was one of the first, if not the very first female to perform Hijrah to Yathrib.

Banu 'Abd ad-Dar:

Nadr ibn al-Harith

He was the chief of Banu 'Abd ad-Dar. He was a man who had travelled extensively through Persia and Syria. He had learned of the stories and legends of other cultures and continued to use these to interrupt the Recitation of the Qur'an. He was an inveterate opponent of Prophet Muhammad (ﷺ) who stopped at nothing to try to turn people aside from the path of guidance. He would hire songstresses and poets to distract people whenever the Messenger (ﷺ) would preach. He would also torture many of the Believers. He was thus condemned in several Verses (including 8:31, 31:6, 104:1). He and 'Uqbah ibn Abi Mu'ayt went to Yathrib to ask the Rabbis difficult questions to overcome the Prophet (ﷺ) and some Verses of Surah Kahf were revealed in response. He was one of the main instigators of the Boycott against Banu Hashim. He was the one who demanded a punishment to descend on him and some Verses of Surah Ma'arij (70:1-2) was revealed in response. He was among those who plotted to assassinate him on the Night of Hijrah. He was one of the commanders of the pagans in the Battle of Badr and was captured whilst fighting. It has been said that the Messenger of Allah (ﷺ) ordered 'Ali ibn Abi Talib to execute only Nadr ibn al-Harith and 'Uqbah ibn Abi Mu'ayt on account of their crimes. All of the other seventy prisoners were treated well and released after ransom. This is sufficient to show the evil and irredeemable nature of Nadr.

Bagheed ibn 'Amir

He was a son of 'Amir ibn Hashim ibn 'Abd Manaf ibn 'Abd ad-Dar. His name is most famously mentioned as Bagheed, which carries the meaning of "hateful". However, some sources have referred to him as 'Ikrimah ibn Hashim or as Mansur ibn 'Ikrimah. He was the man who wrote down the Pact of the Boycott against the Banu Hashim. It is said that after the Messenger of Allah (ﷺ) prayed against him, Bagheed's hand became paralysed. It is not clear whether he ever accepted Islam, although most sources say that he did not. And Allah (ﷻ) knows best.

Nahdia

She and her daughter were slaves owned by a cruel woman from Banu 'Abd ad-Dar. She was among the early Believers. She was tortured by that mistress as well as by 'Umar ibn al-Khattab prior to his acceptance of Islam. Nahdia was set free by Abu Bakr.

Umm 'Ubays

According to some sources, this was the name of the daughter of Nahdia - however other sources say Umm 'Ubays was another slave girl, not related to Nahdia. In any case, neither of them would leave Islam despite the severe torture they were subjected to. Umm 'Ubays was set free by Abu Bakr, who also freed many other slaves.

Mus'ab ibn 'Umayr

He was an extremely handsome youth who belonged to a wealthy family from Banu 'Abd ad-Dar. His father was 'Umayr ibn Hashim and his mother was Khunnas bint Malik. Although he grew up surrounded by luxury and was known for his love of fine clothing and perfume, Mus'ab was actually a very astute and intelligent young man with a deep yearning for truth. When he heard about the Message of Islam, he did not hesitate to try and learn more. He attended the gatherings at the house of Al-Arqam and soon became a Muslim. He initially kept his new Faith a secret, but when the news of it eventually reached his mother, she rebuked him and tried to make him recant. Even after being chained and deprived of food, he refused to return to polytheism. His mother eventually threw him out of her home, and he was forced to live a difficult life. After experiencing much persecution, he was advised by the Prophet (ﷺ) to emigrate to Abyssinia for a time. He later returned to Makkah and was sent to Yathrib by the Prophet (ﷺ) to teach Islam to its people. Mus'ab was thereafter known as the "First ambassador of Islam". He had a welcoming demeanour, a loveable personality and a excellent manner of communication. By the Grace of God, through his efforts, the majority of the people of Yathrib ended up embracing Islam, and the city was renamed to *Madinatun-Nabi.* Mus'ab fought in the Battle of Badr and was martyred in the Battle of Uhud. The Messenger of Allah (ﷺ) performed his burial, testified to his faith and martyrdom, and prayed for his forgiveness.

Banu Sahm:

Al-'Aas ibn al-Wa'il

He was the chief of Banu Sahm. He was among the most relentless enemies of the Messenger of Allah (ﷺ), and was counted among the mockers. It was he who first began referring to Prophet Muhammad (ﷺ) as *Al-Abtar* (the one who is cut off), following the death of his son. Thus the last Ayat of Surah Al-Kawthar (108:3) was revealed as a response to him. On another occasion, he refused to pay Khabbab ibn al-Aratt money that he owed him, unless the latter would renounce Muhammad (ﷺ) and Islam. Khabbab would not, and so Al-'Aas told him he would pay him then when he was resurrected as he was sure to be given a great deal of wealth. A Verse of Qur'an (19:77) was also revealed criticising him in this regard. When his son Hisham became a Muslim, Al-'Aas took pride in imprisoning and torturing him for the sake of the idols. Al-'Aas was one of the five mockers who were referred to in Surah Hijr (15:95). The Angel Jibreel (ع) pointed to his instep and this ended up becoming the cause of his death later. A thorn entered his foot which subsequently became infected, and he died from sepsis, before the time of Hijrah.

'Amr ibn al-'Aas

He was the son of Al-'Aas ibn Wa'il and An-Nabighah bint Harmalah. Like his father, 'Amr was also initially very active in opposing Islam. He has been described as being short and stocky in appearance, with a wide forehead. He was known for his cunning and skills of persuasion, and was thus sent to Abyssinia to try to negotiate the return of the Muslim emigrants. However, his tricks did not work on that occasion so he returned unsuccessful. He continued to oppose Islam in word and deed for a number of years. He eventually embraced Islam after the Treaty of Hudaybiyyah. Under the first caliph, he was involved in the conquest of Syria. Later in life, he became a key figure in the conquest of Egypt and chief advisor to Mu'awiyah ibn Abu Sufyan, the founder of the Umayyad Caliphate. He was one of the commanders against 'Ali ibn Abi Talib in the Battle of Siffin, where at one point, he narrowly escaped being killed by him. He eventually became the governor of Egypt. He died a wealthy man at the age of ninety, during the early part of the rule of Mu'awiyah: to the extent that he was reported to have left behind seventy sacks full of gold dinars in his house.

Hisham ibn al-'Aas

He was the son of Al-'Aas ibn Wa'il and Umm Harmalah al-Makhzumi. He was persecuted by his father and his older brother, 'Amr, for his Faith. It is said that he emigrated to Abyssinia but returned to Makkah a few years later. He was imprisoned and prevented from performing Hijrah to Yathrib as he had intended, but after the Battle of Khandaq he was able to emigrate to the city now known as Madinah. He was killed in either the Battle of Yarmouk or Ajnadayn.

'Abdullah ibn Ziba'ra

He was a pagan poet who opposed the Prophet (ﷺ) during his years in Makkah. He composed many poems against Islam. He had some knowledge of the Scriptures. It is said that he eventually became a Muslim, although details regarding his life are limited.

Nabih ibn al-Hajjaj

He was the son of Al-Hajjaj ibn 'Amr. He was one of the notable men of Quraysh with considerable wealth and family support. He was a polytheist who aggressively opposed Islam and tried to turn people away from the Messenger of Allah (ﷺ). Eventually, he was involved in the plot to kill the Messenger (ﷺ) on the Night of Hijrah. He later fought in the Battle of Badr on the side of the pagans and was killed.

Munabbih ibn al-Hajjaj

He was the son of Al-Hajjaj ibn 'Amr and the brother of Nabih. He was one of the pagans who would mock the Messenger and the Believers. He was involved in the plot to kill the Messenger (ﷺ) on the Night of Hijrah. He participated in the Battle of Badr where he challenged and was killed by 'Ali ibn Abi Talib.

Khunays ibn Hudhayfah

He was one of the earliest Believers from Banu Sahm and was a righteous man. He emigrated to Abyssinia along with thirteen other members of his clan including his brother Abdullah and Qays. He returned to Makkah three years later. He then married Hafsah bint 'Umar. He performed Hijrah to Madinah. He fought in Badr. He died in Madinah later that year due to wounds he had sustained. He was buried at Al-Baqi. Some time afterwards, Prophet Muhammad (ﷺ) married his widow in order to provide support and assistance to her.

Banu Jumah:

Umayyah ibn Khalaf

He was the chief of Banu Jumah. He was a wealthy merchant and slave owner, described as being very fat. He displayed a great deal of cruelty to the Believers, especially towards his slave Bilal when he had discovered he had become a Muslim. Umayyah tortured him in various ways including by flogging him, placing a heavy rock on him and leaving him to burn in the midday sun. Abu Bakr interceded on the order of the

Prophet (ﷺ) and bought Bilal's freedom. Umayyah had been a long-time friend of 'Abdu 'Amr, who later became known as 'Abdur Rahman ibn Awf. He refused to call him by his new name as he would not recognise the Name of 'Ar-Rahman'. Even so, the two remained on relatively good terms with one another. Umayyah was killed in the Battle of Badr by Bilal and a group of the Ansar. 'Abdur Rahman had tried his best to protect his friend and sustained an injury because of that. After his death, Umayyah's body became bloated and he could not be lifted, so unlike the other pagans who were thrown in a well, his body was buried under some stones.

Safwan ibn Umayyah

He was the son of Umayyah ibn Khalaf. He was a harsh-tempered man who like his father despised Islam. He was involved in the plot to murder the Prophet (ﷺ) on the Night of Hijrah. He did not participate in Badr himself, but was enraged when he learnt that his father and brother had been killed. He therefore arranged for his cousin 'Umayr ibn Wahb to assassinate the Prophet (ﷺ) in Madinah. However, 'Umayr ended up accepting Islam instead. Safwan was one of the leaders in the Battle of Uhud, where he reportedly killed some Believers. He also on other occasions killed Believers that he captured. He remained active in his animosity, drumming up support for the Battle of Khandaq. He fled after the Conquest of Makkah but was intercepted by his cousin 'Umayr ibn Wahb who gave him a token of safety from the Prophet (ﷺ) and convinced him to return. He eventually accepted Islam. He fought on the side of the Muslims in the Battle of Hunayn and the Siege of Ta'if. After this, he was among those whom the Prophet (ﷺ) gave a gift of a hundred camels to reconcile their hearts. He remained in Makkah for the rest of his life where he died during the last year of Uthman's rule.

Abul Ashaddayn

It is said his real name was Usayd ibn Kaladah. He was a very physically powerful and muscular man. He was renowned for his strength, to the extent that it was said about him that if he sat down on a piece of leather, ten men would not be able to remove it from under him without it being torn to shreds. He was among those who mocked the Verses of the Qur'an with great arrogance. He declared at one point that if there were only nineteen angels guarding the Fire of Hell, he would be able to handle seventeen of them by himself and he just needed the rest of Quraysh to take care of the remaining two. It has been reported that on one occasion he attempted to kill the Messenger of Allah (ﷺ) by throwing a spear at him but did not succeed. It has been said that several Verses of the Qur'an make reference to him and his pride in his own strength and creation (such as 37:11). He died as a Disbeliever.

'Umayr ibn Wahb

He was the first husband of Arwa bint 'Abdul Muttalib, whom he later divorced. He remained a staunch enemy of the Prophet (ﷺ) throughout the period of his preaching in Makkah and was involved in persecuting the Believers. He participated in the Battle of Badr and managed to escape but his son Wahb ibn 'Umayr was captured. 'Umayr ibn Wahb secretly conspired with Safwan ibn Umayyah, then went to Madinah with the intention of assassinating the Prophet (ﷺ). However when he met with him, claiming to have come for his son, the Prophet (ﷺ), through Divine inspiration miraculously related to him his true purpose and the entire apparently unwitnessed and confidential conversation he had had with Safwan in Makkan. 'Umayr was amazed and ended up accepting Islam instead. He then sought the Prophet's (ﷺ) permission to return to Makkah and invite people towards Islam. Several people embraced Islam at his hands and emigrated to Madinah. After the Conquest of Makkah, 'Umayr went after his cousin, Safwan ibn Umayyah who had fled and convinced him to return to the Messenger of Allah (ﷺ). Soon after this, Safwan also ended up accepting Islam.

Tulayb ibn 'Umayr

He was the son of 'Umayr ibn Wahb and Arwa bint 'Abdul Muttalib. Tulayb was among those who became Muslim in the house of Al-Arqam. He was around 15 years old at that time. He was outspoken and open in practising his Faith which made him a target for persecution. He performed Hijrah to Abyssinia, and then later performed Hijrah to Madinah. He fought in the Battle of Badr and other battles. Two years after the Prophet (ﷺ) passed away, Tulayb was killed in the Battle of Ajnadayn against the Romans at 35 years of age.

Abu Fukhayah

He was at the time of the start of the Prophetic Mission, a man of advanced age. He had formerly been a slave of Safwan ibn Umayyah. His real name is said to have been Yasar. He was considered to be of no importance by the Quraysh. However, he was among the early Believers who were persecuted for their Faith. He was severely beaten on several occasions. He likely died at some point prior to the Hijrah. His children included Fukhayah and Baraka who both emigrated to Abyssinia.

Bilal ibn Rabah

He was the son of Rabah, an Arab slave who belonged to Banu Jumah, and Hamamah, an Abyssinian woman who had been captured and enslaved, following the conflict in the Year of the Elephant. Bilal was raised as a slave in the household of Umayyah ibn Khalaf who frequently mistreated him. Bilal was one of the first to accept Islam and was severely tortured by Umayyah for this – yet he did not relent even when he had a heavy rock placed on his chest in the burning sun. The Messenger (ﷺ) sent Abu Bakr to purchase Bilal's freedom at that time. The pagans regarded Bilal as inferior not only due to his dark skin but also because his mother wasn't an Arab. Bilal emigrated to Madinah where he was appointed by the Prophet (ﷺ) as the first Mu'adhin (Caller to Prayer) as he has a very beautiful voice. He was also placed in charge of the Public Treasury (*Bayt al-Mal*). He participated in the Battle of Badr where he killed Umayyah, and was also present in all the subsequent battles. He chose to step down from his role as Mu'adhin after the death of the Prophet (ﷺ). He died at around the age of sixty in Syria during the caliphate of Umar.

'Uthman ibn Maz'un

He and his wife Khawlah were among the earliest Believers. They accepted Islam in the house of Al-Arqam. 'Uthman ibn Maz'un was a very devout man who used to pray a lot. He was the leader of one of the groups of the emigrants to Abyssinia. He later returned to Makkah, and then performed Hijrah to Madinah. He died in the third year after Hijrah and was the first of the Muhajireen to be buried in Al-Baqi. Years later, 'Ali ibn Abi Talib named his son, 'Uthman ibn 'Ali, after him.

Banu 'Amir ibn Lu'ayy:

'Amr ibn 'Abdu Wadd

He was a famed warrior who had proven himself with incredible feats of courage. He once was attacked in a valley by a group of bandits. All of his companions fled but 'Amr remained behind and defeated all the bandits whilst on horseback. He was thereafter regarded as one of the most dauntless knights of Quraysh. They considered him as being worth a thousand men. He did not accept Islam and was one of the diehard followers of Abu Jahl. According to some reports he was present at Badr and retreated after seeing the Angels. During the Battle of Khandaq, he managed to cross the ditch surrounding Madinah and challenged the Muslims for a one-on-one-duel. No one besides 'Ali dared to confront him. The Prophet (ﷺ) referred to this as "the Entirety of Faith going against the Entirety of Disbelief." Ali called on him to accept one of three choices, in accordance with a vow he had made long ago. 'Amr refused to accept Islam when invited to do so, nor was he willing to retreat because of the shame he felt it would bring him. Therefore, he accepted the third of the three choices and dismounted to fight on equal terms. After a fierce battle, 'Ali managed to defeat 'Amr ibn 'Abdu Wadd by cutting off his leg. 'Amr spat in 'Ali's face as he was about to finish him, so 'Ali went away to control himself and returned only when he was sure that he was striking him for the sake of Allah (ﷻ), and not for any other reason. That strike of Ali on the Day of Khandaq was greatly praised by the Messenger of Allah (ﷺ). After 'Amr's death, the strength of the pagans dissipated and the

Battle of Khandaq was soon over. That marked a turning point as the pagans of Quraysh were now on the back foot after this point.

Suhayl ibn 'Amr

He was from Banu 'Amir ibn Lu'ayy on his father's side, and Banu Umayyah on his mother's side. He was known as the "*Khatib* (orator) of Quraysh" due to his rhetorical skill and persuasiveness. He was among the bitterest of enemies of the Prophet (ﷺ) for a long time. Some of his children accepted Islam before him and were among the emigrants to Abyssinia. It was he who slapped Sa'ad ibn 'Ubadah when he was captured after the Second Pledge of Al-'Aqabah. He fought in the Battle of Badr on the side of the pagans and was subsequently captured. 'Umar ibn al-Khattab wanted to pull out his incisor teeth so as to ruin his ability to speak eloquently but the Messenger of Allah (ﷺ) forbade any form of mutilation, and furthermore predicted that Suhayl would do something more pleasing to him in future. Suhayl was the negotiator of the pagans during the Treaty of Hudaybiyyah and he pushed for terms that were seemingly unfavourable to the Muslims. This also upset 'Umar. However, the Qur'an declared it a "Manifest Victory" and it was soon proven to be. Suhayl became Muslim after the Conquest of Makkah and he was among the ones that the Messenger of Allah (ﷺ) gave a gift of a hundred camels to help reconcile their hearts. He eventually was endeared to the Faith and became a Believer. During the caliphate of 'Umar, Suhayl fought in the Battle of Yarmouk against the Romans and many battles against the Persians. He died from the plague in Palestine during the caliphate of 'Uthman.

Sahlah bint Suhayl

She was the daughter of Suhayl ibn 'Amr. Unlike her father, she was among the early Believers. She was married to Abu Hudhayfah ibn 'Utbah. Due to both of them belonging to families who were very antagonistic towards Islam, they were forced to emigrate to Abyssinia in order to continue to practise their religion in peace. They later returned and performed Hijrah to Madinah.

Umm Kulthum bint Suhayl

She was the daughter of Suhayl ibn 'Amr. Like her sister Sahlah, she was an early Believer, and emigrated to Abyssinia after experiencing abuse from her family.

Banu Khuza'ah:

'Amr ibn Luhay

Not to be confused with 'Amir ibn Lu'ayy, who was the progenitor of one of the clans of Quraysh. 'Amr ibn Luhay was a chief of the tribe of Banu Khuza'ah, who were the custodians of Makkah prior to the Quraysh. 'Amr was an influential man, known for feeding people generously from his wealth. It was he who turned the people of Makkah away from the monotheistic Faith of Ibrahim, about three hundred years prior to the birth of the Prophet (ﷺ). 'Amr travelled to Syria for trade one year and was impressed by the idols worshipped by some people, so he brought a few back including a figure named Hubal.   He followed the advice of soothsayers who were in communion with some satanic jinn, and dug up the idols that had been formerly worshipped by the people of Nuh (ؑ), such as Wadd, Yaghut, Ya'uq, Nasr and Suwa. He is said to have also placed the two idols called Isaaf and Na'ilah upon Mount Safa and Mount Marwah. The people of Makkah followed 'Amr, and soon the majority of subsequent generations became polytheists. During the Mi'raaj, the Messenger of Allah (ﷺ) was shown 'Amr ibn Luhay dragging his intestines in the Fire as indication of his final state.

Umm Anmar

She was from the tribe of Banu Khuza'ah and was the slave-owner of Khabbab ibn Al-Aratt. She was a sadistic and merciless person who hated Islam. She would be frequently torture Khabbab; sometimes having him beaten with metal bars, other times placing heated pieces of iron upon his head until he fainted, or making him lie down on live cinders. He endured this kind of treatment from her for years. Finally, at the time of Hijrah, she acquired a severe sickness for which no cure was known. It involved the worst headaches. The only treatment that she could make use of involved her head being cauterised with heated pieces of iron. The pain of it was immense, even exceeding that of the sickness itself. She died in that state, still adamant upon disbelief.

Siba'a ibn 'Abd al-'Uzzah

He was the brother of Umm Anmar. Urged by his sister, he inflicted a great deal of torture on Believers, especially Khabbab ibn Al-Aratt. He used to speak with him harshly, beat him, and place metal armour on his body then leave him in the heat of the blazing sun. Siba'a was an extreme polytheist who desired nothing more than to eradicate Islam. He fought on the side of Abu Sufyan in the Battle of Uhud and was killed by the "Lion of God", Hamza ibn 'Abdul Muttalib, just prior to the latter's own martyrdom in that battle. Khabbab was present also and witnessed the end of his former tormentor.

Al-Harith ibn at-Tulatilah

He was one of the most persistent of the pagans in their mockery of the Messenger (ﷺ). He attended every gathering voicing his opposition to Islam and did not refrain from evil acts against the Messenger (ﷺ). Finally, when he had crossed all limits, the Angel Jibreel (ع) pointed to his head: it soon became swollen with pus, and he died from it.

Khabbab ibn Al-Aratt

He was a young man from Banu Tamim. He had been captured from his homeland of Al-Yamama in Najd and brought to Makkah as a slave. He was bought by Umm Anmar, a woman from Banu Khuza'ah. He trained as a blacksmith and became skilled at the art of crafting fine swords. Umm Anmar soon became wealthy through his efforts. When the Prophet (ﷺ) announced his mission, Khabbab was one of the first to respond. He did not attempt to conceal his Faith when he was asked, so he was tortured severely by Umm Anmar, her brother Siba'a and their people from Banu Khuza'ah. He bore this patiently for many years, even though his body had become scarred and burnt from all their abuse. Then when Umm

295

Anmar contracted a severe illness, Khabbab was able to perform Hijrah to Madinah. He fought in the Battle of Badr and thereafter at Uhud where he saw the tyrannical Siba'a meet his end at the hands of Hamza. Khabbab eventually began to prosper in Madinah and would give his wealth to the needy generously. He even left money in an open part of his house and allowed anyone who wished to take it without seeking permission. When he died, 'Ali stood at his grave and testified to his deep conviction and faith.

Banu al-Harith:

Abu 'Ubaydah ibn 'Abdullah al-Jarrah

He was a merchant from Banu al-Harith. His real name was 'Amir. He was one of the first to accept Islam on the invitation of Abu Bakr. His clan remained opposed to Islam and he faced a great amount of backlash and abuse from them. He was among those who migrated to Abyssinia. After the Hijrah, he moved to Madinah. He took part in the Battle of Badr where he is reported to have reluctantly fought and killed his own father who had been a pagan and had insisted on fighting him. He also fought at Uhud, Khandaq, Khaybar, Hunayn, Tabuk and the expedition against Banu Qurayzah. He was present at the Treaty of Hudaybiyyah and the Conquest of Makkah. After the Prophet (ﷺ) passed away, Abu 'Ubaydah was one of the very first to pledge his allegiance to Abu Bakr. He was known to be a skilled warrior and took part in several battles. Later on, 'Umar appointed him to command the armies in the campaigns against the Persians and Romans. He was affected by a plague that had broken out in Syria, and eventually succumbed to its effects. He was buried at Jabiyah.

The People of Yathrib:

Banu Khazraj:

As'ad ibn Zurarah al-Khayr

He was among the first six to accept Islam among the people of Yathrib, and the first to preach it to them. He was the chief of the subclan of Banu Najjar of Khazraj. He was a reportedly a monotheist during the Jahiliyyah times, and he helped destroyed the idols of Yathrib after Islam. He was a loyal and sincere man who was present at each of the pledges of Al-'Aqabah, where he was appointed as one of the twelve representatives (*An-Nuqaba*) responsible for propagating Islam. Soon after the Hijrah, As'ad passed away from an illness. His was the first funeral prayer that the Prophet (ﷺ) performed in Madinah, and he was buried in the graveyard of Al-Baqi.

Al-Bara' ibn Marur

He was one of the twelve representatives chosen by the Prophet (ﷺ) at Al-'Aqabah. He was among the foremost of Believers, blessed with insight and certainty. He worked tirelessly to spread Islam among the people of Yathrib, until it became known as *Madinatun-Nabi*. He became sick and passed away just before the Prophet (ﷺ) performed Hijrah. He asked to be buried facing the Kaaba as he had been unable to fulfil his promise of returning to visit Makkah during the next Hajj season. When the Prophet (ﷺ) arrived in Madinah, he prayed the funeral prayer over his grave.

Sa'ad ibn Rabi

He was one of the twelve representatives chosen by the Prophet (ﷺ) at Al-'Aqabah. He was a virtuous man of excellent character. The Prophet (ﷺ) established brotherhood between him and 'Abdur Rahman ibn 'Awf. Sa'ad took him into his own home, and treated him generously offering to give him half of all what he owned. He was martyred in the Battle of Uhud. With his last breaths he exhorted his people to ensure the safety of the Prophet (ﷺ).

Rafi ibn Malik

He was a man who was humble and generous in spirit. He was one of the first six men from Khazraj who went to Makkah and accepted Islam. He returned and began preaching to his people. He was later one of the twelve representatives chosen by the Prophet (ﷺ) at Al-'Aqabah. After the Hijrah, he was made the brother of Sa'eed ibn Zayd. Although he did not participate in the Battle of Badr, his son Rifa'a ibn Rafi did, and Rafi would consider this a greater honour than being present at Al-'Aqabah. Rafi ibn Malik was martyred in the Battle of Uhud.

'Abdullah ibn 'Amr

He was the son of 'Amr ibn Haram. He was a brave and honourable man. He was one of the twelve representatives chosen by the Prophet (ﷺ) at Al-'Aqabah. He was around forty years of age at this time. He continued preaching among his people with constancy. He fought in the Battle of Badr and was among the first to be martyred at Uhud. The Prophet (ﷺ) ordered for him to be buried in the same grave as his close friend 'Amr ibn al-Jamuh who had also been martyred. 'Abdullah's son was the famous Jabir ibn 'Abdullah al-Ansari, who reached a great age and became one of the last surviving companions of the Prophet (ﷺ).

Al-Mundhir ibn 'Amr

He was the son of 'Amr ibn Khunays. He was a dignified man possessing patience and a resolute will. He was one of the twelve representatives chosen by the Prophet (ﷺ) at Al-'Aqabah. He was captured by the Makkans along with Sa'ad ibn 'Ubadah, but managed to escape from them. He fought alongside the Messenger of Allah (ﷺ) at Badr and Uhud. He was sent to the people of Najd and martyred at Bir Ma'una along with seventy others in 4 AH.

'Abdullah ibn Rawaha

He was one of the twelve representatives chosen by the Prophet (ﷺ) at Al-'Aqabah. He was a man of considerable intelligence and learning. He was a poet, and was able to write unlike many of his contemporaries. He used to pray a lot and was among the most obedient of people to the Messenger of Allah (ﷺ). He had raised Zayd ibn al-Arqam as an orphan child. He defended the honour of the Prophet (ﷺ) when 'Abdullah ibn Ubayy, the Leader of the Hypocrites, insulted him. He was a brave warrior who longed for martyrdom. He was the third in command in the Battle of Mutah, after Zayd ibn al-Haritha and Ja'far ibn Abi Talib and was martyred after them.

Sa'ad ibn 'Ubadah

He belonged to the subclan of Banu Sa'ida. Sa'ad was the overall chief of Khazraj and one of the most influential men in Yathrib. He was one of the first to accept Islam among the Ansar, and after he broke the idols of his clan, many followed him. He was one of the twelve representatives chosen by the Prophet (ﷺ) at Al-'Aqabah. He was captured and beaten by the Makkans, but he did not reveal any information to them. He was subsequently released on account of his trade relations with Jubayr ibn Mut'im and Al-Harith ibn Harb. Sa'ad was a man who was very well-known for his generosity, as well as his physical prowess and archery skills. He used to pay off the debts of the needy and feed whoever wanted to be fed. He was also known to have a hot temper. He was unable to fight in Badr but fought in most other battles including Uhud, Khandaq, Khaybar, the Conquest of Makkah, Hunayn and Ta'if, and he was often the standard bearer of his clan. He had some differences with Usayd ibn Hudayr, the leader of the Aws, which nearly led to conflict, until the Prophet (ﷺ) calmed the situation down. After the Prophet (ﷺ) passed away he was nearly appointed as the Caliph. He was among those who did not give the pledge of allegiance to Abu Bakr, when he became the first Caliph. He left Madinah for Syria during the caliphate of 'Umar, and was killed by the arrow of an unknown assailant.

'Ubadah ibn as-Samit

He was the son of As-Samit ibn Qays. He was one of the twelve representatives chosen by the Prophet (ﷺ) at Al-'Aqabah. He participated in almost all the battles alongside the Prophet (ﷺ) including Badr and

Uhud. He was present also in *Bayat ar-Ridhwaan.* He was a dark-skinned and muscular man with an impressive physical appearance and a sombre personality. He was both a fearless warrior and a capable general who led armies to many victories during the conquests under the caliphates of Abu Bakr, 'Umar and 'Uthman. He was well-informed about the Qur'an and used to teach its interpretation. He also narrated many hadith, had knowledge of jurisprudence and architecture and built mosques. He refused to take any positions of authority over the people out of fear of being questioned on the Day of Judgement for not fulfilling his duty appropriately. 'Ubadah had his differences with Mu'awiyah ibn Abi Sufyan who had been placed by the Caliph 'Umar ibn al-Khattab as the Governor of Palestine. Finally after much criticism of the Governor's conduct, 'Ubadah refused to live in the same land as him and returned to Madinah. 'Umar sent him back and informed Mu'awiyah that he was not to rule over 'Ubadah as 'Ubadah was "a commander of himself." 'Ubadah ibn As-Samit died during the caliphate of 'Uthman ibn 'Affan and is buried in Palestine.

'Abdullah ibn Ubayy

He was a prominent chief among the Banu Khazraj. He had not participated in the Battle of Bu'ath in which the majority of Al-Aws and Khazraj were embroiled. He also had close ties with the various Jewish tribes of Yathrib, especially Banu Qaynuqa'. He was at one point widely regarded as the best man to end the conflict and the people were on the verge of crowning him as their king, but this did not come to fruition because they ended up pledging allegiance to Prophet Muhammad (ﷺ) instead. 'Abdullah ibn Ubayy later outwardly accepted Islam when the Prophet (ﷺ) arrived in Madinah, realising that he would lose his position and prestige if he didn't, but inwardly he bore an intense grudge against the Messenger of Allah (ﷺ) from preventing him from his ambition of kingship. He and a group of similarly inclined hypocrites plotted against the Believers and worked secretly with their enemies for their destruction. His true nature was exposed after several such incidents and remarks and Verses of the Qur'an were revealed condemning him and his followers.

He was thereafter known as, "the Leader of the Hypocrites." Even so, the Prophet (ﷺ) was lenient with him and prevented people from harming him. He had nine children, all of whom became Muslims and were not thought to be hypocrites. When Ibn Ubayy died, the Prophet (ﷺ) as an act of mercy gave his own shirt for 'Abdullah ibn Ubayy to be buried in, and spent a long time praying for his forgiveness. He only stopped when Divine Revelation ordered him to stop, and stated that 'Abdullah ibn Ubayy was one of the confirmed inhabitants of Hell, in its lowest level. This caused the Messenger of Allah (ﷺ) much grief as he did not wish that fate for anyone.

Banu al-Aws:

Suwayd ibn as-Samit

He was the son of As-Samit ibn 'Atiyyah. He was a noble man from Al-Aws who met the Prophet (ﷺ) in Makkah. He was a poet who was familiar with the sayings of Luqman and read them to him. The Prophet (ﷺ) then recited the Qur'an which greatly impressed Suwayd. He said he would return to give his allegiance the coming year. He was killed by Al-Mujadhir ibn Ziyad in the Battle of Bu'ath which was part of the ongoing conflict of between Al-Aws and Khazraj. Some of his family members said that Suwayd had accepted Islam before his death. And Allah the Exalted and Merciful knows best.

Abul Haytham ibn at-Tayyihan

His real name was Malik. He was a man of great dignity and courage. He was among the first six to accept Islam from among Al-Aws in Yathrib. He is said to have been a monotheist during the Jahiliyyah times. He was present at the First and the Second Pledges of Al-'Aqabah. After the Hijrah, the Prophet (ﷺ) selected him to be the brother of 'Uthman ibn Maz'un. He fought in several battles during the life of the Prophet (ﷺ) including Badr, Uhud, Khandaq, and Mutah. He fought in Jamal, and was killed in the Battle of Siffin, fighting on the side of 'Ali ibn Abi Talib.

Sa'ad ibn Khaythamah

He was among the first of the Believers among Al-Aws in Yathrib. He was a man full of Faith and sincerity. He was present at the Second Pledge of Al-'Aqabah, where he was appointed as one of the twelve representatives responsible for propagating Islam. He was killed in the Battle of Badr, reportedly at the hands of Tu'aymah ibn 'Adiyy and 'Amr ibn 'Abdu Wadd.

Rifa'a ibn 'Abdul Mundhir

He was among the first of the Believers among Al-Aws in Yathrib. He was a courageous man who was truthful to his promise. He was present at the Second Pledge of Al-'Aqabah where he was appointed as one of the twelve representatives responsible for propagating Islam. He obeyed the Messenger (ﷺ), fought in Badr and he was martyred at Uhud.

Usayd ibn Hudayr

He was one of the most prominent men among Al-Aws, famed for his skills in swimming and archery. His father had been killed in the Battle of Bu'ath. He accepted Islam on the invitation of Mus'ab ibn 'Umayr who was sent to Yathrib before the Hijrah. Usayd was one of the twelve representatives chosen by the Prophet (ﷺ) during the second pledge of Al-'Aqabah to spread Islam in Yathrib and he performed this duty with great passion and diligence. After the Hijrah, the Prophet (ﷺ) selected him to be the brother of Zayd ibn al-Haritha. He participated in most of the battles and carried the banner of his clan. After the Prophet (ﷺ) passed away, Usayd as Chief of Al-Aws, was instrumental in getting the Muslims to accept Abu Bakr as their caliph, and was one of the first to give him allegiance. He died during the caliphate of 'Umar and was buried in Al-Baqi.

The People of Other Regions:

Banu Ghifar:

Abu Dharr al-Ghifari

His real name was Jundub ibn Junadah. He was described as being tall and emaciated in appearance. He was from the tribe of Ghifar: a people who were known for being bandits and highwaymen. However, Abu Dharr, despite his poverty, chose to live as a shepherd instead. He was known for being a very truthful man who did not fear the blame of anyone. When he heard from his brother, Unays, the news that a claimant of Prophethood had appeared in Makkah, he travelled to the city, and sought out the Prophet (ﷺ) himself. He was among the very first to accept Islam. He was beaten by the pagans when he announced his belief. The Prophet (ﷺ) instructed him to return to his clan, where he spread the teachings of Islam. He travelled to Madinah after the Hijrah. He fought in Badr, Uhud, and other battles. After the Prophet (ﷺ) passed away, he lived a simple life. He never hesitated to stand up for what he believed in, which caused friction between him and various holders of authority. He was eventually exiled to the desert of Ar-Rabadha, east of Madinah, where he died.

Banu Tamim:

'Abdullah ibn al-Mas'ud

He was a shepherd from Banu Tamim described as a thin, short man with dark skin. He lived in Makkah and used to work for 'Uqbah ibn Abi Mu'ayt. One day whilst out grazing his flock, he met Prophet Muhammad (ﷺ), who recited to him the Qur'an. The words had profound effect on his soul, and he embraced Islam on the spot. He kept his Islam secret for a time. When it became known that he was a Muslim, he was often the victim of persecution from the pagans. Abu Jahl in particular, would attack him and other Believers who did not have strong family support. One day, Ibn Mas'ud recited Surah Ar-Rahman to the Quraysh in front of the Kaaba. He was severely beaten by the pagans, but this did not deter him from his faith. Later, he was among those who emigrated to Abyssinia, and afterwards returned to Makkah. He was a witness to the miracle of the moon being split. After the Hijrah, he fought at Badr. It was he who finally killed Abu Jahl after he had been wounded. He took part in many other battles including Uhud, Khandaq, Khaybar and he went to Tabuk. He possessed a great deal of knowledge and was regarded as an authority on the Qur'an. During the caliphate of 'Uthman, he passed by the desert of Ar-Rabadha, and found Abu Dharr's family was burying him. He wept at that, and took part in his funeral rites. 'Abdullah ibn Mas'ud died in Madinah during the caliphate of 'Uthman and was buried at Al-Baqi.

Nafisa bint Umayyah

She was the daughter of Umayyah bint Abi ibn 'Ubayd from the Banu Tamim. She lived in Makkah and belonged to a family that were allies of Al-Harith ibn Nawfal ibn 'Abd Manaf ibn Qusayy. Nafisa was a close friend and confidant of Khadija, and was the one who was sent by her to convey her proposal to Muhammad (ﷺ). It has been reported that she accepted Islam when the Prophet (ﷺ) started preaching. However, further details of her life are limited.

Banu Sa'ad ibn Bakr:

Halimah bint Abi Dhu'ayb

She was from Banu Sa'ad, a bedouin subclan of the Banu Hawazin tribe that lived outside of Makkah: they would be hired to raise the children from the cities in the desert where it was hoped they would grow more healthy and eloquent. Every woman from her tribe had taken a child to foster except for her. The only remaining child was Muhammad (ﷺ), who no one wanted as he was an orphan whose father had died and they feared that they would not be paid properly. Halimah however chose to take him and looked after him until he was five years old. She noticed many blessings from his presence and became deeply attached to him, and so was very reluctant to return him back to his mother Aminah. Halimah accepted Islam after the Battle of Hunayn, moved to Madinah and died there in the year 9 AH. She was buried in Al-Baqi.

Banu Khuza'ah:

Umm Ma'bad

Her real name was said to be 'Aatikah bint Khalid, but she was named Umm Ma'bad after her child. She was an elderly lady who the Prophet (ﷺ) and his companions encountered on his Hijrah to Madinah. She and her husband had two tents and they would often provide hospitality to any travellers. However, at the time when the Prophet (ﷺ) passed by, she had nothing to offer, as her husband had taken the entire flock out to their pastures, except for a goat that produced no milk. The Prophet (ﷺ) recited the Name of Allah (ﷻ), and wiped his hands on its udders, and it began to produce a large quantity of milk, enough to satiate all of them and still fill the containers she had. When her husband returned she informed him of what had happened. He asked her to describe the man who had come. Her poetic description of the Prophet (ﷺ) has become very famous and beloved. Her husband informed her who that man was, and they both accepted Islam at that time. She later emigrated to Madinah where she died.

Abu Ma'bad

It is said his real name was Hubaysh. He belonged to a bedouin branch of the Banu Khuza'ah, related but separate from those who lived in Makkah. He and his wife Umm Ma'bad lived in a tent in the area near the Valley of Qudayd. One day he returned from taking his sheep out for pasture. After learning from his wife that a "blessed man" had passed by, he recognised him as being the Prophet (ﷺ) that the Quraysh had been talking about. At that, Imaan entered his heart. He went after him and caught up with him at the Valley of Reem, where he professed his Belief. He emigrated to Madinah. It is said he died during the lifetime of the Prophet (ﷺ).

Banu Azd:

Dhamad the Exorcist

His name was Dhamad ibn Tha'labah and he was from the tribe of Banu Azd of Shanu'ah. He was a man who was known for treating various illnesses and performing exorcisms. He came to Makkah and heard people claiming that Muhammad (ﷺ) had become insane or was possessed, so he met with him intending to cure him. The Prophet (ﷺ) however ended up being the one to cure him of his ignorance and Dhamad accepted Islam during their very first meeting.

Other:

Abraha al-Ashram

He was a Christian ruler in Yemen from 525-570 AD. He had been a commander in the army of King Kaleb of Axum against the tyrannical Dhu-Nuwas, a Jewish ruler in Yemen who was oppressing Christians. However, once he gained victory, Abraha seized power for himself as a King in Yemen. He built a magnificent church in Sana'a, and plotted to destroy the Kaaba with a huge army that included war elephants. However, Abraha and his army were destroyed by a flock of birds sent by Allah (ﷻ) before they could do anything.

Companions of the Cave, The

They were a small group of Believing youth who sought refuge in a cave from their oppressive pagan folk. God caused them to sleep for a certain length of time and when they awoke, hundreds of years had passed and the society had now become monotheistic. In Christian tradition they are often identified as the "Seven Sleepers of Ephesus".

Some Muslim scholars have suggested that they were Christians who lived during the Diocletian persecution of 303 AD (or the earlier Decian persecution of 250 AD) and they awoke during the rule of the now-Christian Roman Emperor, Theodosius II. The Qur'an relates their story in Surah Kahf: it does not actually specify their number or the exact duration of time they slept but quotes the various opinions of others, and states that Allah (﷽) knows better what the truth of the matter is.

Devil, The

Also known as Satan, Shaytan, or Iblis. He was not a fallen angel but a jinn who was once devout in obedience to God, and was therefore raised to a position of honour among the inhabitants of the Heavens. However, he had arrogance in his heart and he refused to bow before Adam (ﷻ) as instructed by God and declared his belief in his own superiority. He was therefore expelled, but not before he vowed to take revenge on the children of Adam, and make his life's work their misguidance. He was allowed respite until the Day of Judgement. He appeared at several points trying to incite the Disbelievers against the Prophet (﷽). It was he who gave Abu Jahl the idea to attempt to kill the Prophet (﷽) on the Night of Hijrah. He was also there on the Day of Badr, but fled when he saw Jibreel (ﷻ) and the Angels.

Dhul-Qarnayn

A title for a ruler whose story is mentioned in Surah Kahf in response to a question posed by the Rabbis of Yathrib. It literally means "the one with two horns". All the evidence points to him being Cyrus the Great, the Persian King who liberated the Israelites during their period of Babylonian Captivity. He had a crown with two horns, conquered lands East and West, was a monotheist, was famed for his justice and was mentioned favourably in previous Scriptures.

Idris (ﷻ)

He was a Prophet who was sent to mankind in the time between Adam (ﷻ) and Nuh (ﷻ). He is generally identified as Enoch (ﷻ). It has been said that he was commanded by God to teach mankind the knowledge of writing.

Fir'aun (The Pharaoh)

He was the tyrannical ruler of Egypt who oppressed the Bani Israel in various ways. Prophet Musa (ﷺ) was sent to guide him but he rejected all the clear Signs he was shown. He was a polytheist who also claimed that he himself was god. He pursued Musa and the Bani Israel with his army, even after he witnessed the sea splitting for him. The Bani Israel were all saved while Fir'aun and his followers were all drowned. He is generally identified as the Pharaoh Ramses II.

Haman

He was the Vizier of Fir'aun (The Pharaoh) and it is in part due to his evil advice and goading that the latter refused to believe even after being confronted with clear Signs. On one occasion Fir'aun asked him to build a tall tower so he could "see the Lord of Musa" (ﷺ). They were both drowned in the Red Sea with their army after they pursued Musa (ﷺ)

Harun (ﷺ)

He was the elder brother of Musa (ﷺ), and was appointed after him to Prophethood in order to support him in his mission. He accompanied him to the Court of the Pharaoh, speaking on his behalf, and was with him in every challenging situation thereafter. He was left in charge of the Banu Israel when Musa (ﷺ) went up to Mount Sinai to receive the Ten Commandments, and opposed their worship of the golden calf. He died before Musa (ﷺ).

Heraclius

The Christian ruler of the Eastern Roman Empire from 610-641 AD. He re-organised and expanded the Empire and changed its official language from Latin to Greek. After initial defeats, he gained victory against the Persians. When he received a letter from the Messenger of Allah (ﷺ), he treated it with respect, although he did not accept Islam as he was invited. He later fought against and lost territory to the Arabs.

Jibreel (ع)

The Arabic word for Gabriel, the greatest Angel of God. Jibreel (ع) is known by the title "*Al-Amin*" which means "The Trustworthy". He is tasked with conveying the Message of God to the human Messengers. Through him came the Revelation of the Injil, Taurat and Qur'an. He was sent to Mary in the form of a human man, to give her the news of the birth of Jesus (ع). He has been the supporter of every prophet including Prophet Muhammad (ﷺ). He also has been ordered to destroy various disbelieving nations.

Khosrow "Parviz" II

The Zoroastrian ruler of the Persian Sassanid Empire from 590-628 AD. He was arrogant, extravagant and tyrannical. He promoted the creation of Fire Temples and waged a war against the Romans. When he received a letter from the Messenger of Allah (ﷺ), he ripped it up and made threats against him. Khosrow was eventually overthrown and executed by his own son, Sherow.

Luqman

Luqman was a servant of the Prophet Dawud (David) (ع) most likely of Abyssinian origin. He was known for his wisdom, although he was not a prophet himself. Many of his sayings were passed down across cultures and the Arabs had heard of them too. Therefore when the Qur'an was revealed, some wondered whether it was from the sayings of Luqman. However, it soon became clear that the Qur'an was something far greater and was being revealed contemporaneously in response to the exact situations the Prophet (ﷺ) was facing. One of the chapters of the Qur'an is named after Luqman and recounts some of his advice to his son.

Maryam (Mary)

She was the daughter of Imran and Hannah. Prophet Zakariyyah (ع) was her uncle and Yahya (John the Baptist) (ع) was her first cousin. On account of her exceptional piety and purity, Mary has been named by Prophet Muhammad (ﷺ) as one of the greatest four women of all time.

The Qur'an has an entire chapter named after her and her story. She had been dedicated by her mother in service to God, and she spent her time in a private chamber in the temple, visited only by her uncle Prophet Zakariyyah (ع). There, she would be provided fruits from Heaven, miraculously outside of their normal season. Although she was not a Prophet herself, the Angels spoke to her, and Jibreel (ع) himself descended in order to give her the good news of a son who would be born miraculously, although she had never been touched by any man. Within an impossibly short space of time, she found herself heavily pregnant and so left the city and just outside of it, under a date palm tree, gave birth to Prophet Jesus (ع). She returned to the city and was maligned by the people accusing her of indecency. However, the newly-born Prophet Jesus (ع) spoke, announced his Prophethood and exonerated his mother.

An-Najashi (The Negus)

His real name was Ashamah or Armah. He was the Christian ruler of the Kingdom of Axum, Abyssinia from 614-631 AD. He was an equitable, humble and pious man who provided sanctuary to the Believers who had emigrated to his Kingdom. He performed the marriage ceremony of the Prophet (ﷺ) with Umm Habiba. It is said he himself accepted Islam, although his people opposed him in this regard. When he died, the Messenger of Allah (ﷺ) prayed for him.

Suhayb ar-Rumi

He was the son of Sinan al-Malik: an Arab who was a governor of a Persian city in Iraq. Suhayb, aged five, was captured by some Roman soldiers while he was out at a picnic with his mother. He then spent the next twenty years living as a slave in the Byzantine lands, speaking Greek. He eventually managed to escape and found his way to Makkah. There, he met Abdullah ibn Jada'an, and became wealthy through associating with him in trade. People called him *Ar-Rumi* (the Roman) because of his blonde-haired appearance and foreign accent. When he heard about the Messenger's (ﷺ) preaching, he came to the house of Al-Arqam and became a Muslim. He was persecuted for his Faith like most of the early Believers. He was prevented from performing Hijrah alongside the Messenger (ﷺ), but some time later found an opportunity. The pagans pursued but Suhayb gave up his entire wealth to them in order to leave peacefully. In later life, Suhayb remained close to 'Umar ibn al-Khattab. He was chosen to lead prayers in Madinah for the duration of time between Umar's stabbing and Uthman's appointment as caliph. After 'Uthman's killing, Suhayb avoided taking any side in the ensuing tribulations: he did not give allegiance to the caliph 'Ali ibn Abi Talib but did not oppose him. Suhayb died in Madinah during his caliphate and was buried in al-Baqi.

Yahya (John the Baptist/Yohannan).

He was a Prophet from among the Bani Israel, born miraculously to parents who were both advanced in age. He was the son of Prophet Zakariyyah (ؑ) and the answer to his prayers for someone to inherit and succeed him. He had a soft and loving nature with a tender heart. He was obedient to his parents and did not cause them any inconvenience. Yahya (ؑ) was appointed to Prophethood when he was only two-years old and was among the most humble and God-fearing of people. He would weep intensely whenever he remembered the Hereafter. He wore the simplest clothing, he had very little material wealth and he did not eat, sleep or rest except a little. He invited people to the path of righteousness and spoke against injustice and indecency for many years. His main role was to prepare the way for Prophet 'Isa (ؑ), who was his cousin. Shortly before the latter was raised to Heaven, Yahya (ؑ) was imprisoned and beheaded on the orders of Herod Antipas the tyrannical ruler. The killing of Prophet Yahya ؑ) was one of the greatest enormities on earth as he had been sinless and innocent of any wrongdoing.

Glossary

Abraham's Station

In Arabic it is known as *Maqam Ibrahim*. It is a rock sent down from Heaven that Prophet Ibrahim (ع) stood on while he was building the upper parts of the Kaaba. It contains an imprint of his footprints, as the rock became soft when he stood on it. After completing the Tawaaf around the Kaaba, a pilgrim must perform two units of prayer at Maqam Ibrahim (see Qur'an 2:125)

Abu, Abi

An Arabic word which means "Father of". In Arabian culture, many people are addressed by their Teknonymic title, especially in relation to their eldest child. It is also used in a figurative sense to suggest a connection between them and some particular quality or thing.

Abu Duwaymah, The Path of

Ri' Abu Duwaymah is a dust covered stony path which is located between the Pass of al-Murar and the Path of Humayyah.

Abu Qubays

One of the prominent Mountains of Makkah. Mount Safa is connected to (and may be considered part of) it.

Ahmad

One of the other names of Prophet Muhammad (ﷺ). It means "the Praised one" or "the one who praises the most". It is by this name that the Prophet Jesus (ع) referred to him (See Qur'an, 61:6).

Ahya, The Spring of

Maa' Ahya is a verdant area of pasture and fresh water near to the Pass of Al-Murar.

Allah (﷾)

This is the name used in Arabic to refer to the Creator and Sustainer of all things. It was used by the monotheistic Hunafa and the Arab-speaking Jews and Christians. Even most of the polytheists of Quraysh recognised and referred to Allah as their Creator, although they falsely associated others with Him. It is said to derive from the words *Al-Ilaah*, meaning "The God".

Al-'Aqabah

A mountain pass located about 3 miles away from Makkah. It is most famous for the First and Second Pledges of Al-'Aqabah that were made there by the Ansar in the eleventh and twelfth years of the Prophetic mission.

Alif. Laam. Meem.

These are part of the mystical disjointed letters called the *Muqatta'at* in Arabic. They are found at the start of some Surahs of the Qur'an. The meaning is only known to Allah, the Exalted and Wise.

Al-'Aqeeq, The Valley of

It is near to the neighbourhood of 'Usbah and contains numerous sources of fresh water.

Al-Aqsa

Another name for Jerusalem. It is a blessed city associated with many Prophets and Messengers including Abraham, Isaac, Moses, Joshua, Solomon, David, Samuel, Daniel, Elisha, Ezekiel, Ezra, Zakariyyah, John the Baptist and Jesus (peace be upon them all). Masjid al-Aqsa is located within it.

Amj, The Village of

A small settlement northwest of the town of 'Usfan.

Angels

These are creations of Allah (ﷻ) made out of light. They do not possess free will but do exactly what they are ordered to do by God. Various classes of them exist, including Angelic Messengers, the Angel Scribes that write down deeds, Angels of death, Angels that question in the grave, Angels tasked with controlling the winds, the Guardians of Hell, Angels that guard the Believers, and many more types.

Ansar, The; Ansari

A title which literally means the Helpers. It refers to the people of Banu Qaylah (Al-Aws and Khazraj) who helped the Prophet and the rest of the Emigrants from Makkah.

Al-Arj

This is the name of both a village and the valley around it. It is a somewhat difficult route to traverse due to its narrow and meandering course.

Awal

It was the name of an idol that was worshipped by some of the pagans, especially among the people in the region of Bahrain. It has been described as resembling the form of an ox.

Axum

The name of an influential kingdom in Abyssinia, ruled by An-Najashi.

Ayr, Mount

A dark coloured Mountain, marking the southern edge of the Sacred Area (*Haram*) of Madinah.

Bayt-ul-Mamur

It is the original Kaaba, located in the Seventh Heaven, built for the worship of Allah (﷾) among the inhabitants of the Heavens. Its name literally means the "Frequented House". Each day seventy thousand new angels take their turn to make a visitation to it, and they will not get another chance until the Day of Judgement. It is one of the incredible sights Prophet Muhammad (ﷺ) witnessed during the Mir'aaj.

Believers, The

They are called "*Al-Muminoon*" in Arabic, which literally means "Those who have been made secure". These are the people who willingly submitted to the Will of Allah (﷾) so they were given security in their Faith and on the Day of Judgement.

Bethlehem

Known as "*Bayt al-Lahm*" in Arabic. It was a small village, famous due to its association with Prophet Jesus (ع). During the Night Journey, Prophet Muhammad (ﷺ) is reported to have stopped at this place.

Bushaymat mountains

This is a chain of mountains near Makkah.

Buraaq

One of the creations of Allah (﷾). It is a beautiful white winged steed. It was brought down from the Heavens by the Angel Jibreel (ع) in order to carry Prophet Muhammad (ﷺ) during the Night Journey (*Al-Isra*) and Ascension (*Mi'raaj*). It could travel so fast that each step it took would take to the extent of its vision.

Companions of the Elephant, The

This is a reference to Abraha and his army, which consisted of at least one elephant and according to some sources as many as fifteen.

Dar an-Nadwa

It literally means, "The House of Assembly". It was a house that was built by Qusayy ibn Kilab. It was later used by the chiefs of Quraysh as a place to meet together and make important decisions. The usual rule was that no one under the age of thirty could be admitted to these meetings; however two famous exceptions to this were Hashim ibn 'Abd Manaf and 'Amr ibn Hisham (Abu Jahl).

Dhil-Majaz

A place near Mount Arafat where there would be a popular yearly market fair in the pre-Islamic period of *Jahiliyyah*.

Dhul-Hijjah, Dhil-Hijjah

The twelfth month of the Islamic calendar. It is the month during which the Hajj, or Holy Pilgrimage takes place, on its eighth, ninth and tenth days each year.

Dirham

Pieces of silver of fixed weight that were used as currency. These were not necessarily in the form of coins at that time.

Disbelievers, The

They are called, "*Al-Kafiroon*" in Arabic, which literally means, "Those who deliberately conceal and cover up". The implication is that these are not merely people who simply do not believe, but they are a special class of people who have recognised the Truth, but consciously chosen to openly reject it and to attempt to turn others away from it also. Such a people qualify for the worst punishment and it is they who the various Verses of the Qur'an refer to in their condemnation.

Faith

In Arabic it is called *Al-Imaan*, which also carries the connotation of "Security". The one who has it is called a *Mu'min* (Believer) and will be secure of the Day of Judgement, *Insha'Allah*.

Fijar War

Harb al-Fijar literally means the Sacrilegious war, as it took place during the sacred months when fighting was usually prohibited. This was a war that took place at Ukaz between the Quraysh and their allies and the Hawazin and their allies. It began when a man of Banu Kinanah in a state of anger attacked a man from Banu 'Amir. There were eight days of fighting over the course of four years. Muhammad (ﷺ) was present during some of it as a teenager but did not personally fight. He collected arrows for his uncle Abu Talib. There were no real victors in the end, but the side that had less casualties paid for the blood money of the other side.

Gate of Banu Shaybah, The

This was the gate located at the northeast entrance to the Sacred Mosque, near the path between As-Safa and Marwah. It was thus named because it passed through the habitations of Banu Shaybah, a subclan of Banu Abd ad-Dar who held the keys to the Holy Kaaba.

Ghadir Khumm

Located near Juhfah, it was a generally barren area where there was a seasonal pond. It is famous because Prophet Muhammad (ﷺ) chose to make one of his final major public sermons at this place.

Al-Ghamim

Kura' al-Ghamim is a lava spur. It is located north of *Thaniyyat al-Murar* and northeast of Jeddah.

Hadhrami cloak

A traditional cloak made in the region of Hadhramaut in Yemen.

Hafr, Valley of

It is a short valley of about 4 miles in length that connects the Valley of Ar-Ras to the Valley of Reem.

Hajj

The Divinely ordained pilgrimage to Makkah, and surrounding regions in the month of Dhil-Hijjah. It consists of various rites and practices whose purpose is to bring one closer to God. These include Tawaaf, Sa'i between As-Safa and Marwah, stoning the Devil, praying on Mount Arafat and sacrificing an animal. It began with Prophet Ibrahim (ﷺ). The pre-Islamic Arabs used to perform the rituals but with some distortions.

Ha-Meem

These are part of the mystical *Muqatta'at* (disjointed letters) whose meaning is perhaps known only to Allah (ﷺ).

Hamra al-Asad, Mount

A reddish mountain located about 8 miles away from Madinah. It has an elevation of 940 metres. The Expedition of Hamra al-Asad took place here the day after the Battle of Uhud in 3 AH.

Hashimi, Hashimite

A member of the tribe of Banu Hashim – the descendants of Hashim ibn 'Abd Manaf.

Hijrah

An Arabic word which means "emigration". It refers to the emigration of Prophet Muhammad (ﷺ) and his followers (ﷺ) from Makkah to Yathrib (which was then renamed 'Madinah') in the year 622 CE, or 1 AH. That event marks the beginning of the Islamic calendar.

Hijr Isma'il

Also known as *Al-Hateem*. It is the semi circular area next to the Kaaba. It was originally part of the Kaaba but when the Quraysh rebuilt it, they did not have enough funds acquired from pure money to complete it. Praying in this area has great rewards. It was called Hijr Isma'il because this was the place where Prophet Ibrahim (ﷺ) had made a shelter for Isma'il (ﷺ)

and his mother. Some say that Isma'il and Hajrah are actually buried here, but this is unproven.

Al-Hudaybiyyah

A place near to Makkah, located on the caravan route. It is most famous for the treaty of Hudaybiyyah that the Prophet (ﷺ) made with the Quraysh there in 6 AH: something that the Qur'an refers to as "a Manifest Victory."

Humayyah, The Path of

A well-established route with sparse herbage alongside the stony mountains. Trade caravans have travelled this way for centuries.

Al-Hutamah

One of the levels of Hell. It is a place of great violence which crushes and shatters bones. Its fire has been described as burning right up to the hearts. It is reserved for a particularly egregious class of criminals among the disbelievers.

Ibn

An Arabic word which means 'the son of'. It is used to indicate the lineage of a person, which was one of the most important ways of identifying people in Arabian society at the time.

Ibrahim, Valley of

Also known as the Valley of Makkah. It is named after Prophet Ibrahim (ﷺ) who passed through this way.

Isfahan

A cultural and religiously diverse city in central Persia. Many Jews settled there during the time of Cyrus the Great as a result of his policies of tolerance. Later during the Sassanid dynasty, it was a place of great architectural projects. Due to its strategic location, it also became a military base for use against campaigns against the Romans. The name Isfahan literally means "Standing place of the army."

Jahannam

One of the names of Hell in Arabic. A place of great torment for the oppressors and unbelievers.

Jannah

An Arabic word which literally means "Garden". It refers to the Garden of Paradise. It is a place of serenity and reward for the righteous.

Jinn

A race of creatures created by Allah (ﷻ) prior to the creation of mankind. They were made from smokeless fire, and are not normally visible to our eyes. Like mankind they possess free will and were placed on Earth to be tested. There exist among them different communities and faiths. Some are Disbelievers, some follow the Torah and the teachings of Judaism, others are Christian, and some became Muslim.

Juhfah

A place where a lot of people passed through, being both a busy trade caravan stop and the specified halting place (Miqat) for pilgrims from Syria and Egypt, headed towards Makkah.

Jumdan, Mount

A dark coloured mountain located near to the village of Amj. *Jabal Jumdan* is among the mountains that the Messenger of Allah (ﷺ) has spoken of with praise.

Kaaba

The oldest House built on Earth for the worship of God. Its foundations and original construction were laid by Adam. Its walls were later built up by the Prophets Ibrahim and Isma'il. During Hajj, an important rite is to perform Tawaaf - the act of ritualistically circling around it seven times, whilst reciting words of Divine praise.

Khandama, Mount

It is one of the largest of the mountains of Makkah. It is located to the west of Mount Marwah.

Kharrar, The Valley of

A valley between the Valley of Kulayyah and Juhfah.

Al-Khatir

A busy place with many wells which were often used by travellers to water their animals.

Al-Khulaysah, The Tract of

Harrat al-Khulaysah is a lava tract which speckles the edge of the valley of Qudayd with black volcanic rocks. It is also known as *Al-Bakkawiyah*.

Kulayyah, The Valley of

Wadi Kulayyah is an open and sandy area located after the Tract of Al-Mushallal. It is here that Suraqah ibn Malik caught up with the Prophet (ﷺ) during the Hijrah.

La ilaaha il-Allah

An Arabic expression that means, "There is no god but Allah." This is one of two sentences that must be uttered with sincerity, in order for a person to be considered a Muslim. The other sentence is *"Muhammadur-RasulAllah"*, which means "Muhammad is the Messenger of Allah."

Al-Lat

This was an idol that had been worshipped by many of the pagans of Arabia including the Quraysh and especially the Banu Thaqif. They claimed this was a "daughter of Allah" who was a goddess of warfare and prosperity. The name al-Lat was derived by taking the Name 'Allah' (The God) and feminising it. There was a famous temple for al-Lat in the city of Ta'if, which eventually destroyed in the year 8 AH (630 AD).

Liqf, The Valley of

Wadi Liqf is a long valley between mountain ranges. It is where the Prophet (ﷺ) camped on the third night of the Hijrah journey.

Madyan

A city in North-western Arabia where Prophet Musa (﷿) settled after his first escape from Egypt. Prophet Shu'ayb (﷿) was sent to these people, to warn them against their evil practices of polytheism, short-changing in trade and their ambushing of people along the roadways. Despite years of constant preaching, only a minority of the people believed. These were saved alongside their Prophet; while all of the others were destroyed when the promised Divine Punishment overtook their city.

Majannah

This was a place near Makkah that used to host a yearly market fair near the time of Hajj.

Makkah

A city in the region of Hijaz in Arabia and the holiest place in the entire world for Muslims. The Kaaba is located here. Makkah was the birthplace of Prophet Muhammad (ﷺ) and the place where he began his preaching. Most of the Qur'an was revealed in Makkah.

Manat

This was an idol that has been worshipped by many of the pagans of Arabia especially Al-Aws and Khazraj. They claimed this was a "daughter of Allah" who was a goddess fate, fortune and time. There was a famous temple for Manat at Al-Mushallal, which was eventually destroyed in the year 8 AH (630 AD).

Maarib Dam

One of the engineering wonders of the ancient world. It allowed the Kingdom of Saba to turn the deserts of Yemen into a fertile oasis full of greenery and fruits by means of a complex irrigation system. However, the people became ungrateful and disbelieved. The destruction of the Dam is referred to in the Qur'an (Surah 34:15-17). Afterwards all that remained were a few sparse trees and bitter fruits: migrations and the end of the Kingdom followed.

Marwah

One of two prominent hills surrounding the city of Makkah. The house of Prophet Muhammad (ﷺ) and Khadija was located near to Mount Marwah.

Masjid al-Aqsa

It literally means "the Furthest Mosque". A place of worship in Jerusalem. It is the third most sacred mosque after *Masjid al-Haram* (the Sacred Mosque) in Makkah and *Masjid an-Nabawi* (The Prophet's Mosque) in Madinah.

Mina

A place near Makkah where important rituals during the Hajj take place including the ritual stoning of the Devil (*Rajm ash-Shaytan*).

Mijah, Valley of

Located between the Valley of Far' and the Valley of Qaha. It is a wide sandy area surrounded by towering mountains on all sides.

Mi'raaj, The

It literally means "Ascension". It refers to the miraculous event where the Messenger of Allah (ﷺ) was made to ascend from the Foundation Stone in Jerusalem to the Heavens by means of a Divinely-sent 'Stairway' to the Heavens. It was a physical ascension and not a spiritual one nor was it a dream.

Mudhammam

It literally means "the condemned one" or "reprobate". It is one of the insulting names that the pagans came up with to refer to the Prophet (ﷺ), in contrast to his actual name which means "The Praiseworthy one".

Muhajiroon

The Arabic term for the Emigrants, meaning in this context, the Believers who performed *Hijrah* from Makkah to Madinah.

Muharram

The first month of the Islamic calendar. It is one of the four sacred months during which fighting is prohibited.

Al-Mulaysa, Mount

Jabal al-Mulaysa is a smooth grey-white mountain near to the Valley of Liqf. It is also known as *Sakhrat Akha*.

Al-Murar, The pass of

Thaniyyat al-Murar is a narrow region located between two mountains: Jabal Mukassir and Jabal Daf. It is on the route towards al-Hudaybiyyah.

Al-Musaydirah

Tal'at al-Musaydirah is a watercourse formed by the passage of water through the mountains.

Al-Mushallal, The tract of

Harrat al-Mushallal is a lava tract located on the Northern part of the Valley of Qudayd. It is near to the trade caravan route, which passes alongside it. The pagan shrine of Manat was located in nearby Al-Mushallal.

Mustandhar

Also later on known as *Abyad*. One of the many mountains of Makkah, located to the west of Mount Marwah. Along with Mount Khandama it forms the northern periphery of the Valley of Banu Hashim. It is famous for the Well of Badhdhar that was dug at its base by Hashim ibn 'Abd Manaf.

Mustazilat, Mount

Khushum al-Mustazillat is a group of yellow-brown foothills which are located near to the valley of Liqf.

Nakhlah Valley

An area located between Makkah and Ta'if. It marks the boundary of the sacred valley of Makkah. In the pre-Islamic era, the pagan shrine of al-'Uzzah was found here. In the second year after Hijrah, the Raid on Nakhlah took place here.

Nasibin

Also known as Nusaybin. A city variously identified as being in Iraq, Turkey or Yemen. A group of Jinn came from this place to investigate what had changed in Makkah. They heard the Qur'an and became Muslims.

Nasr

This was the name of an idol that is said to have been formerly worshipped by the Himyar of Yemen, before they converted to Judaism. It is also the name of an idol worshipped by the polytheists among the people of Noah (ع) before them. It has been described as resembling the form of an eagle or a vulture.

Night of Decree, The

Laylatul Qadr is the most sacred night of the year It is the night in which the Qur'an was revealed, prayers are answered and all major decisions for the coming year are decreed by God. This one night is greater than a thousand months. It can be found in one of the odd numbered last ten nights of the month of Ramadhan. The knowledge of the exact night has been hidden from us in order to encourage worship throughout all the nights.

Night Journey, The

Al-Isra was the miraculous journey that the Messenger of Allah (ﷺ) made from *Masjid-ul-Haram* in Makkah to *Masjid-ul-Aqsa* in Jerusalem in a single night by means of the *Buraaq*.

Night Vigil

Qiyam al-Layl, also known as *Tahajjud* was the practice of the Messenger (ﷺ) and some of the Believers, in rising to establish supererogatory prayers in the hours of the night.

Ninawa

Located in Northern Iraq, it is the place where the Prophet Yunus i.e. Jonah (﷙) was sent. It is a city the Qur'an describes at that time as having a population of "a hundred thousand or more."

Noon

The letter ن in Arabic. It is one of the Muqatta'at (Disjointed Letters) that some Surahs begin with. Its meaning is known only to God.

People of the Book, The

Ahlul Kitab is the term used in the Qur'an for the monotheistic adherents of Scripture, specifically the Jews, Christians and Sabians.

Qaha, Valley of

It is a very long valley, more than 45 miles in total length. It was a well-established route for the trade caravans, and was also an ancient pathway used by countless pilgrims and Prophets on their way to Makkah, which is why it is also known as "*Darb al-Anbiyah*", or "Path of the Prophets".

Qiyamah

One of the names for the Day of Judgement. Its full form "*Yawm-ul-Qiyamah*" literally means "The Day of Standing".

Quba

A neighbourhood on the outskirts of Yathrib. It was the first place the Prophet (ﷺ) stayed after his Hijrah. It was here that he established the first public Masjid which is known as Masjid al-Quba.

Qudayd

It is both the name of a busy town and the nearly 100-mile-long valley which stretches from it to the Red Sea.

Qur'an

It literally means, "The Recitation". It is the Divine Revelation sent down onto Muhammad (ﷺ) in the Arabic language. It is the direct unaltered word of God delivered by the Angel Jibreel (ﷺ). The Qur'an was revealed part by part in response to questions and circumstances faced by the Prophet. Most of it was revealed in Makkah over a period of thirteen years, while the rest was revealed over the next ten years in Madinah. In total it consists of 6236 Verses divided into 114 chapters.

Rabbis

Religious scholars of the Jewish faith. A great number of them had settled in Yathrib because they were awaiting the advent of the Final Prophet who had been described in their books.

Ar-Rahman

One of the Beautiful Names of God, found throughout the Qur'an. It literally means "The Merciful One". The pagans of Quraysh disliked this Name because it was similar to the Name *Rahmanan* used by some of their rivals from Yemen like the Himyar. They therefore refused to acknowledge it.

Rakubah

This is both the name of a Mountain and its valley. Mount Rakubah is located in the Valley of Reem, near to Mount Warqan.

Rajab

The seventh month of the Islamic calendar. It is one of the four sacred months during which fighting is prohibited.

Revelation, The

In Arabic, *Tanzil*. It means the sacred and secure communication that has come down sequentially from God to his Prophets or Messengers. Sometimes it may refer to Scripture in general, or to the Qur'an in particular, or it may even be other non-scriptural knowledge or information that descends upon them.

Recitation, The

See the Qur'an.

Reem, Valley of

It is a more than thirty mile long area well-frequented by travellers. It is here that Abu Ma'bad finally caught up with the Prophet (ﷺ) to testify and accept Islam.

Rijalayn, Pass of

Maqrah ar-Rijalan is a mile long route leading to the Valley of Hamidah, which is on the route towards the Valley of Liqf. It was a burial site for some ancient people and traces of their graves can still be seen today.

Remembrance, The; The Reminder

In Arabic it is called *Ad-Dhikr*. It can refer to either the Qur'an or the Messenger of Allah (ﷺ) depending on the context.

As-Safa. Mount

One of two prominent hills surrounding the city of Makkah. Hajrah, the wife of Ibrahim and mother of Isma'il, ran seven times between this hill and the nearby hill of Marwah searching for water. Sa'i, a ritual that is performed during Hajj is performed in commemoration of that struggle and perseverance that Lady Hajrah demonstrated that day. It was from upon Mount As-Safa that Prophet Muhammad (ﷺ) made his first public call.

Salaam

The greeting of peace in Islam, said by one Muslim to another using the Arabic phrase *"As-Salaamu 'Alaykum"* which means "Peace be unto you."

Saqar

One of the levels of Hell, that has been mentioned in the Qur'an. Its flames burn the flesh and leave nothing behind.

Sanctuary, The

Al-Haram refers to the Sacred area of Makkah where the Kaaba and Masjid al--Haram is located.

Sawa, Lake

A large body of water in Persia. It was worshipped by some of the pagans. It famously dried up at the time of the birth of Prophet Muhammad (ﷺ). Geographers have described it as being located between Rey and Hamazan. However, there is also a similarly named lake in the south of Iraq.

Shaddad, The Well of

Bir Shaddad is an area with palm trees and a water well, near Yathrib.

As-Shu'aybah

Located along the Red Sea coast, it was the main port used by the people of Makkah at the time for sea journeys. The Emigrants crossed over to Abyssinia from here.

Sidratul Muntaha

"The Furthest Lote tree" is a place referred to in the Qur'an (53:14). It is the utmost boundary of Paradise beyond which not even the Angel Jibreel (ﷺ) was permitted nor able to cross. However, Prophet Muhammad (ﷺ) alone on account of his superior rank above all creation, was permitted to cross beyond this to an exalted place of proximity to The Almighty. Such proximity does not mean in a physical sense as God is not temporally nor spatially bound but what is meant is proximity in a spiritual sense.

Sinai

Both the name of a sacred mountain in Egypt and the valley surrounding it. This is the place where Moses (ﷺ) was appointed to his mission as the Messenger of God.

Stern Guardians

In Arabic they are called *Az-Zabanniyah*. They are the nineteen angels guarding the Fire of Hell, tasked with punishing the criminals.

Straight Path, The

As-Siraatul Mustaqeem is a term used throughout the Quran for the Path that leads to the Favour of Allah and avoids his Punishment. It is the path of the Prophets and the righteous Believers.

Surah

A chapter of the Qur'an (singular *Surah*, plural *Suwar*, although the anglicised word Surahs is commonly used). There are 114 Surahs in total, most of which were revealed in Makkah.

Suwa

The name of an idol worshipped by some of the Banu Lihyan, and by the polytheists among the people of Noah (ع) before them. It has been described as resembling the form of a woman.

Ta'if

Some seventy miles east of Makkah, it was a powerful city with vast gardens of roses, grapes, figs and pomegranates. Due to its wealth, the influence of the Banu Thaqif who lived there, and the fact that the grand temple dedicated to the pagan idol al-Lat was located there, Ta'if was considered second only to Makkah in importance. This is the city where the Prophet (ﷺ) was stoned when he went there to preach. A few months after the Siege of Ta'if in 10 AH, the people of Ta'if became Muslims.

Ta-Ha

These two letters are part of the Muqatta'at (Disjointed letters). In this case it appears to be a title of Prophet Muhammad (ﷺ) but Allah (ﷻ), knows best what it means.

Tawaaf

The ritual circumambulation around the Kaaba. Sets of seven Tawaafs are performed at various points during the Hajj.

Taybah

Another name for Yathrib, the city that would later be known as Madinah.

Thawr, Mount

A mountain located about five miles away to the South of Makkah. With an elevation of 750 metres, it takes about 2 hours to ascend. There is a small cave on Mount Thawr where Prophet Muhammad (ﷺ) and Abu Bakr sought refuge during the Hijrah and remained within it for three days.

Trinity, The

A belief not taught by Jesus or his disciples, but held by later Christian communities, made mainstream after the Council of Nicaea in 325 AD. It is the claim that God consists of three entities - The Father, represented by the God of the Old Testament; the Son, represented by Jesus, and the Holy Spirit represented by Angel Gabriel. Not all Christians hold this belief.

Tuwa, Valley of

Located between the mountains within the Sinai peninsula in Egypt. It is here where Moses (ع) was appointed to his Prophetic mission when he climbed Mount Sinai.

Ukaz

It was a place between Nakhlah and Ta'if, where a popular yearly market fair was held during the month of Dhil-Qa'dah. There would be various stalls for trade, sporting events, poetry competitions and social gatherings.

Al-'Usbah

One of the first neighbourhoods that the Prophet (ﷺ) passed through as he entered the main part of Madinah. It was inhabited by the Bani Jahjaba, a subclan of Banu Aws. He drank from a well there named Al-Hajeem which still exists until today.

'Usfan, town of

It is a busy town located on the trade caravan route, about 48 miles away from Makkah.

Ummi

An-Nabiyy-ul-Ummi is a reference to the Prophet as found in the Qur'an (7:157). It literally means "from the mother", and it can either be taken to mean "unlettered" or "the one who is from Ummul Quraa'".

Ummul Quraa'

It literally means, "The Mother of Cities". It is one of the titles of the city of Makkah, as found in the Qur'an (6:92), signifying both its historical importance and as its importance in the spread of Islam.

Unseen, The

Al-Ghayb refers to what is not usually perceived by the senses or conceived by the mind alone. Its knowledge belongs to Allah the Exalted alone and He reveals it to whomsoever He wishes to whatever extent He wishes. The Unseen includes all hidden matters, the realms parallel to or beyond our own, and knowledge of the future and the undocumented past. Mankind has been given some knowledge of this by means of Prophets and Messengers who are informed of this via Revelation. However, this only comprises a very small part of the entire Unseen.

Al-'Uzzah

This was an idol that had been worshipped by many of the pagans of Arabia including the Quraysh. They took the Name Al-Aziz (The Mighty), and feminised it. They claimed this was a "daughter of Allah" who was a goddess of might, protection and love. There was a famous temple for al-'Uzzah at Nakhlah, which was eventually destroyed in the year 8 AH (630 AD).

Verse(s)

An *Ayat* (plural *Ayaat*) in Arabic literally means sign or miracle. It is the word the Qur'an uses for its Verses.

Warqan, Mount

Jabal Warqan is also known as *Jabal Hamt*. It is a striking reddish mountain in the Valley of Reem. The Prophet (ﷺ) has described it as one of the mountains of Paradise.

Ways of Ascent

Al-Ma'arij means the pathways to and from the Heavens by which the angels ascend. This is not knowledge available to human beings ordinarily. However, the Messenger of Allah (ﷺ) was granted use of one of these during his *Mi'raaj* or Ascension.

Western Wall, The

Also known as the Wailing wall, the Kotel, and *Ha'itul Buraaq*. It is a 2000 year old limestone wall constructed during the reign of Herod I, part of which still remains standing today. It surrounded the site of the ancient Temple Mount and has therefore been regarded with great reverence for this reason. For Muslims, it holds importance as it is the site where Prophet Muhammad (ﷺ) tied the Buraaq to during the Night Journey (*Al-Isra*) while he prayed at the site of *Masjid-ul-Aqsa*.

Yaghuth

It was an idol worshipped by the Banu Murad of Yemen. It was also formerly worshipped by the polytheists among the people of Noah (ﷷ). It has been described as resembling the form of a lion.

Ya'uq

It was an idol worshipped by the Banu Hamdan of Yemen and was formerly worshipped by the polytheists among the people of Noah (ﷺ). It has been described as resembling the form of a horse.

Ya Sabaha

An Arabic expression which was used to alert people to some kind of danger. The Messenger of Allah (ﷺ) made use of it while standing on Mount Safa to gather his people and warn them of Judgement Day.

Yathrib

A city in Arabia, north of Makkah. When Prophet Muhammad (ﷺ) emigrated to it from Makkah, it become the centre of the Islamic movement and its name was changed to *"Madinatun-Nabi"*, meaning "the City of the Prophet".

Zamzam

A famous well in the city of Makkah whose origins are mentioned in the Qur'an. While Lady Hajrah was searching desperately for water, the infant Prophet Isma'il (ﷺ) struck his heels onto the ground and a stream of water began to flow from beneath him. Hajrah made a structure around it which became known as the Well of Zamzam. Centuries later, its location was lost until it was rediscovered by 'Abdul Muttalib – the esteemed grandfather of the Holy Prophet Muhammad (ﷺ). The water of Zamzam which is renowned for its clarity, unique taste and various beneficial properties has continued to flow in abundance up until the present day.

Zaqqum, The Tree of

A terrible plant, which the Qur'an informs us is found in the depths of hell. It bears fruits that are described as being "like the heads of devils". Certain classes from the sinners will be forced to eat it, which is among the severest of punishments. Abu Jahl had mocked this but is one of those who will be subjected to it.

Bibliography

During the research phase of this work, we tried to examine as many different perspectives as possible. We looked at how both primary and secondary sources from a variety of ideological, cultural and religious backgrounds understood and explained different aspects of the story. We also analysed depictions in other media forms in order to better understand what the general public may already have in mind as a reference.

It should be recognised that no one reads or writes anything in a vacuum and understanding the background and social milieu of each author is paramount. At times, we were inspired by some aspects, and other times we differed with them and sought to clarify the matter in this work. Within each of these sources can be found some benefit; whether it be in their unique content, style, structure or comments. At the same time, some of them (especially the work of the Orientalists) might also include what we have considered to be conjecture, bias, uncharitable opinions, baseless assertions, artistic licence or even outright falsehood in stark contrast to the well-established historical reality of the matter. This has not prevented us from reading and analysing their work: taking what is best from it, and leaving what has no proof.

The following list of our sources is therefore not to be necessarily taken as an absolute endorsement or recommendation of any of these works or their authors, but rather an acknowledgement that our writing was in some way influenced by their efforts. It may also serve as a starting point for others who wish to delve deeper.

Books:

Biographies:

The Life Of Muhammad (*Seerat RasulAllah*)
Muhammad ibn Ishaaq (d. 767)
Partially reconstructed and translated by Alfred Guillame (1955)

The Life of the Prophet, (*As-Seerat an-Nabawiyyah*)
'Abd al-Malik ibn Hisham (d. 833)

The Book of the Major Classes (*At-Tabaqat al-Kabir*)
Muhammad ibn Sa'ad (d. 845)

History of the Prophets and Kings (*Tarikh ar-Rusul wal Muluk*)
Muhammad ibn Jarir at-Tabari (915)

Healing by the Recognition of the Rights of the Chosen One
(*As-Shifa bi-Ta'rif Huququl Mustafa*)
Qadi Iyad (d. 1149)

The Life of the Prophet (*As-Seerat an-Nabawiyyah*)
Isma'il ibn Kathir (d. 1373)

Life of the Hearts, Vol. II (*Hayat al-Qulub*)
Muhammad Baqir al-Majlisi (d. 1699)

Abridged Biography of Prophet Muhammad (*Mukhtasar Seerat ar-Rasul*)
Muhammad ibn 'Abdul Wahhab (d. 1792)

The Life of Mohammed:
Founder of the Religion of Islam, and of the Empire of the Saracens.
George Bush (1831)

The Life of Mohammad From Original Sources
Aloys Sprenger (1851)

The Life of Muhammad and History of Islam to the Era of the Hegira,
William Muir (1861)

Mercy for Mankind (*Rahmatulil 'Aalameen*)
Muhammad Sulaiman Mansoorpuri (1911)

The Life of Mohammad, The Prophet of Allah
Etienne Diner, Sliman Ben Ibrahim (1918)

Al-Amin, A Life-Sketch Of The Prophet Muhammad,
Muhammad Marmaduke Pickthall (1930)

The Life of Muhammad *(Hayat Muhammad)*
Muhammad Husayn Haykal, (1933)

Mohammed: the man and his faith
Tor Andrae (1936)

Muhammad at Mecca,
William Montgomery Watt (1953)

The Life of the Prophet *(Seerat an-Nabi)*
Shibli Noumani and Sulaiman Nadvi Muhammad, (1918-1955)

Muhammad (*Mahomet*)
Maxime Rodinson (1960)

The Life of The Holy Prophet of Islam
Sa'eed Akhtar Rizvi (1971)

Twenty three years: a study of the Prophetic career of Mohammed
Ali Dashti (1973)

The Sealed Nectar (*Ar-Raheeq al-Makhtum*)
Safiur Rahman Mubarakpuri (1976)

Understanding the Life of the Prophet (*Fiqh Us-Seerah*)
Muhammad al-Ghazali as-Saqqa (1976)

The Prophet of Mercy *(As-Seerat an-Nabawiyyah)*
Abul Hasan 'Ali Nadwi (1978)

The Benefactor Of Humanity *(Mohsin e-Insaniyat)*
Naeem Siddiqui (1979)

Muhammad, Man of God
Hossein Nasr (1982)

Muhammad, His life based on the earliest sources
Martin Lings (1983)

The Message *(Farugh Ibdiyat)*
Ja'far Subhani (1984)

The Life of Muhammad
Tahia al-Isma'il (1988)

Muhammad: A Biography of the Prophet
Karen Armstrong (1991)

Muhammad the Prophet
Muhammad 'Ali (1993)

Muhammad: man and prophet, a complete study of the life of the Prophet of Islam
'Adil Salahi (1995)

A Restatement of History of Islam and the Muslims
Ali Asghar Razwy (1996)

The Biography of the Prophet, and the Orientalists
Muhammad Mohar Ali (1997)

The Life of Muhammad
Baqir Sharif al-Qurayshi (2003)

The Prophet Muhammad: A Biography
Barnaby Rogerson (2004)

The Noble Life of the Prophet
'Ali as-Sallabi (2005)

In the Footsteps of the Prophet: Lessons from the Life of Muhammad
Tariq Ramadhan (2006)

The First Muslim: The Story of Muhammad,
Lesley Hazleton (2014)

Muhammad: Prophet of Peace Amid the Clash of Empires
Juan Cole (2018)

Muhammad, the World-Changer: An Intimate Portrait
Mohamad Jebara (2021)

Ahadith (Traditions):

Sahih al-Bukhari
Muhammad al-Bukhari (d. 870)

Sahih Muslim
Muslim ibn al-Hajjaj (d. 875)

Sunan Ibn Majah
Muhammad ibn Yazid ibn Majah (d. 889)

Sunan at-Tirmidhi
Muhammad at-Tirmidhi (884)

As-Shamail al-Muhammadiyya
Muhammad at-Tirmidhi (d. 892)

Al-Mustadrak 'alaa al-Sahihayn
Muhammad al-Hakim an-Nishapuri (1002)

Riyaad us-Saliheen
Yahya ibn Sharaf an-Nawawi (d. 1277)

Al-Khasais ul Kubra
Jalaluddin as-Suyuti (d. 1505)

Muhammad the Merciful
Muhammad Tahir ul Qadri (2013)

Tafasir (Commentaries of the Qur'an):

Asbab an-Nuzul
'Ali ibn Ahmad al-Wahidi (d. 1075)

Tafsir al-Qur'an al-'Adheem
Isma'il ibn Kathir (d. 1373)

Prolegomena to the Qur'an
(*Al-Bayan Fi Tafsir al-Quran*)
Abul Qasim al-Khoei (d. 1992)

Tafhim ul-Quran
Abul 'Aala Mawdudi (1972)

Tafsir al-Mizan
Sayyid Muhammad Husayn Tabataba'i (1976)

An Enlightening Commentary into the Light of the Holy Qur'an
Sayyid Kamal Faqih Imani, et al (2003)

Translations of the Qur'an:

The Meaning of the Glorious Qur'an
Muhammad Marmaduke Pickthall (1930)

The Holy Qur'an: Translation and Commentary
'Abdullah Yusuf Ali (1940)

The Qur'an
"Mohammed Habib Shakir" (c. 1980)

The Holy Qur'an
Saheeh International (1997)

Other reference books:

The Book of idols *(Kitab al-Asnam)*
Hisham ibn al-Kalbi (d. 819)

Lives of the Companions *(Hayat as-Sahabah)*
Muhammad Yusuf al-Kandihlawi (d. 1965)

The Qur'an in Islam, its Impact and Influence on the Life of Muslims
Sayyid Muhammad Husayn Tabataba'i (d. 1981)

Men and women around the Messenger
Khalid Muhammad Khalid (2012)

From Makkah to Madinah:
A photographic journey of the Hijrah route
Dr. 'Abdullah H. Alkadi (2013)

Makkah in the time of the Prophet: An illustrated reference with maps of key
homes, mountains and other landmarks
Binimad al-Ateeqi (2020)

History:

History of the Sasanian Empire: Annals of the New Persian Empire
George Rawlinson (1875)

A History of Rome to 565 A. D.
Arthur Edward Romilly Boak (1921)

History of the Arabs
Philip Khuri Hitti (1937)

A History of India
Burton Stein (1998)

Articles:

Statistical analysis about the order of Quran's revelation, *Digital Scholarship in the Humanities*: April 2019, M. Reza Mahmoudi, Ali Abbasalizadeh,

Rahman' before Muhammad: A pre-history of the First Peace (Sulh) in Islam, Sigrid K. Kjær, Cambridge University Press: May 2022.

Further Resources

Films and TV series:

The Message, (1976)
Filmco International Productions Inc.
Directed by Moustapha Akkad

Muhammad, The Last Prophet (2002)
RichCrest Animation Studios
Directed by Richard Rich

Muhammad: The Final Legacy (2008)
Media Link International
Directed by Najdat Anzour

Omar series, episodes 1-17 (2012),
MBC Group, Qatar TV
Directed by Hatem Ali

Muhammad, the Messenger of God (2015)
Noor-e-Taban Film, Infinite Production
Directed by Majid Majidi

Websites:

www.quran.com
www.sunnah.com
www.altafsir.com

لَا إِلٰهَ إِلَّا ٱللَّهُ مُحَمَّدٌ رَسُولُ ٱللَّهِ

Laa ilaaha il-Allah,

Muhammadur-Rasulullah.

There is no god except Allah.

Muhammad is the Messenger of Allah.